Legal Information

© 2024
Author and Editor: M.Eng. Johannes Wild
Author Reference: A94689H39927F
Email: 3dtech@gmx.de

The complete imprint of the book can be found on the last pages!

This work is protected by copyright

Thank you so much for choosing this book!

Table of Contents

Foreword

Thank you very much for choosing this book!

Are you interested in using CAD software with which you can create technical drawings (DXF, SVG, PDF format) of mechanical components, floor plans of apartments, wiring diagrams for electrical engineering and other 2D drawings as well as isometric 3D views?

Then you've come to the right place! I am an engineer and would like to teach you in a simple and easy to understand way how to use the free software "LibreCAD". In this course, you will learn everything you need to know to create technical drawings for mechanical components, architecture, DIY projects and much more.

This comprehensive and detailed course is aimed particularly at beginners and shows you from the ground up what CAD is, how to use the software and how to create technical drawings. You don't need any previous knowledge for this book, as everything is explained step by step and in detail. This book is also ideal for advanced users, who just want to switch from another CAD program to "LibreCAD".

"LibreCAD" is ideal for hobbyists, students, technicians, architects, craftsmen, and freelancers who are looking for a good and free alternative to expensive CAD software such as "AutoCAD". With detailed step-by-step instructions, numerous illustrations and practical examples, this book will teach you the basics of "LibreCAD" through to advanced commands and drawing techniques in a simple way. After completing the course, you will be able to create components, floor plans and other technical drawings with ease and precision and print them to scale.

"LibreCAD" offers a wide range of functions that can also be found in commercial programs. Whether you want to draw parts for model making, a furniture design, architectural plans or mechanical engineering parts, "LibreCAD" provides the necessary tools for professional results. And this course gives you a comprehensive insight into the tools of the software.

Let's get started now! Enjoy drawing!

1 What is CAD and why "LibreCAD"?

What is CAD?

CAD stands for "Computer-Aided Design". With the help of such software, engineers, constructors, architects, designers, craftsmen and other users can create and edit their designs on the computer. Floor plans of houses, designs of mechanical components as well as furniture and other objects were designed and drawn entirely on paper a few decades ago. Particularly in the professional field of architecture and mechanical engineering, this was done in large drawing rooms and with classic drawing boards. Nowadays — at least in the professional environment — most designs are created exclusively on a PC and with CAD software.

Working with CAD software has revolutionized traditional drawing on paper by not only speeding up drawing and simplifying changes, but also allowing complex models to be designed, analyzed, simulated and visualized in different perspectives in both 2D and 3D.

There are many CAD programs from which the user can choose. Most of them are subject to a fee, only a few of them — such as "LibreCAD" — are completely free of charge. The decision for a specific CAD software depends on various factors, including professionalism, functionality, price, licensing and, above all, the respective area of application.

Why "LibreCAD"?

"LibreCAD" is open-source software and is therefore provided <u>completely free of charge</u> by the development community. This software was specially developed for the creation of 2D CAD drawings, but 3D views (e.g., isometric views) can also be drawn with it. "LibreCAD" is platform-independent, so it can be used under Windows, macOS, and Linux.

Another major advantage of "LibreCAD" is the intuitive and simply designed user interface. The software offers a solid selection of tools required for 2D drawings, including commands for creating lines, arcs, circles, hatching, dimensions and many more. Despite its simplicity, "LibreCAD" offers a good range of functions and enables a high level of precision when drawing.

Who is this software suitable for and what are the possible applications?

"LibreCAD" offers a wide range of possible applications for the most diverse target groups. The variety of possible applications ranges from architecture and construction to mechanical engineering and hobby applications. The software can also be used very well as a teaching aid for pupils and students in the field of CAD and technical drawing.

Architects, master bricklayers and civil engineers

One of the main target groups of "LibreCAD" are architects and civil engineers, who can use this software to create 2D floor plans of objects as well as sections and elevations for construction projects. "LibreCAD" offers all the essential tools for creating technical drawings quickly and efficiently.

One example of the use of this software in architecture is the planning of a house or apartment. Architects can use it to draw floor plans, add room layouts and dimensions and visualize the placement of doors, windows, and furniture. The software allows the use of layers, whereby different elements such as the building, the electrical installations and the water pipes can be organized separately. But more on this later.

Mechanical engineers and designers

"LibreCAD" also offers a cost-effective and powerful solution for creating technical drawings in the field of mechanical engineering and design. Designers require detailed technical drawings of 3D components for transfer to production. "LibreCAD" offers the option of creating technical drawings in 2D as well as isometric 3D views. Dimensions, angles, tolerances, annotations, etc. can be added to the technical drawings in the software.

One example of this is the creation of an exploded drawing of a simple gearbox. "LibreCAD" makes it possible to display the various components such as gears and shafts true to scale and to illustrate their positions in the assembled state.

Electrical engineers

You can also design detailed circuit diagrams for electronic systems in "LibreCAD". The CAD software can be used to create precise circuit diagrams for industrial systems, control systems or circuits, for example. A library with numerous ready-made electronic circuit symbols (capacitors, coils, diodes, antennas, speakers, microphones ...) is already integrated in "LibreCAD". The software can be used to display both the position of components and their connections in precise circuit diagrams.

Students and educational institutions

Students in the fields of engineering, architecture or design are another important user group of "LibreCAD". As the software is available free of charge, it is ideal for use in educational institutions and for self-study. Teachers can use this program to teach their pupils and students the basics of technical drawing.

A typical example of the use of "LibreCAD" in education is a basic technical drawing course, in which students learn to draw and dimension simple mechanical components. The software provides a user-friendly and simple environment to learn the basic CAD techniques without having to purchase expensive licenses or making the course too complex.

Hobbyists and DIY enthusiasts

Not only professional users benefit from "LibreCAD" — hobbyists and DIY enthusiasts in particular can also use the software to design their own components and plan projects. Whether it's building a model airplane, constructing furniture yourself or planning a garden shed, "LibreCAD" offers the necessary tools to create precise 2D plans.

One example would be the planning of a garden shed. With "LibreCAD", the dimensions of the shed, the position of the windows and doors as well as the required material quantities can be easily calculated and visualized. This considerably simplifies the planning of a DIY project.

Small companies, freelancers and other craftsmen (locksmiths, carpenters, electricians, etc.)

"LibreCAD" is also an excellent choice for small businesses as well as freelancers and craftsmen who are looking for free and simple CAD software.

An example would be a freelance industrial designer who creates product designs for his customers. With the help of "LibreCAD", he can quickly create conceptual 2D designs. This makes it possible to work efficiently and cost-effectively on projects.

Another example would be a carpenter who can use "LibreCAD" to create detailed plans for pieces of furniture. The CAD software can be used, for example, to precisely define the dimensions of a bookshelf, the layout of the compartments and the placement of connectors and screws. A true-to-scale drawing can be created that not only shows the size of the shelf, but also the positions of the shelves, support struts and the back panel. This precise planning can reduce production time and facilitate furniture construction.

Another example would be an electrician who wants to use "LibreCAD" to create detailed circuit diagrams for electrical installations. The CAD software can be used to precisely plan and neatly display the positions of cables, sockets, switches, and fuse boxes in a building, for example. As already mentioned, there is a library with many ready-made electrical and electronic circuit symbols in "LibreCAD", which considerably simplifies the creation of circuit diagrams.

A final example would be a locksmith who can use "LibreCAD" to create precise drawings for metal structures such as railings, gates or steel beams. The software makes it possible to specify the dimensions and material thicknesses of the individual parts as well as the positions of connecting elements such as weld seams or screws. This true-to-scale planning simplifies the production of metal parts and speeds up assembly on site.

What are the essential differences to other CAD software?

"LibreCAD" is — as already mentioned — primarily designed for the creation of 2D drawings. Although isometric 3D views can also be drawn, this software cannot be used to create or edit components and objects directly in 3D. In comparison to other — mostly fee-based — programs, which also offer the creation of 3D models, the assembly of individual parts into modules, simulations and advanced design tools, "LibreCAD" is mainly limited to the 2D area. For many applications, particularly in the fields of architecture and construction as well as for simple parts in mechanical engineering and for the creation of technical drawings, this is perfectly adequate. However, if you need 3D models or simulations and work in a professional environment, you should use other programs such as "FreeCAD", "Fusion 360", "SolidWorks", "Catia", "AutoCAD" and so on. Apart from "FreeCAD", however, these are only available for a fee and are usually very expensive.

Nevertheless, "LibreCAD" can be warmly recommended, especially for absolute beginners in the field of CAD. The simplicity of the software combined with its wide range of functions is not overwhelming but offers quick and good learning success. This course will provide you with a simple, step-by-step introduction to CAD and the "LibreCAD" software. This will enable you to learn the basics of 2D design and use them as a basis for more advanced software if required. With "LibreCAD", technical drawings can be saved in DXF format. This is a widely used format and is therefore supported by all common CAD programs. This means that projects can be easily imported into other programs if you decide to use more complex software later.

So, let's learn the basics of CAD together using the software "LibreCAD" and create the first components, floor plans and projects. In the next two chapters, we will start by installing the software and then familiarize ourselves with the user interface and basic settings.

1.2 Installing the Software

As already mentioned, the software "LibreCAD" is an open-source project and can therefore be downloaded free of charge. If you wish, you can voluntarily donate a small amount to the developer community for the further development of the software. The download and installation procedure for both Windows and macOS operating systems is described step by step below.

Open your preferred Internet browser and go to the official website: https://www.librecad.org. In the middle section of the website, you will find the available download options. Here you can click on "from SourceForge" ① in the macOS or Windows area, and you will be redirected to the file hosting service "SourceForge", where the current version of the software is available for download. Alternatively, "GitHub" is also available as a file hosting service.

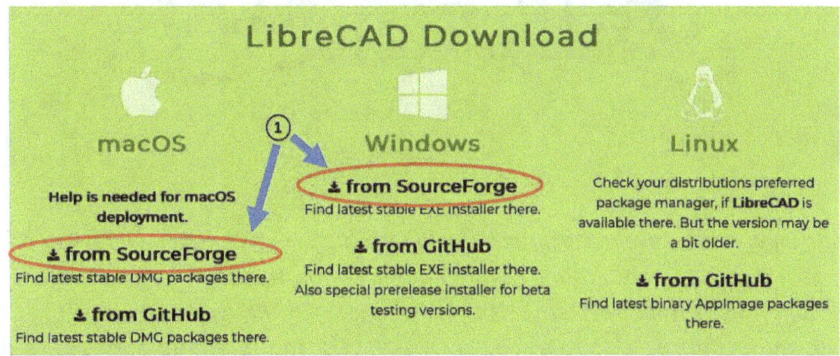

Then look for a green download button on the "SourceForge" website labeled "Download Latest Version" ② and click on it. The download will now start.

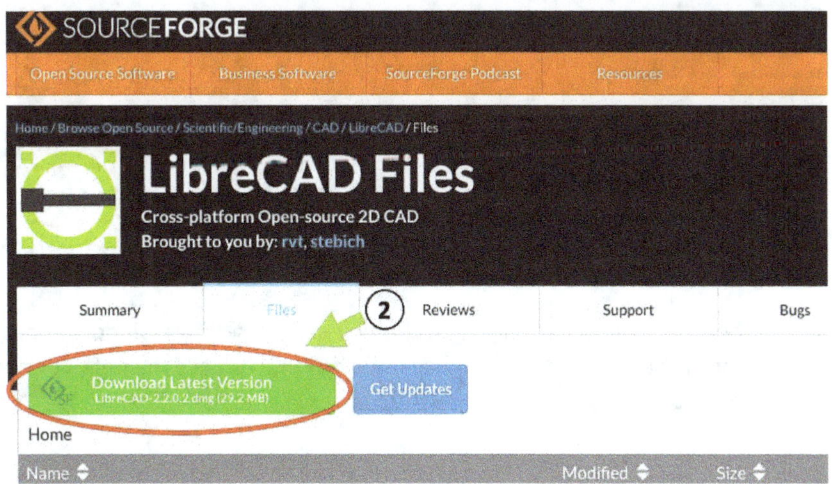

Windows only: *If you have a Windows PC, you will be warned in the first installation step that this app has not been verified by Microsoft. This is the case with many programs that are not in the App Store. Simply click on "Install anyway" and then follow the further installation steps by clicking through the installation process.*

Mac only: *If you have a Mac, the downloaded file may be blocked when you open it, as it does not come from a verified developer. In this case, you must scroll to "Security" in the Mac's system settings (Apple icon) at "Privacy & Security" ① and click on the button "Open Anyway" ②. Note: For this button to appear, the file must have been opened once beforehand and thus blocked.*

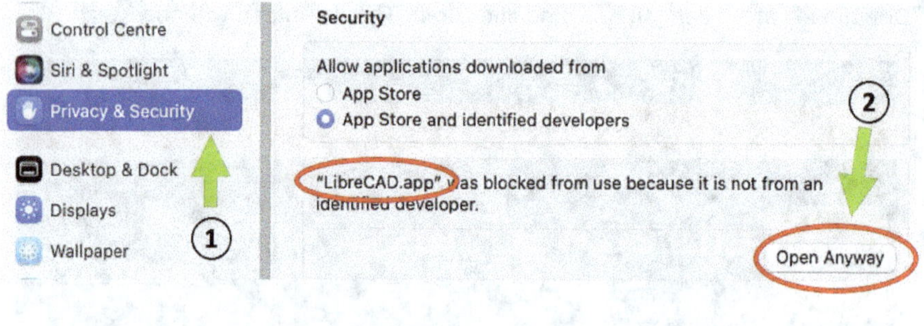

You can then start the program and in the first step, a settings window appears asking us for the default unit and language. We can simply leave the default values as they are, as we will look at all the settings in detail later.

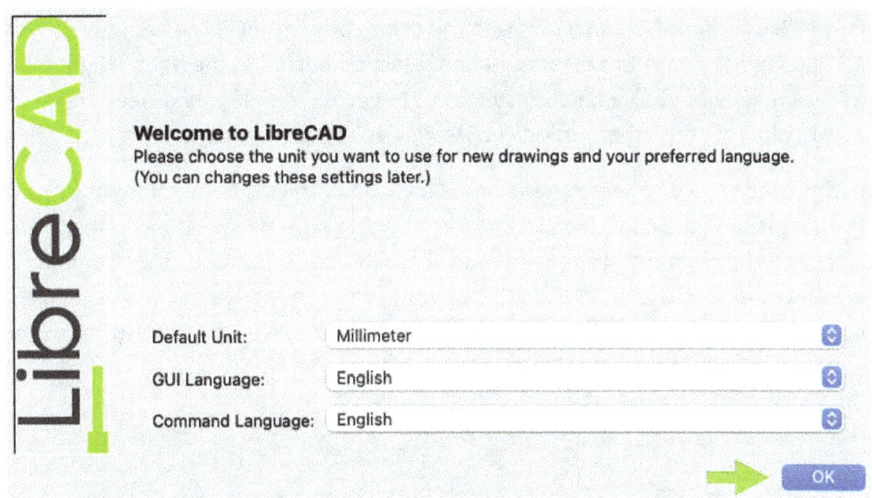

1.3 First Steps with "LibreCAD"

After installation, we will first look at the basic settings of the software. To do this, we select "Application Preferences" ② from the "Options" ① tab in the menu bar.

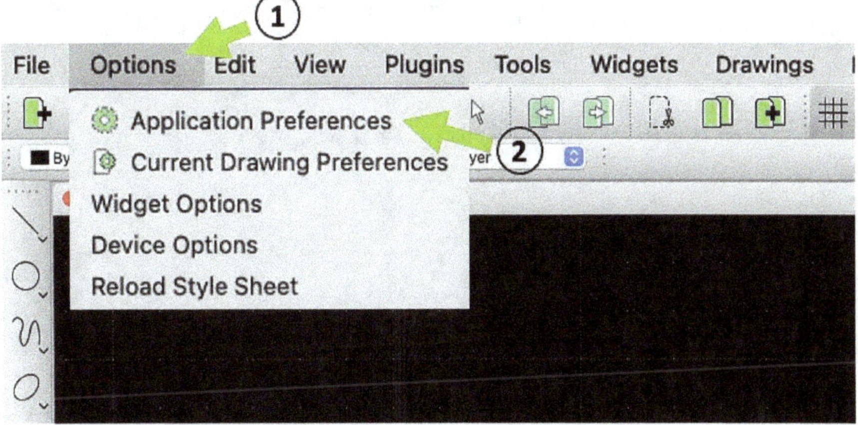

A window opens in which we can make adjustments to the appearance of the graphical user interface in the "Appearance" tab. Here we can set the display of grid lines and change colors for various elements such as the background and the grid. Language options for the user interface and commands can also be configured.

The background in "LibreCAD" is colored black by default. I clearly prefer the color white as a drawing background. If you feel the same way, you can make this setting in the "Background" area by entering the color code "#FFFFFF". Alternatively, you can also select a different color using the selection button to the right. A light blue, for example, would also be very suitable. However, you may then need to assign other colors for the other options to create a contrast.

In this window, we can also change the language of the user environment ③ and the language of the command line ④. You should always leave the command line language ("Command Language") in English, as otherwise the commands presented later in this course would not work. You can change the language of the user environment if necessary. However, in this course, we will also leave the setting at "GUI Language" at "English".

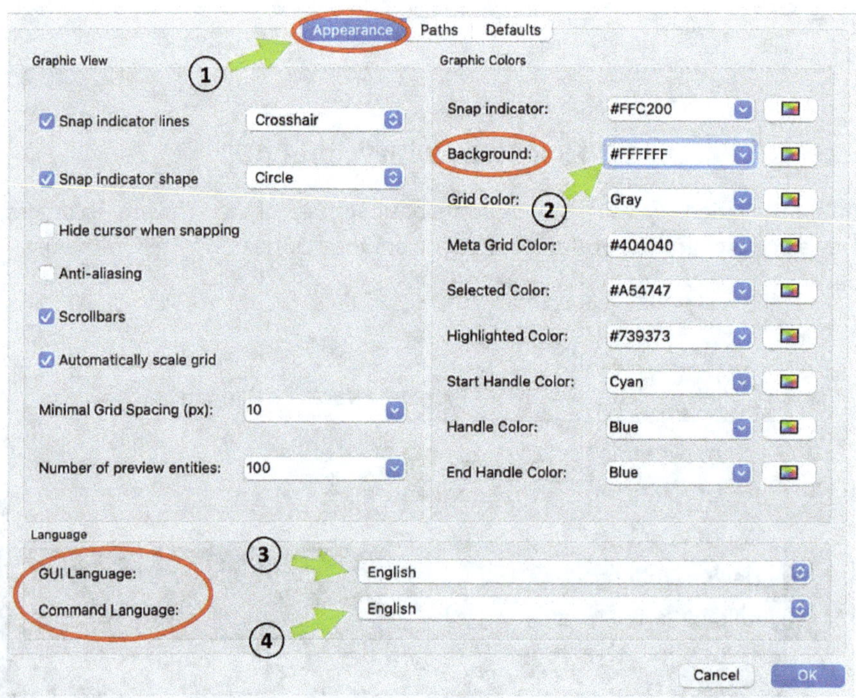

After clicking on the tab "Defaults" ①, we can define the standard units of a drawing document. Here we can leave the millimeter setting ②. We can also set the time interval for the "Auto backup" function ③ here. If you prefer to use "LibreCAD" later with the default settings — as when you first started it — you could reset all previously made settings in the area ④ or alternatively only the layout settings. However, we do <u>not</u> do this.

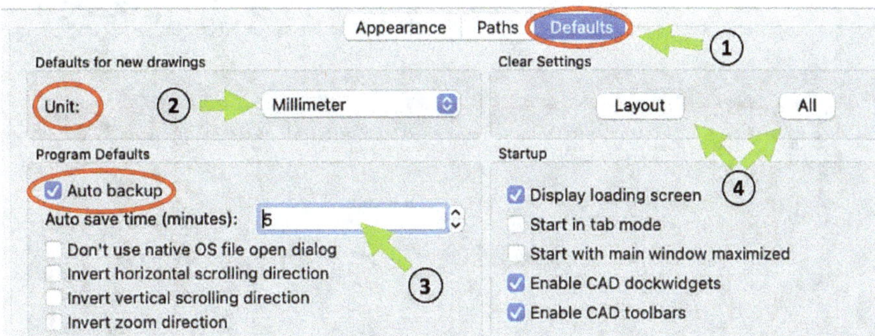

Then click on the "OK" button at the bottom of the window to accept the settings and close the window.

The user environment of "LibreCAD" can be divided into several areas. Let's familiarize ourselves with the software by taking a brief look at each area. More detailed examples will follow later on.

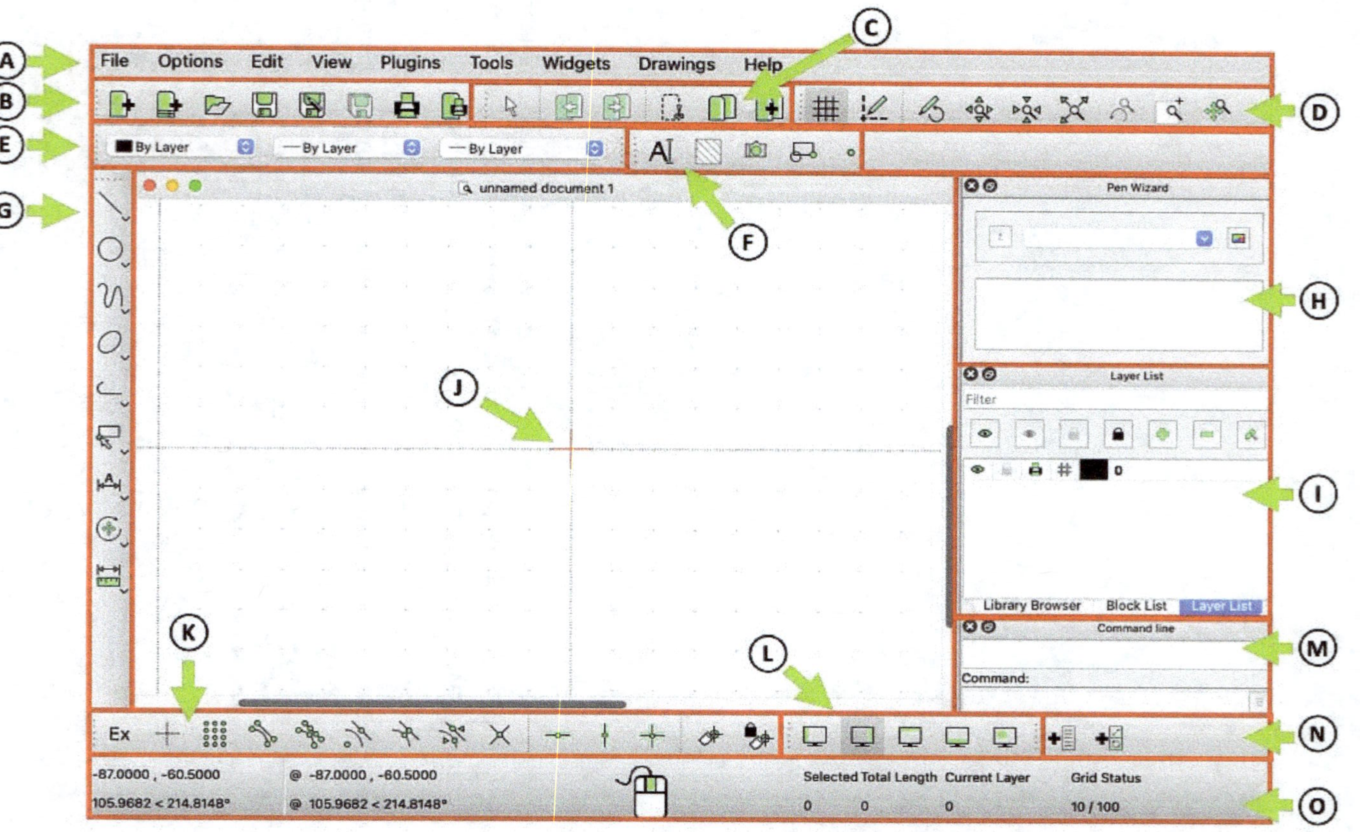
File   Options   Edit   View   Plugins   Tools   Widgets   Drawings   Help
By Layer
By Layer
By Layer
unnamed document 1
Pen Wizard
Layer List
Filter
0
Library Browser   Block List   Layer List
Command line
Command:
Ex
-87.0000 , -60.5000
105.9682 < 214.8148°
@ -87.0000 , -60.5000
@ 105.9682 < 214.8148°
Selected Total Length   Current Layer
0   0   0
Grid Status
10 / 100

Depending on the version of the software, the individual areas may be in a different position. This is possible because almost all bars can be moved by clicking on them and dragging them with the mouse. You are welcome to try this out. Do not be confused by the different positions of the individual areas, but simply look at the symbols below to recognize the respective area. Menu bar **A** (at the top) contains all the commands from "LibreCAD". Many of the commands can also be found in the following toolbars as separate buttons, so we will look at these in more detail later. In addition to the system settings and advanced functions (e.g., "Plugins"), you will also find the menu items "Widgets" and "Drawings", which we will take a closer look at now.

File   Options   Edit   View   Plugins   Tools   Widgets   Drawings   Help

In the menu item "Widgets" ① you can activate and deactivate menu bars under "Toolbars" ②. So, if you are missing a menu bar, you can search for it here. And in the menu item "Drawings" ③ you can switch between the "Tab mode" and the "Window mode" ④. If you have several documents (drawings) active in "LibreCAD", you can choose either tab mode or window mode here and arrange the windows as required (e.g., stepped, tiled) with "Arrange" ⑤.

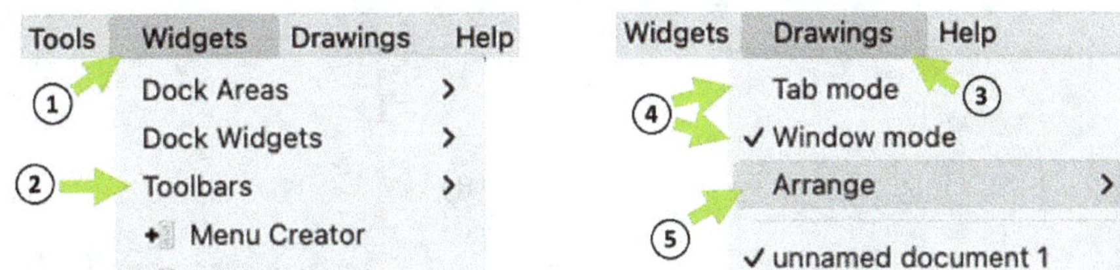

The toolbars **B** ("File toolbar"), **C** ("Edit toolbar") and **D** ("View toolbar") are located directly below this menu bar.

The icons in section **B** can be used to create a new document, save a document and print it. The print preview can also be found here. Section **C** contains further general program commands such as undo, redo, cut, copy and paste. Section **D**, on the other hand, contains program-specific functions. Here you can show or hide the drawing grid ("Grid"), switch to "Draft" mode and execute some zoom commands. The "Draft" mode is particularly useful for complex drawings, as it simplifies computationally intensive geometries and representations. This is helpful for efficient, fluid work with limited computing power and is also less distracting. Below this is the pen selection toolbar **E** ("Pen selection toolbar") and the "DefaultCustom" toolbar **F**. With the "Pen selection toolbar" you can define the line color, line width and line type (continuous, dashed ...) for the next geometry. The setting options "By Layer" and "By Block" mean that the respective attribute (e.g., line color) is taken from the setting of the layer or the block. We will learn what these two terms mean later. You can use the symbols in bar **F** to create a multi-line text, a hatching, a block, and a point, as well as to insert an image into the drawing layer.

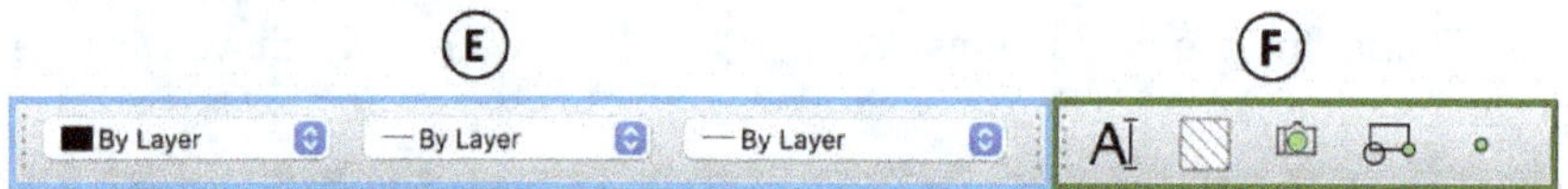

Now let's move on to the middle area of the program window. The vertically arranged CAD toolbar **G** is located on the left-hand side. This contains the most important drawing tools for creating technical drawings. All common geometries such as lines, circles, curves, ellipses, polygons and many more can be found here. The four symbols at the bottom of the bar are used to select, modify and dimension geometries that have already been created. Each icon can be clicked to open a submenu, each of which contains a variety of additional commands.

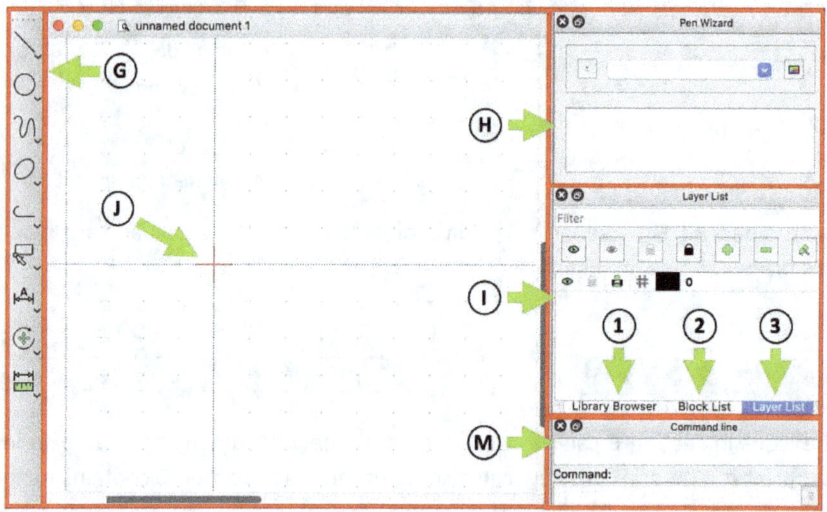

On the right-hand side of the software environment are the windows **H** ("Pen Wizard"), **I** ("Layer List", "Block List", "Library Browser") and **M** ("Command line"). Depending on the version of the program, these can also be arranged differently, and you can also rearrange them yourself by clicking on a window and dragging it at the same time. If a window is not required, you can close it.

In the "Pen Wizard" (**H**) window, you can select pen colors and save them in a list. This is useful if you repeatedly use several line colors in a document or, for example, want to apply a color to several geometries. The list of colors is retained even after a program restart.

Window **I** contains the three sections "Library Browser" ①, "Block List" ② and "Layer List" ③. In the "Layer List" and the "Block List", you can create and edit the previously mentioned layers and blocks. These two functions allow you to work in an organized and structured way.

In "LibreCAD", a layer can be imagined as a transparent film on which you draw and then hold up to a light source (the principle of the daylight projector). You can create several layers and draw a different category on each layer. For example, you can draw all geometries on layer 1, all dimensions on layer 2 and all texts on layer 3. If you now position all of these layers on top of each other on a light source, the information is superimposed, and you obtain an overall image with all the details. However, if you remove a slide, you can easily hide a specific category. This function (hide) is also available in "LibreCAD".

With the term "block" you can save a self-drawn geometry of several shapes as a kind of grouped file in "LibreCAD". As an architect, for example, you can draw a piece of furniture in "LibreCAD" to illustrate the furnishing of a house. The piece of furniture could, for example, consist of several lines and the architect would also like to use it in other floor plans. He would then have to redraw the piece of furniture in each file, which would take a lot of time if there were several objects. However, if he saves the piece of furniture as block, he can select it again and again from the "Block List" and insert it with one click. Blocks can be exported and imported into other drawings and changed centrally.

In the "Library Browser" you can select from predefined blocks and insert special geometric shapes, arrows, electronic circuit symbols and other geometries into your drawing.

The **M** window ("Command line") contains a command line, with which you can draw using the keyboard by entering commands. We will take a closer look at this later. Area **J** contains the drawing layer of the current file. This can be imagined as a sheet of paper containing a grid and a coordinate origin (small red cross). The grid can also be hidden. The desired technical drawing is drawn in this area using the geometric shapes from area **G**.

Before we take a more detailed and practical look at the individual functions of the program and create the first drawings in the next chapter, let's take a look at the lower area of "LibreCAD". Here we find the toolbars "Snap Options" (**K**), "Dock Areas" (**L**) and "Creators" (**N**) and below them the status bar (**O**).

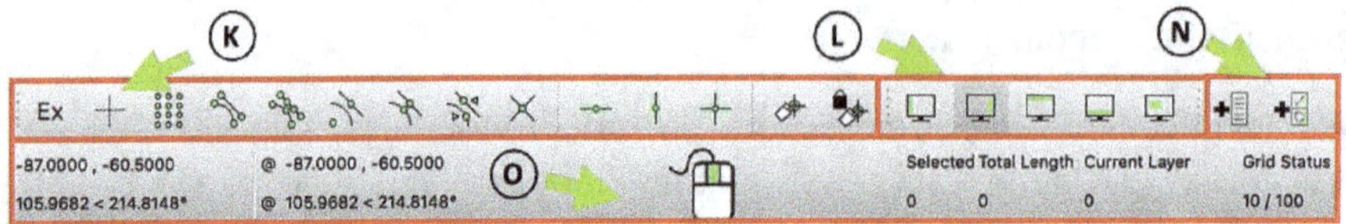

With the "Snap Options" symbols from area **K**, you can select a specific snap mode that facilitates the exact placement of geometry elements. For example, you can select that the starting point of a new line should snap exactly to the center of an existing line.

The "Dock Areas" in the **L** area can be used to determine in which areas of "LibreCAD" windows are active. Currently, for example, the right-hand window area is active, which contains windows **H**, **I** and **M**. These windows can be shown and hidden quickly by clicking on the icon. With the two icons from the **N** area ("Creators"), advanced users can create their own menus and toolbars by selecting their favorite commands. You can also assign individual names here.

The status bar **O**, which is located at the very bottom of the "LibreCAD" area, is an essential bar. The left-hand area shows the current coordinates of the mouse pointer, the middle area shows the image of a PC mouse, and the right-hand area shows other important information, details of which will be provided later. In the PC mouse area — after selecting a command — a very brief explanation is given to the left and right of the two mouse buttons of what is possible for a command. Whenever we don't know what to do with a command, we can get brief help here.

2 Basics of Using "LibreCAD"

2.1 Creating Simple Geometries

In this chapter, we will look at the basic operation of "LibreCAD". We will start by drawing the first simple geometries and then learn how to use the user interface.

Let's draw a circle as our first geometry. We do this by clicking on the circle icon ① in the CAD toolbar, which is located on the left-hand side of the program window by default. This opens a submenu in which a variety of circle-related geometries can be selected. We click on "Center, Point" ② and can then click slightly to the right above the coordinate origin ④ in the drawing plane to determine the center point ③ of the circle. Now we drag the circle to any size with a mouse movement and click again in the drawing plane. This creates the circle.

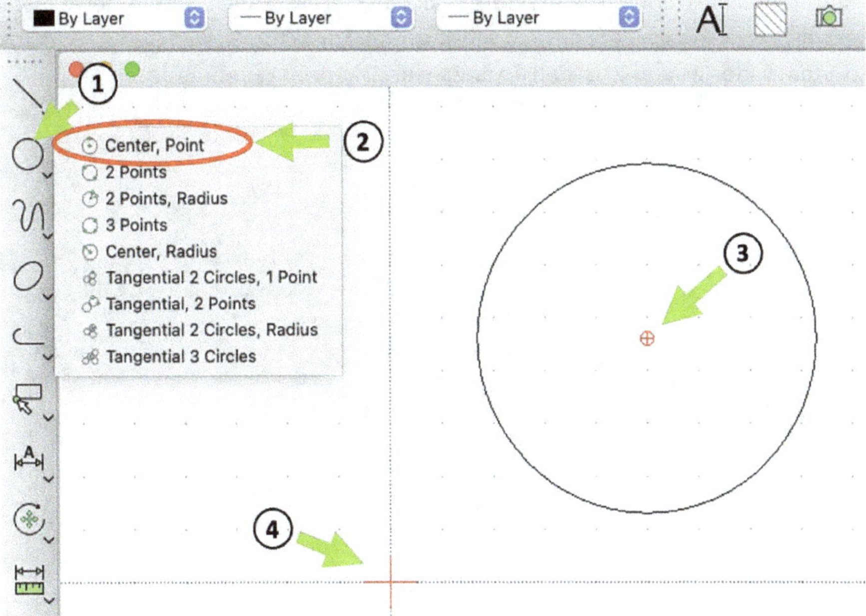

We are now still in the "Center, Point" command and could therefore immediately draw another circle. This can be recognized by the fact that the crosshairs ① are still active. We can end the command by pressing the ESC key.

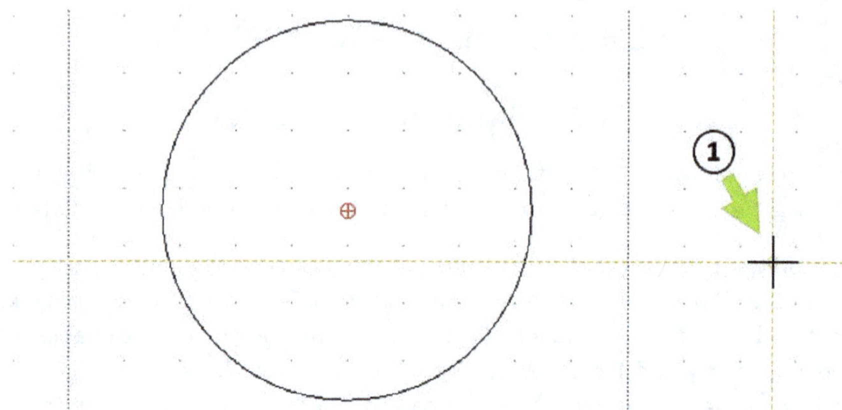

The second geometry we want to create is a rectangle. Before creating this geometry, we change the line color, line width and line type in the "Pen selection toolbar" so that we also learn how to use this toolbar. Clicking on the respective buttons for line color ①, line width ② and line type ③ opens a drop-down menu in which we can select the desired specification. For example, we select a red color, a 1 mm wide line and a dashed appearance.

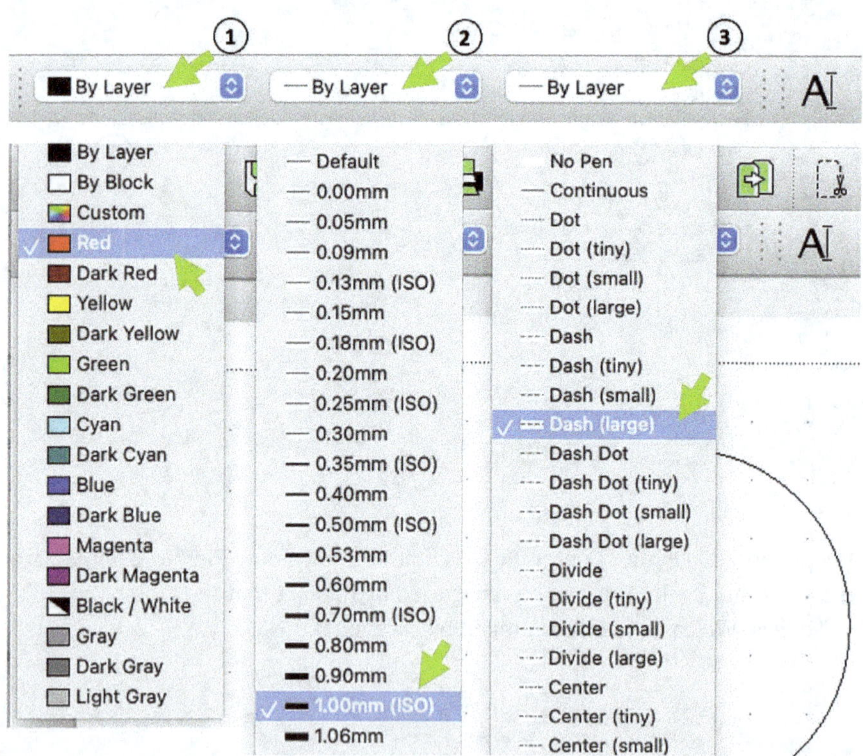

The settings in the "Pen selection toolbar" then affect the subsequently drawn geometries until a change is made to these settings. If the selection options "By Layer" or "By Block" are active, the global settings of the layer or block for color, width, and type are used.

Now, we can draw the rectangle by clicking on the line symbol ① in the CAD toolbar. This opens another submenu in which a variety of line-related geometries can be selected. We click on "Rectangle" ② and can then click in the drawing plane ③, stretch the rectangle with a dragging movement of the mouse and define the second point of the rectangle ④ with another click. Finally, press the ESC key to exit the command. As we can see, the settings of the "Pen selection toolbar" have been successfully applied to the rectangle.

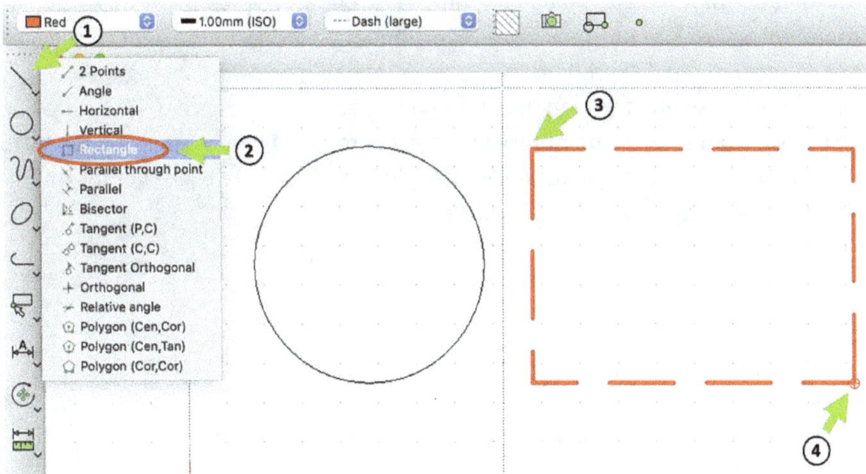

2.2 Coordinate Systems and the Drawing Environment in Detail

Understanding the coordinate system and coordinate origin is essential in CAD and technical drawing. That is why we will now look at this and then get to know the drawing environment of "LibreCAD" in more detail. There are different coordinate systems, including the Cartesian coordinate system (familiar from school) and the polar coordinate system (familiar from school/higher education). In addition to these two systems, there are many other systems, especially in the three-dimensional domain. In this course, we will only deal with the Cartesian coordinate system.

In the Cartesian coordinate system, there is an x-axis (horizontal) and a y-axis (vertical) in 2D space. In the simplest case (positive values only) these axes go to the right and upwards, but normally also to the left and downwards (negative values; shown here with a dashed line) so that a cross is formed. The origin of the coordinates (0,0) is located in the center of the cross (overlap of both axes). Coordinates are provided by first specifying the x-coordinate and then the y-coordinate. The starting point when specifying <u>absolute coordinates</u> is always the coordinate origin. For example, the point at ① has the coordinates (2,1). First, move two graduation marks to the right (x-axis) and then one graduation mark upwards (y-axis). The point at ②, for example, has the coordinates (6,5). The connection of the two points then results in a line. This is also how it works in "LibreCAD".

The drawing plane in "LibreCAD" can be imagined as a white sheet of paper with a coordinate system (grid). When drawing a line, you set the start and end points of the line in the drawing plane by clicking with the mouse, and "LibreCAD" notes the coordinates of the two points in the background. The point at ③ has the coordinates (2,-2), as here you move two graduation marks to the right (positive x-axis direction) and then two graduation marks downwards (negative y-axis direction). The point at ④, on the other hand, has the coordinates (-2,3). Here you first move from the zero point (origin of the coordinates) two graduation marks to the left, i.e., in the negative x-axis direction, and then two graduation marks upwards, i.e., in the positive y-axis direction.

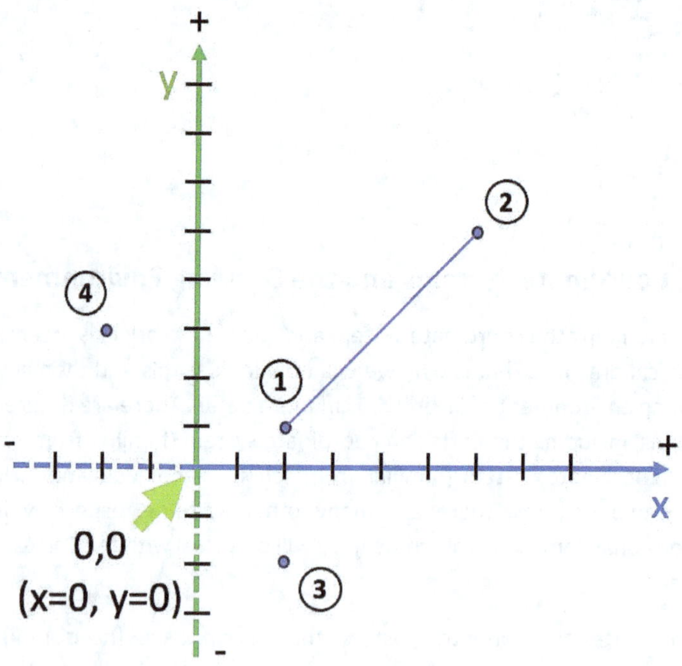

In addition to specifying <u>absolute coordinates</u>, which we have just learned about, "LibreCAD" also offers the option of specifying relative coordinates. <u>Relative coordinates</u> do <u>not</u> refer directly to the origin of the coordinates, but rather to the last point set. You are therefore working <u>relative</u> to the last position. For example, if we have defined the point at ① in absolute coordinates (-2,1), we can determine all other points with relative coordinates starting from this point. To get from point ① to point ② (distance a), we have to move four graduation marks to the right on the x-axis and two graduation marks upwards on the y-axis. The origin of the coordinates (intersection of the axes) also counts as a graduation mark. We place an @ sign before the relative coordinates in "LibreCAD". The specification of the relative coordinates is therefore @4,2.

Please try to find out the relative coordinates to points 3 and 4 (distances b and c) on your own. Remember that you always refer to the last position. You will find the solution below the illustration.

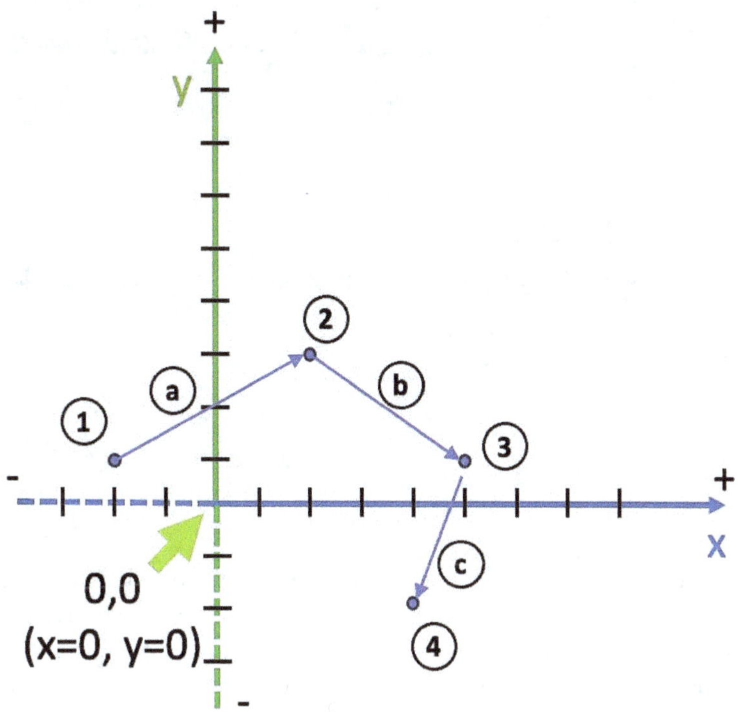

The solution is: From point ② to ③ (line b), go three graduation lines in the positive x-axis direction and two graduation lines in the negative y-axis direction, i.e., @3,-2. For line c, go one graduation mark in the negative x-axis direction and three graduation marks in the negative y-axis direction to get from point ③ to ④, i.e., @-1,-3.

In three-dimensional space, a further axis, the z-axis, is added to the x- and y-axes. Absolute coordinates are specified as follows. The point at ① is reached by moving five graduation marks on the x-axis to the right (positive direction), four graduation marks on the y-axis upwards (positive direction) and three graduation marks on the z-axis forwards (positive direction) from the origin of the coordinates. Do not be confused by the perspective but use the arrows and the dashed line as a guide.

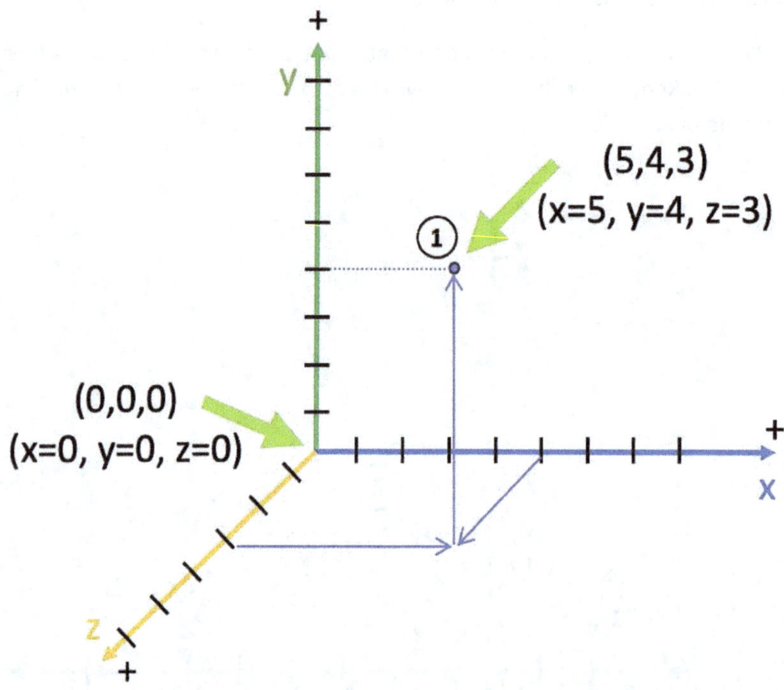

A 3D coordinate system can also have negative axis directions (to the left, to the right, backwards), but this has been neglected here for the sake of clarity. In addition, the orientation of the axes does not have to be as shown above but is made clear in a <u>right-handed</u> coordinate system (standard in mathematics, technology & CAD) by the right-hand rule. Imagine that the thumb of your right hand is the x-axis, the index finger is the y-axis, and the middle finger is the z-axis.

If you now hold these three fingers at right angles to each other, you will obtain a coordinate system. You can rotate the hand as you wish, the axes remain the same relative to each other, but the (absolute) orientation of the axes in 3D space changes.

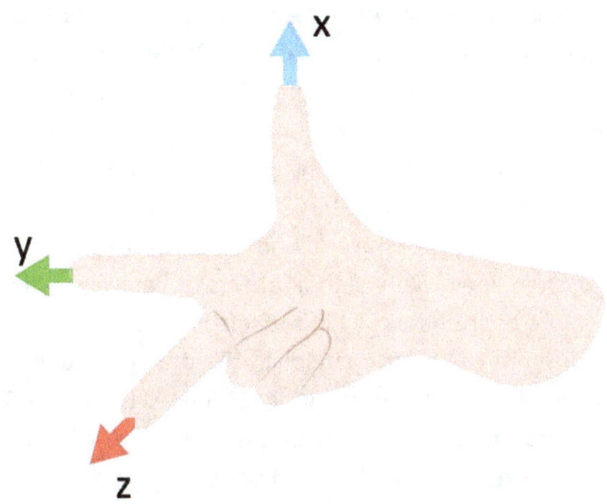

A 3D coordinate system can also be represented as follows. In this orientation, the positive z-axis runs vertically upwards. The orientation of the other two axes is determined by the right-hand rule. You will find this type of orientation in architecture, 3D CAD software, CNC machines, 3D printing, etc., for example. In this case, the z-axis is the height axis, the 2D plane is spanned by the x- and y-axes.

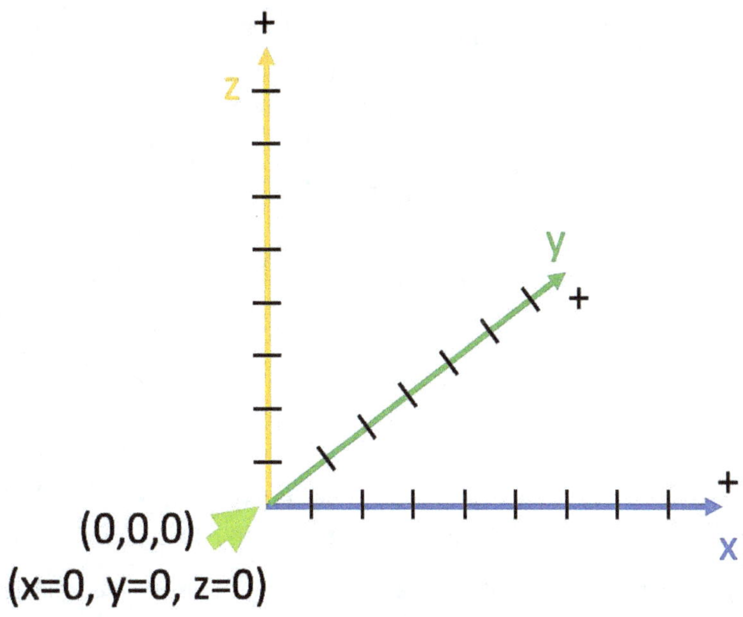

Excellent! Now we have created the basis for taking a closer look at the CAD program "LibreCAD" and its drawing environment in particular.

In the drawing plane of "LibreCAD" there is a red cross ①, which defines the coordinate origin (zero point; coordinates: 0,0). Starting from this, the x-axis extends horizontally to the right in a positive direction and the y-axis extends vertically upwards in a positive direction. If the grid ② is active, you will find dashed lines and points on the drawing plane ③. The "Grid Status" ④ in the status bar is indicated here as "10/100". The first number (10) indicates the distance between two points of the grid and the second number (100) the distance between two dashed lines. We will look at this in detail in a moment. First, let's look at the <u>absolute</u> coordinates ⑤ in the left-hand area of the status bar. Here, the current position of the mouse cursor in the drawing plane is represented by Cartesian coordinates (1st line) and polar coordinates (2nd line). The specification 10.3342, 9.8945 therefore means that the mouse cursor is located 10.3342 units in the positive x-axis direction and 9.8945 units in the positive y-axis direction. If you place your mouse cursor directly over the coordinate origin ①, 0.0 will be displayed here. The <u>relative</u> coordinates ⑥ are also displayed. This can be recognized by the @ symbol. Here too, the first line is in Cartesian coordinates and the second line in polar coordinates.

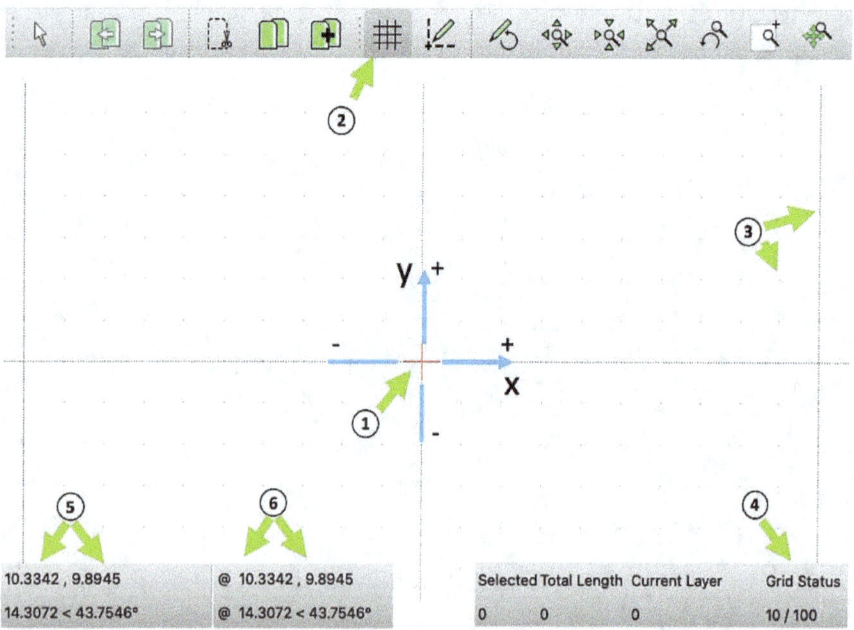

You may notice that the absolute and relative coordinates are identical. However, this is only the case at the beginning when you have not yet drawn anything. For example, if we click on the point symbol ① and place a point ② at any position in the drawing plane, the relative coordinates ④ differ from the absolute coordinates. The drawn point becomes the coordinate origin of its own (relative) coordinate system, which is why "@ 0,0" is displayed at ④ when the mouse cursor is positioned exactly over this point.

As already mentioned in the previous chapter, after selecting a command ①, we can see in area ③ what the left and right mouse buttons do for the current command. This is often very helpful for new commands.

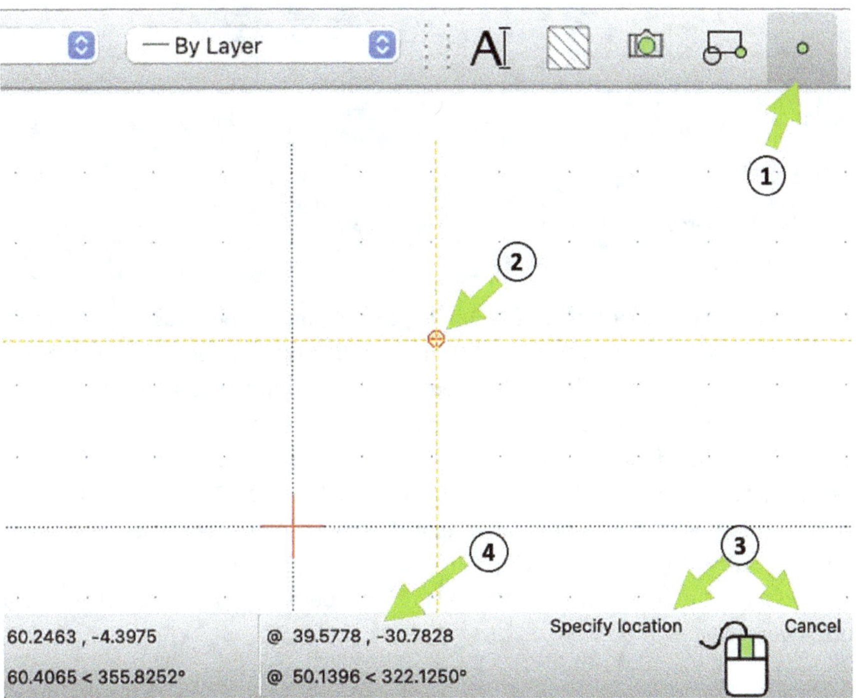

Now back to the grid. As already mentioned, the first number of the "Grid Status" indicates the distance between two points of the grid and the second number the distance between two dashed lines of the grid. The information is always given in the currently set unit of measurement. In one of the previous chapters at "Options" and "Application Preferences", we set millimeters as the default unit. This means that if the specification "10/100" is visible in the status bar at "Grid Status", the distance between two grid points is 10 mm and between two dotted lines (= one grid box) is 100 mm. There are always exactly 10 grid points between two dashed lines. We can also change the unit setting specifically for the active document. To do this, we must go to "Options" and then to "Current Drawing Preferences" ① and switch to the tab "Units" ②. At "Main drawing unit" ③ we can define the desired unit for drawing in the current document. If, for example, we select "Meter" here, the specification "10/100" of the "Grid Status" now means that the distance between two grid points is 10 m and between two dashed lines is 100 m. Existing geometries are not changed, i.e., it makes sense to always set the unit at the beginning. Otherwise, by changing the unit of the grid, a previously 1 mm long line will then be 1 m long, for example.

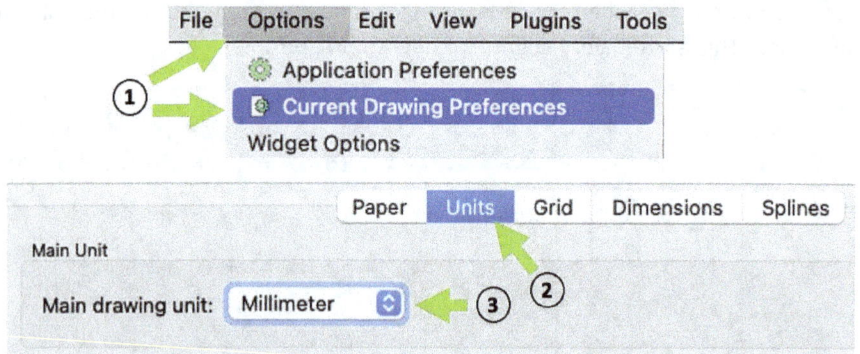

The "Grid Status" is not always "10/100", but changes when you zoom into the drawing plane. You can try this by turning your mouse wheel while the mouse cursor is in the "LibreCAD" drawing layer. If we zoom further and further into the drawing sheet, the "Grid Status" first changes to "1/10", then to "0.1/1" and so on by a factor of 10. If, on the other hand, we zoom out of the drawing sheet, we also see a change by a factor of 10, namely from "1/10" to "10/100" to "100/1000" and so on. The value "0.1/1" would mean that the distance between two grid points is now 0.1 units (depending on which unit was set; e.g., "meter") and between two dashed lines 1 unit, e.g., 1 m. This applies analogously to "1/10", "10/100" and all other values.

Grid Status	Grid Status	Grid Status	Grid Status
0.1 / 1	1 / 10	10 / 100	100 / 1000

Superb! We learned the first important basics. In the following chapter, we will look at navigation within the drawing environment.

2.3 Navigation and Zoom Functions

We have just seen the first way to navigate in "LibreCAD". We can use the mouse wheel to zoom in and out of the drawing plane. This is also possible with the two commands "Zoom in" ① and "Zoom out" ②. If you have zoomed in too far, the command "Auto Zoom" ③ is very helpful. This fits the existing geometries into the active window. Try it out, zoom far into or out of the drawing plane and then press the symbol ③ or alternatively double-click on the mouse wheel. You can return to the previous view with the command "Previous View" ④. The command "Redraw" ⑤ is always helpful if display errors occur (e.g. deleted objects visible, lines duplicated, graphic errors ...). The command updates the drawing area.

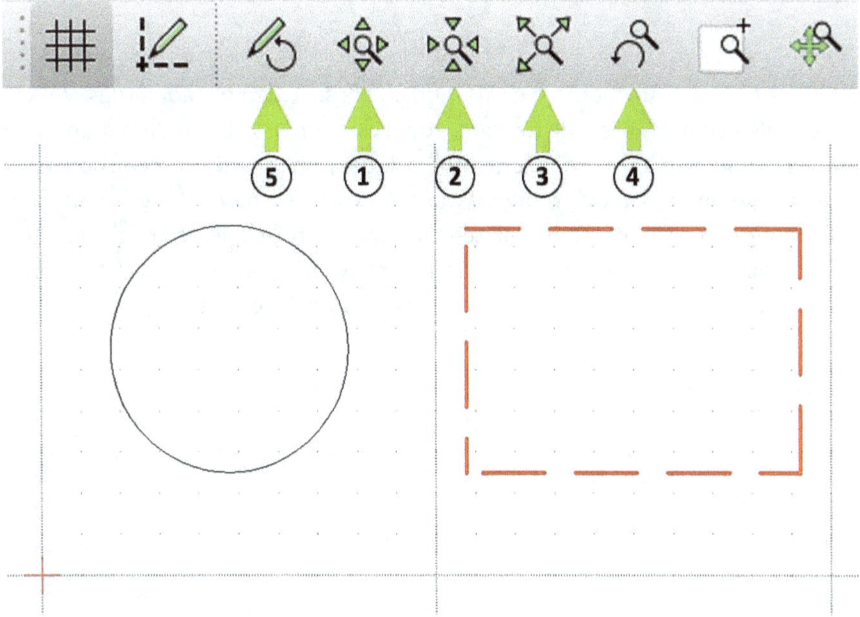

Using the command "Window Zoom" ①, you can use a rectangular selection tool to greatly enlarge a specific area — e.g. the top left-hand corner of the rectangle. This is helpful if you need to work very precisely here, for example.

And with the last command ("Zoom Panning") ② of this toolbar, you can move the drawing layer. You can also do this by holding down the mouse wheel and then moving the mouse. Make a note of this shortcut, as moving the drawing layer is an essential function that you will need regularly.

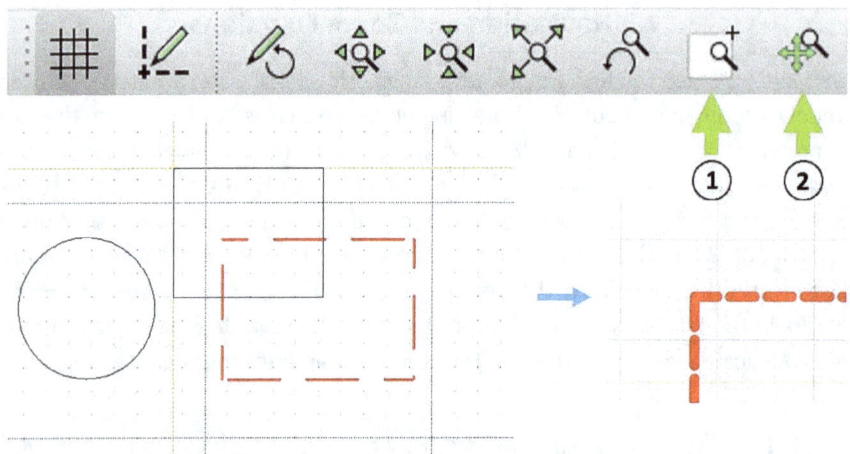

Another essential function is the selection and deselection of geometries. We can select one geometry, e.g. the circle ①, by clicking on it. You can then simply click on the second and any other geometry ② directly afterward. The selection of the previous geometries remains. If you want to deselect a particular geometry, you can simply click on it again. We can see that a geometry is selected by the fact that it then has a dashed line shape. If you want to end the entire selection of all geometries, press the ESC key and all geometries will be deselected.

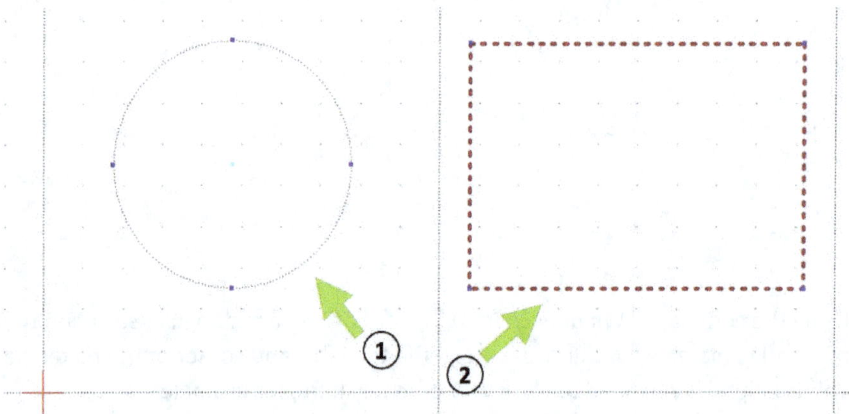

If we want to select many geometries that are close to each other in an area, we can open a selection window. We do this by holding down the left mouse button and then making a dragging movement with the mouse. There are two different options for the dragging movement. If we move the mouse to the right, we get a blue selection window, whereas if we move the mouse to the left, we get a green selection window. These two directions allow a different selection. Moving the mouse to the right (blue window) selects only those geometries that are completely within the blue window. Moving the mouse to the left selects all geometries of which at least one part is located within the green window.

Let's take a look at these different options using examples. If we draw the blue selection window completely around the circle and rectangle (hold down the left mouse button and move the mouse from top left to bottom right), then both geometries ① will be selected. If only the rectangle is completely within the blue selection window ②, then only the rectangle is selected in this case, even if part of the circle is also in the blue window. If none of the geometries are completely within the blue selection window, nothing is selected in this case (③ and ④).

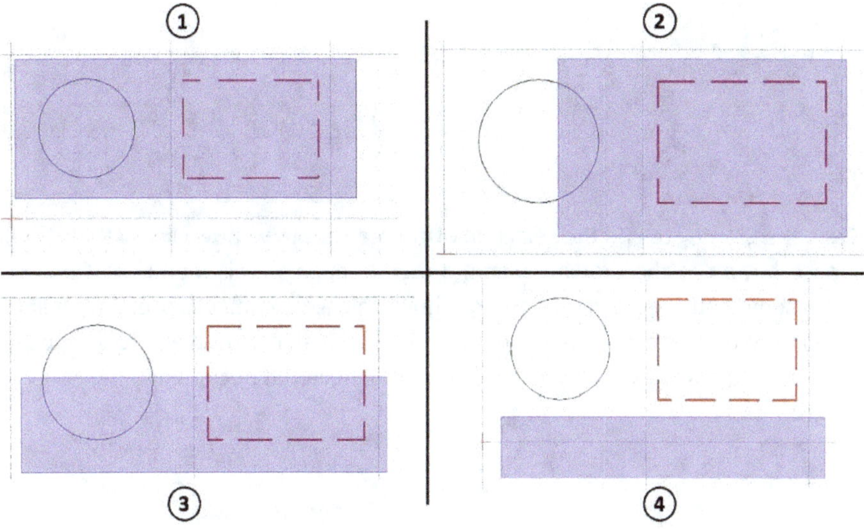

With the green selection window (hold down the left mouse button and move the mouse from bottom right to top left), both geometries are also selected if both are completely within the selection window ①. However, the green window also selects all geometries, of which only one part is in the selection window (② and ③). If there is nothing within the selection window, nothing is selected ④.

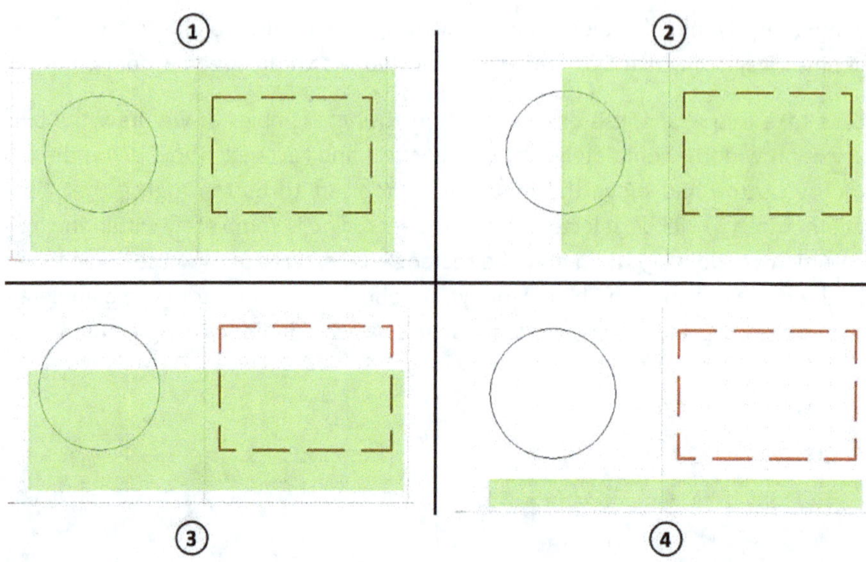

Press the ESC key to end the selection of geometries. If we now click with the right mouse button in the drawing plane, a menu appears. This menu changes with every command executed, as it always shows the last commands used. It is helpful if you want to use several commands in quick succession. However, it only appears if you have already executed a qualified command in the document.

Classic program commands such as cut, copy and paste can be found in the "Edit Toolbar". To copy an already created geometry, we select it ① and then click on the "Copy" icon ②. Now we need to select a reference point for copying the geometry. The reference point will later be used to determine the position of the copy. The center of the circle is a good choice here, so we click on it ③. Then select the "Paste" icon ④ and click again ⑤ to place the copy anywhere on the drawing plane. As you can now see, the circle is positioned based on the center point (previous reference point). This process works identically for the command "Cut" ⑥. The only difference here is that no copy is created, but that the geometry is cut out.

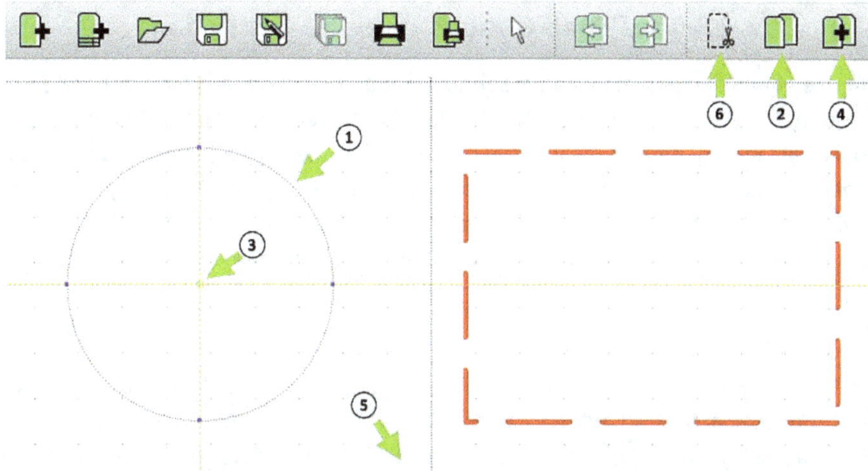

If you use these commands frequently, it is a good idea to memorize the corresponding keyboard shortcuts. The shortcut for copying is CTRL+C, for pasting CTRL+V and for cutting CTRL+X (identical to other programs, e.g. "MS Word"). A reference point must also be selected when using the shortcuts.

Other icons in the menu bar are self-explanatory. However, we will briefly go through them for the sake of completeness. The icons for "Undo" and "Redo" (① and ②) can be used to undo or repeat actions. The cursor symbol ③ can be used to activate the mouse cursor. There are three options for the save process, "Save..." ④, "Save ... as" ⑤ and "Save all" ⑥. You can therefore either save only the active document under the existing name ④, save the active document under a different name ⑤ or save all active documents ⑥ in "LibreCAD". <u>Important note</u>: Save your documents regularly and at short intervals, as "LibreCAD" occasionally crashes.

A new document can be created with the ⑦ symbol, and an existing file can be opened with the ⑧ symbol. The keyboard shortcut for undoing is CTRL+Z, for saving CTRL+S and for opening a file CTRL+O. We will cover the remaining symbols later on.

2.4 The "Snap Options" and the Restrictions

In this chapter, we come to an essential toolbar. Let's take a closer look at "Snap Options" and "Restrictions". This toolbar is located in "LibreCAD" below the drawing layer by default. As already mentioned at the beginning, you can select a specific snapping mode here, which makes it easier to place geometry elements exactly. For example, you can select that the starting point of a new line should snap exactly to the center of an existing line and much more. Let's take a look at this in detail.

The first "Snap Option" is "Free Snap" ①. Activate the option by clicking on the icon ①, it will then become slightly darker. The change in contrast shows that the option is active. Several options can be active at the same time. For example, if you draw a line (② and ③) consisting of two points, you can use "Free Snap" to place these points freely on the drawing plane without the cursor ④ getting stuck on grid points or other geometries.

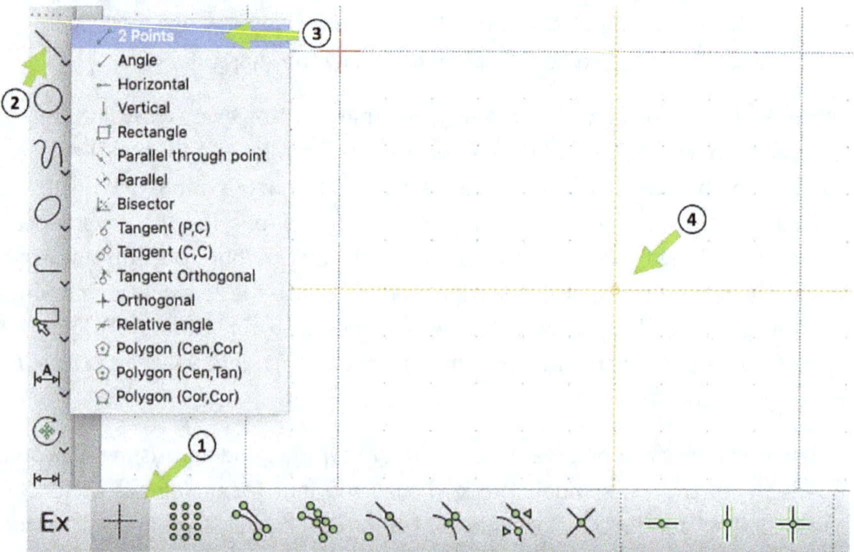

Create the line by clicking twice on the drawing plane at any distance. Then click the right mouse button to remain in the line command, but you can reselect the starting point. Otherwise, the next line would start directly at the end point of the first line. Clicking on ESC would exit the command, but we <u>won't</u> do that for now.

Instead, we now change the "Snap Option" to "Snap on grid" ① by selecting the grid symbol (deactivate the previously activated symbol "Free Snap" by clicking on it). If we are now still in the line command, we can see that the mouse cursor ② remains magnetically attached to the grid points ③ when moving in the drawing plane. We can now only select the grid points, but nothing in between.

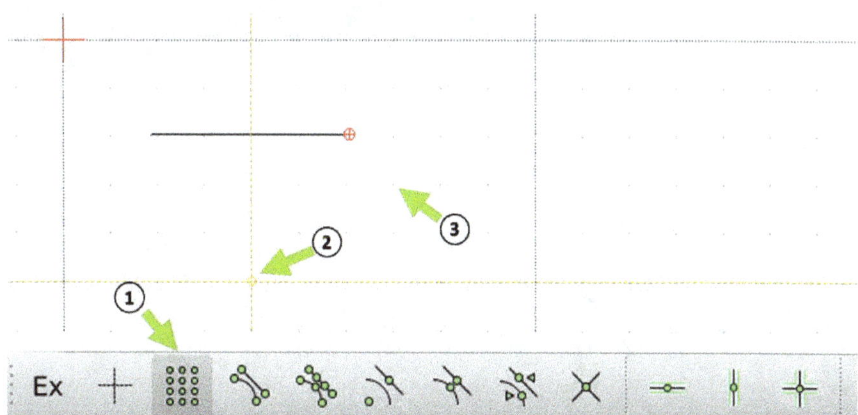

The advantage of this is that we are guided through the grid when drawing. For example, with a "Grid Status" of "10/100", we can easily draw a vertical line three units long by leaving two grid points free between the start and end points of the line. Then right-click again. With "Free Snap", drawing this line would be more difficult, as we cannot hit the grid points so precisely freehand.

The next symbol "Snap on Endpoints" ① activates the magnetic snapping of an endpoint of a geometry. Before we try this option, we deactivate the previous option "Snap on grid". If we now draw a line, we will notice that the mouse cursor only jumps back and forth between the end points of geometries (e.g. lines) when we move it. For example, we can select the end point ② of the horizontal line and the end point ③ of the vertical line. This option is always helpful if you want to select the exact end point of a geometry.

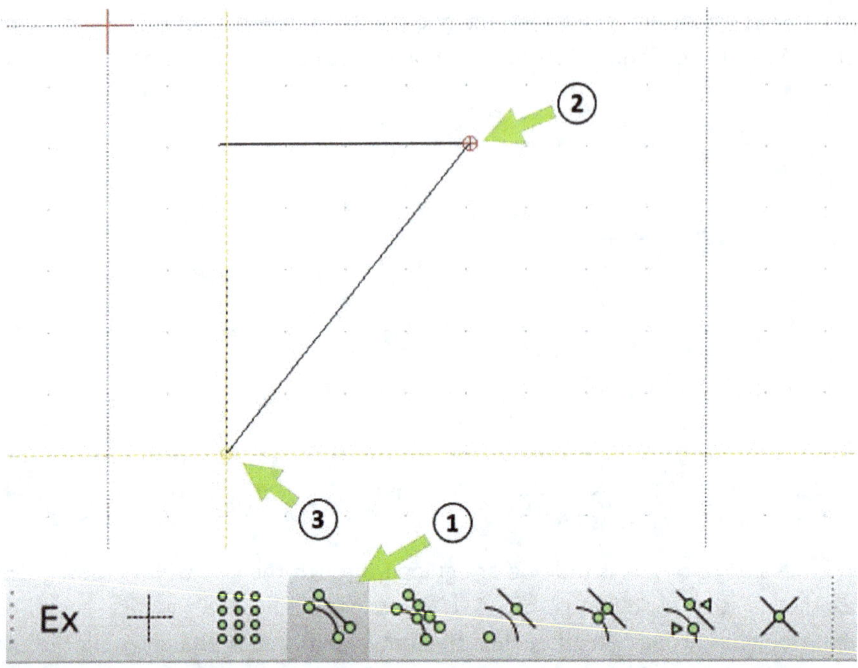

With the "Snap Options", a combination of several options is also possible, e.g. we can select "Free Snap" ②. If we do this, the mouse cursor can be moved freely in the drawing plane again. However, as soon as we come close to an end point of a geometry, the cursor is magnetically attracted to it. Just try it out!

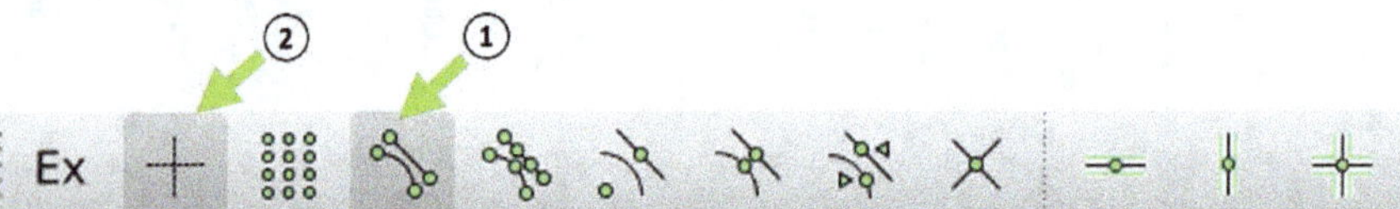

Other important "Snap Options" are "Snap on Entity" ①, "Snap Center" ② and "Snap Middle" ③. If "Snap on Entity" ① is active, the start, and end point of a geometry to be drawn (e.g. line) can only be positioned on the contour of another geometry. Please try this out yourself. If "Snap Center" ② is active, you can only set the start and end point to the center of a geometry. To try this out, you need to draw two circles, for example, then — after activating "Snap Center" — you can connect their midpoints with a line. "Snap Middle" ③ allows you to use the cursor to select the exact center of a geometry (e.g. line) as the start or end point when drawing. Just try this out too! We will skip the remaining two options, "Snap Distance" and "Snap Intersection" as we will only need them in special cases and will come back to them later.

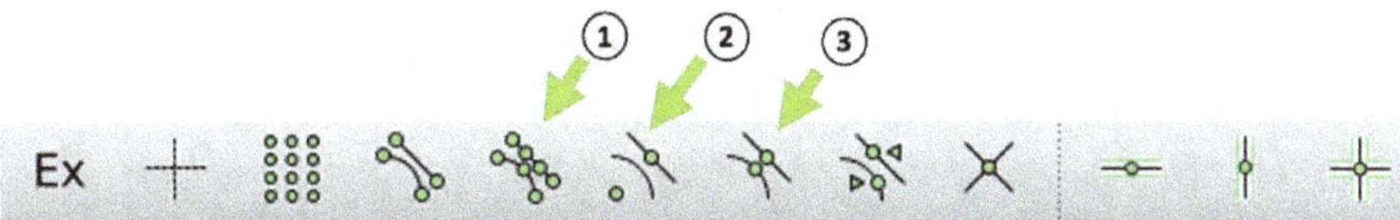

As already mentioned, several options can be active at the same time. Depending on the application and the preferences of the program user, different combinations can be used. **In the following, we will initially continue to work with the following "Snap Options" as the default setting.**

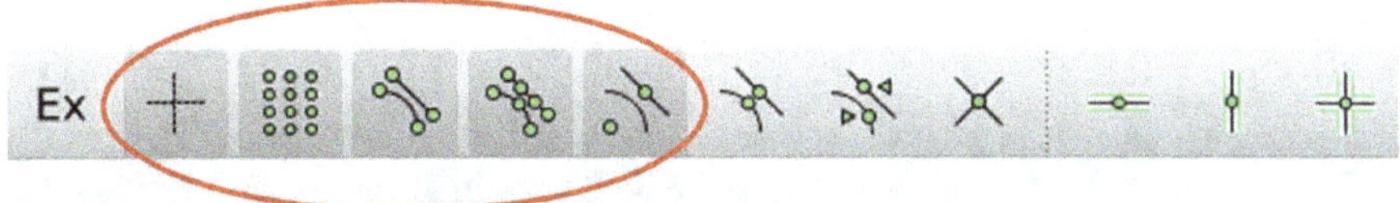

Another special feature here is the "Exclusive Snap Mode" ① (symbol "Ex"). This can be considered a kind of favorites mode. If we activate the mode, we can select a favorite, e.g. the combination of "Free Snap" and "Snap Middle" (② and ③). If we deactivate "Ex", the previously selected standard options become active again. It is a kind of switch for quickly switching between a favorite and the standard selection.

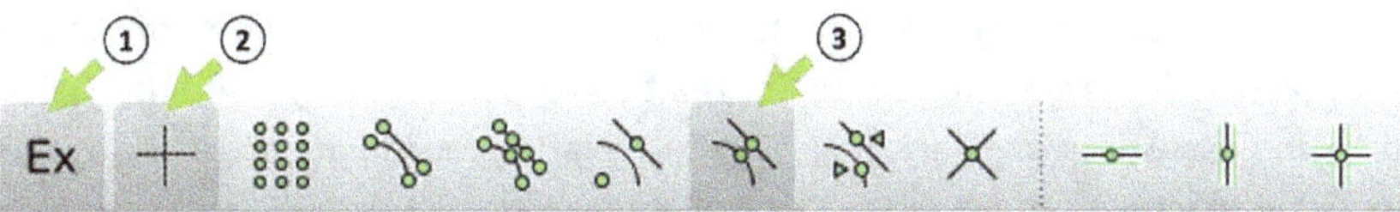

In addition to these "Snap Options", there are also three restrictions in this menu bar: horizontal, vertical and orthogonal. Orthogonal means right-angled, and is simply the combination of vertical and horizontal restrictions.

As the name suggests, these restrictions limit the movement of the mouse cursor during a drawing action. The restriction is always made in relation to the current relative coordinate origin. If, for example, we activate "Restrict Horizontal" ①, we can only move the cursor in a horizontal direction (x-axis direction) to the left or right ③ at the height of the current relative coordinate origin ② when drawing a line (command for line: "2 Points"; *see chapter 2.4*). This also works in the same way with the other two restrictions ("Restrict Vertical" ④ & "Restrict Orthogonal" ⑤).

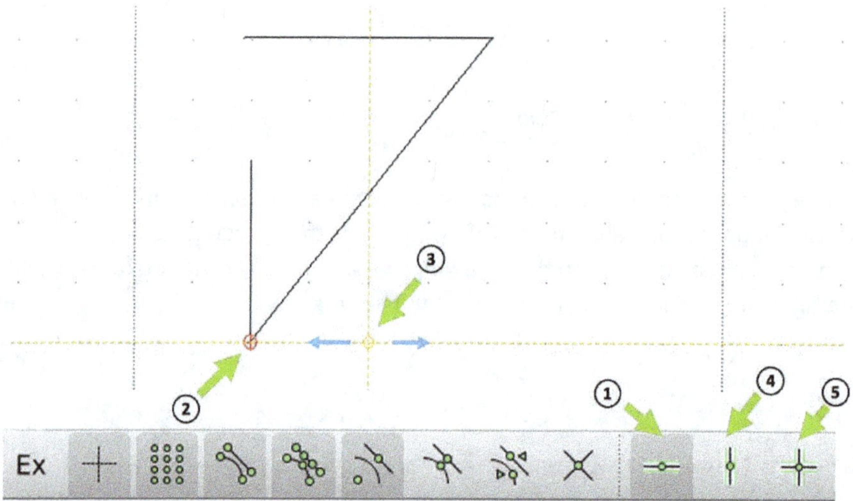

To conclude the chapter, let's take a look at two more symbols that we can also find in this bar — a little further to the right. These are the command "Set relative zero position" ① and the command "Lock relative zero position" ③. With the command "Set relative zero position" we can set the position of the current relative coordinate origin individually.

You may have noticed when drawing the lines that the relative coordinate origin (small red cross with red circle outline) always moves to the end point of the drawn line. If you activate the command "Set relative zero position" ① and then click on any point in the drawing plane (e.g. ②), the relative coordinate origin is positioned here. If you activate the symbol "Lock relative zero position" ③, you can prevent the position of the relative coordinate origin from changing as you proceed.

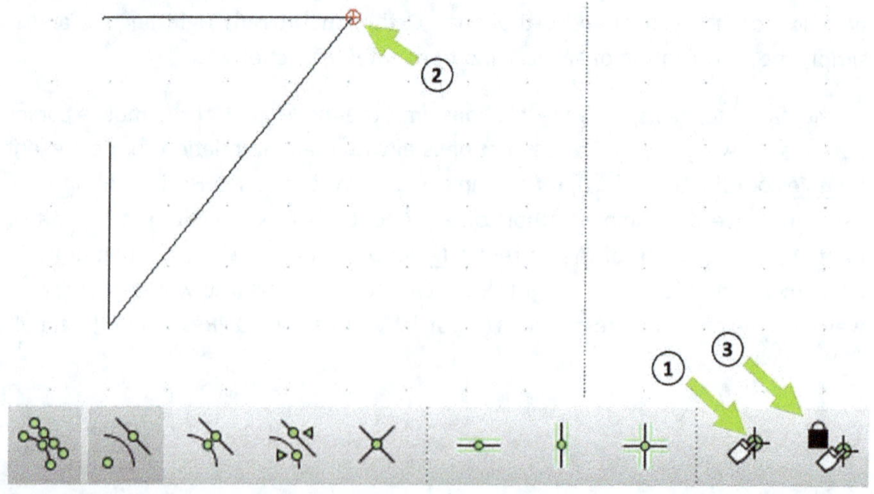

2.5 The "Select" and "Measure" Menus

Let us now look at selected commands in the two menus "Select" and "Measure". These can be found in the CAD toolbar on the left-hand side of the program window.

In the menu "Select" (1), you can select all geometries in the drawing layer (2) and then deselect them again (3). Alternatively, you can use the keyboard shortcut CTRL+A to select and the ESC key to deselect all elements.

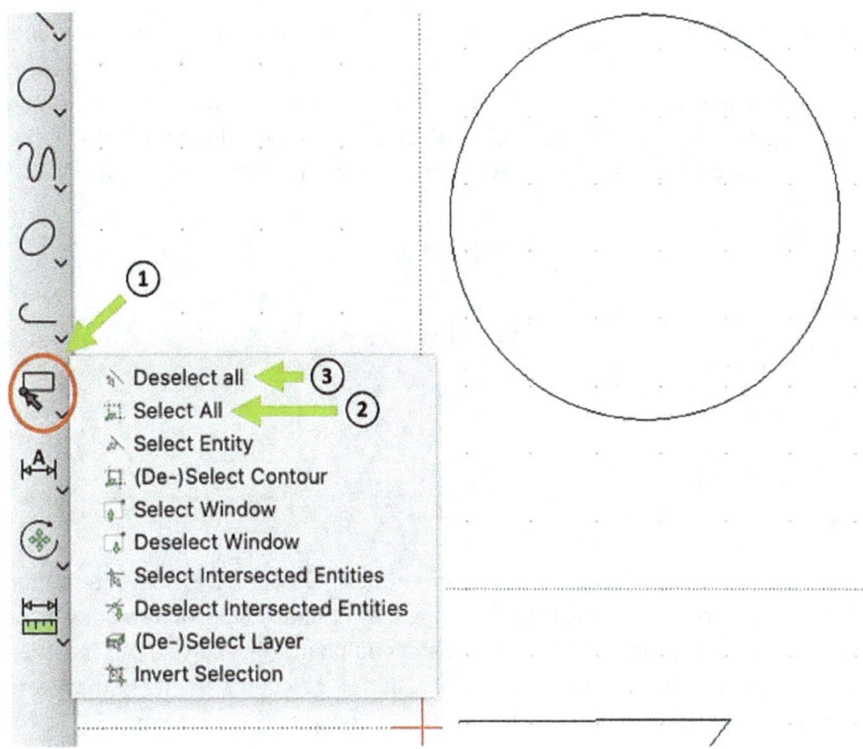

With "Select Entity" (2), you can select a geometry (e.g. a circle, a line). As we already know, this is also possible with a simple click on the geometry — without prior command selection. With "(De-)Select Contour" (3) you can select a contour, e.g. a curve, by clicking on just one line of it. If, for example, you click on a line of a geometry composed of several individual lines after selecting the command, the entire contour (i.e., all lines) is selected. If you were to click on the line without the command, only this particular line would be selected. Try them both out!

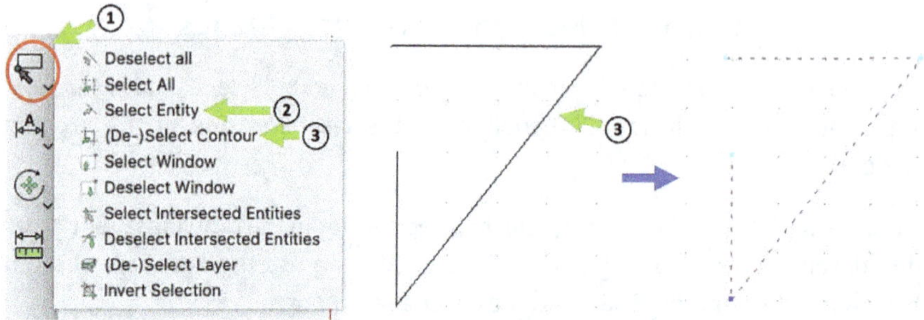

The blue and green selection windows can be created with the two commands "Select Window" ② and "Deselect Window" ③. However, we have already created the selection window ("Select Window") without commands — by simply clicking and dragging with the mouse. What is more interesting here is the option of using these windows to deselect geometry elements ("Deselect Window").

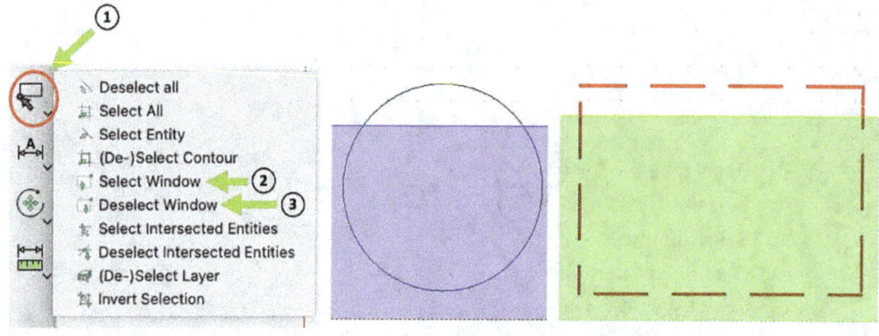

The two commands "Select Intersected Entities" ② and "Deselect Intersected Entities" ③ are interesting. After selecting the command ②, you can draw a line with the mouse using two points (start and end point; ④ and ⑤). After setting the end point, this line disappears again, but all geometry elements that were previously intersected by the line are now selected. The command ③ for deselection works in the same way.

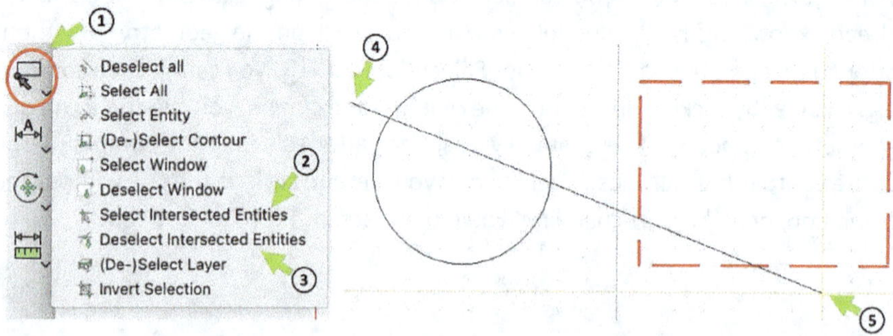

At the beginning of the course, *Chapter 1.3* briefly explained that you can create several layers in "LibreCAD", e.g. to draw a different category on each layer. With the command "(De-)Select Layer" ② you can click on <u>one</u> geometry in the drawing layer and thereby select <u>all</u> geometries on the respective layer. If you click on the selected geometry again, you can deselect <u>all</u> geometries on the layer.

The command "Invert Selection" can also be very helpful ③. If, for example, you want to select all geometries in the drawing layer apart from one or more, proceed as follows. First, click on the geometries <u>that are not</u> to be selected later and then apply the command ③, which exactly inverts the selection of geometries.

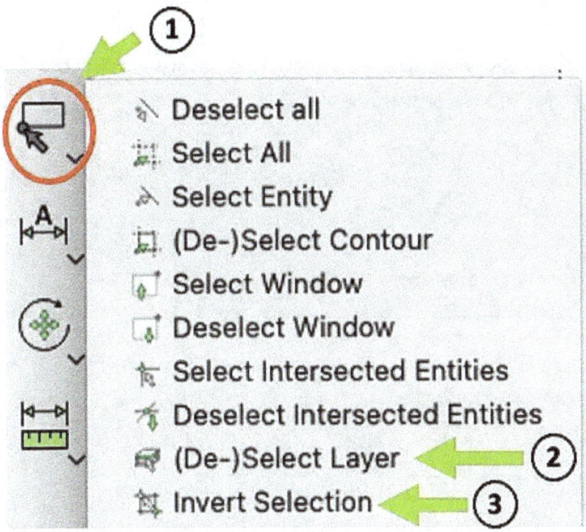

To conclude this chapter, let's look at the commands in the menu "Measure" ①. We need this menu whenever we need a dimension between two geometry elements, an angle, or other dimensional information. This menu can easily be confused with the "Dimensions" ② menu, which we will look at in detail later. The difference is that "Measure" is only used for quick information during the drawing process, and "Dimensions" is used to create actual dimensions on the drawing. Imagine you were measuring on a scaled paper drawing with a ruler or protractor, then you would use the commands from the "Measure" menu. However, if you measure the dimension or angle <u>and</u> then mark it on the drawing with a pencil using dimension lines, you would use the range of functions of "Dimensions".

If we use commands from the "Measure" menu, the information such as length and angle is displayed in the "Command line" window ③, which is located on the right-hand side of the program by default. Let's take a look at how this works.

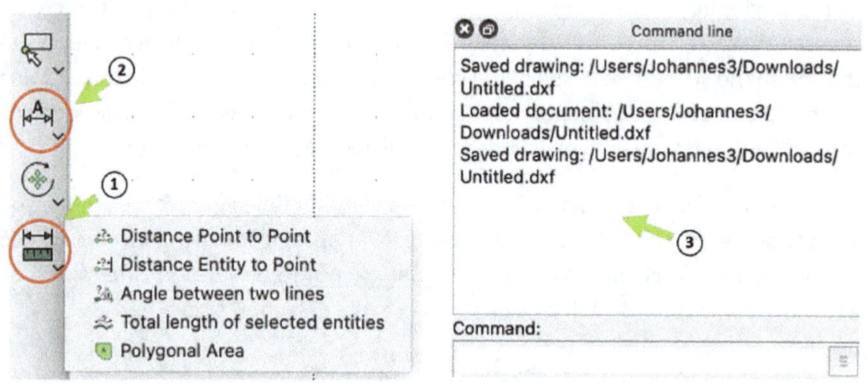

Please draw the following lines and a circle so that we can try out the commands. It is sufficient if it looks something like this.

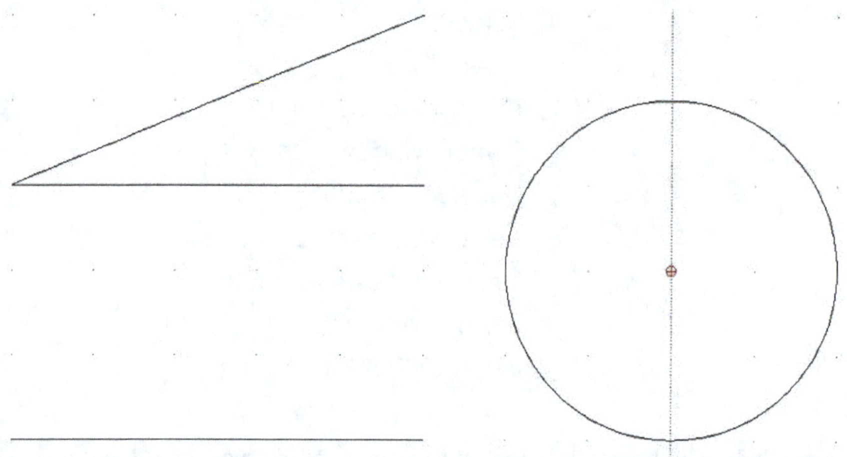

With the command "Distance Point to Point" ① we can measure the distance between two points. The program always gives us the direct distance between the points, i.e., if the points are <u>not</u> aligned, the measurement is diagonal. In our case, however, the points are in a vertical alignment, which is why we get the perpendicular distance here. After selecting the command ①, we simply click on the points (③ and ④) one after the other whose distance we want to measure.

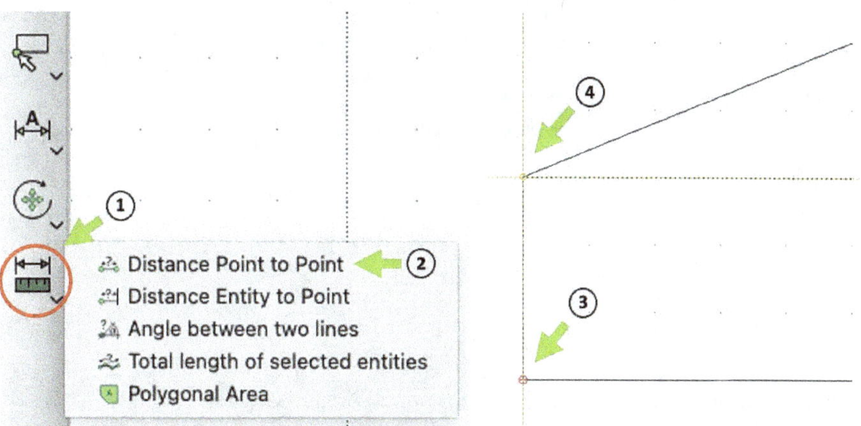

We receive the distance between the two points (longitude) as well as the coordinates in the Cartesian and polar coordinate systems in the next command line. The unit results from the settings (previous chapters).

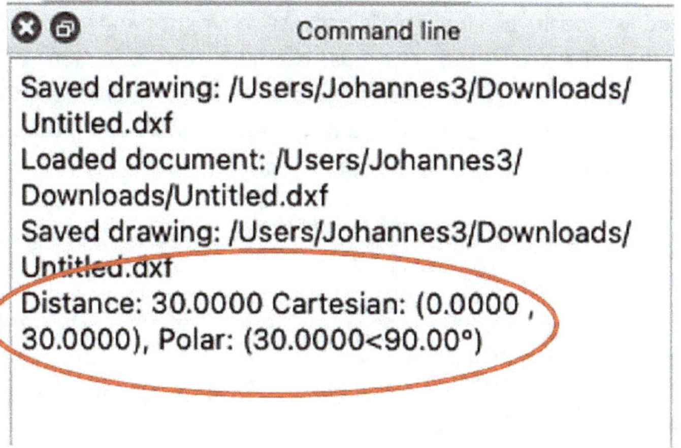

For example, if we need the distance between a geometric object ("Entity"; e.g. circle, rectangle, triangle...) and a point, we select the command "Distance Entity to Point" ②. To apply the command, we first click on the object, e.g. on the contour ③ of a circle and then, for example, on the end point ④ of a line. The shortest distance between the contour of the circle and the end point of the line is then displayed in the command window ⑤ in the next command line (here: "Distance: 16.0555").

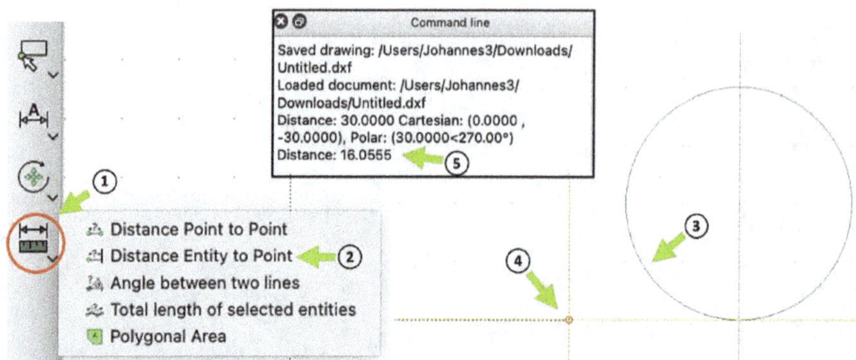

Angles can be measured with the command "Angle between two lines" ②. The click sequence is relevant here. If you click on the upper line ③ and then on the lower line ④ after selecting the command, e.g. clockwise, the value of the internal angle (-21.80°) is displayed as negative and the value of the external angle (338.20°) as positive in the command window ⑤. However, if you first click on the lower line ④ and then on the upper line ③, only the internal angle ⑥ is displayed as a positive value. This is because in a right-handed coordinate system (right-hand rule from the previous chapter), the direction of rotation is counterclockwise ⑦. You can also remember this by stretching the thumb of your right hand towards your body. If you now want to grasp an object with this hand using the other fingers, you will get the direction of rotation.

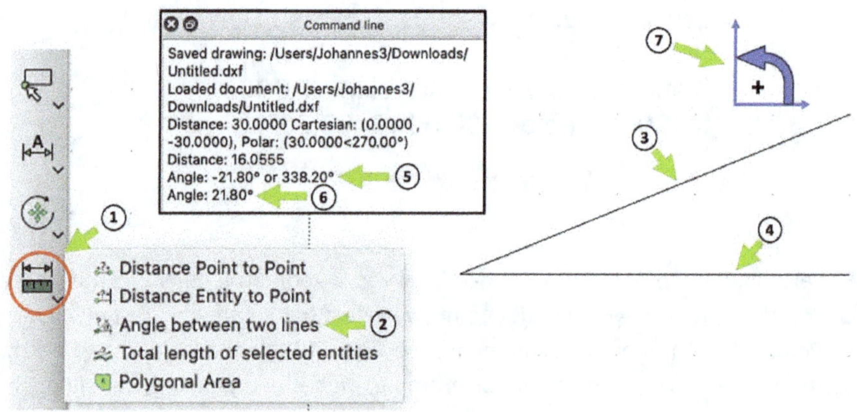

The command "Total length of selected entities" specifies the length or circumference of one or more geometric objects. After selecting the command ② and clicking on an object ③, the total length — in this case the circumference — of the circle contour is displayed in the lower status bar of "LibreCAD". However, this is <u>not</u> displayed in the command bar.

You can also select several objects, in which case the respective lengths of the geometries are added together, and the total is displayed in the status bar.

As you may have noticed, this also works without activating the command (normal selection of a geometry).

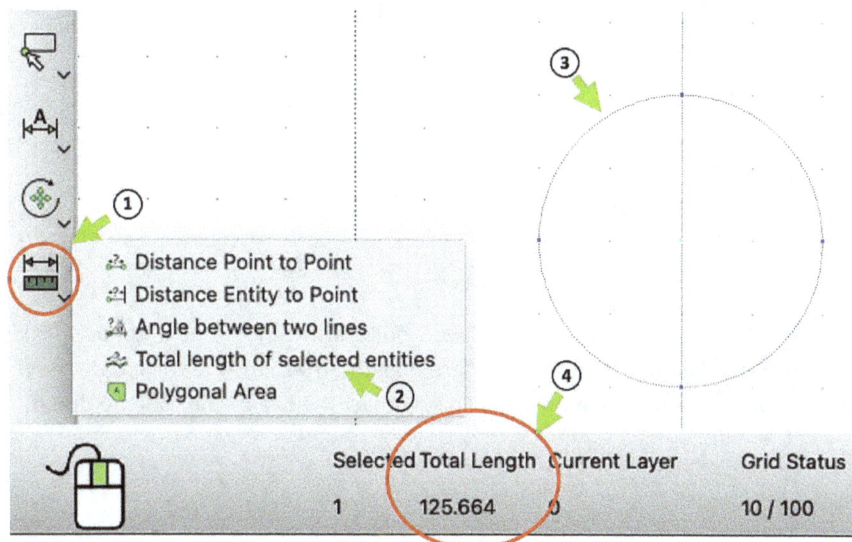

The last command in the menu "Measure" is called "Polygonal Area" ②. This allows you to span a polygon ③ and obtain the area of the polygon and its circumference in the command window ④. The values in the command window ④ change continuously as you draw the polygon.

A polygon is a closed object consisting of several lines and with several corner points. The simplest polygon is the triangle, followed by the quadrilateral, pentagon, hexagon and so on. When you have drawn enough corners, simply right-click and the polygon will disappear, as it only consisted of auxiliary lines for the measuring process.

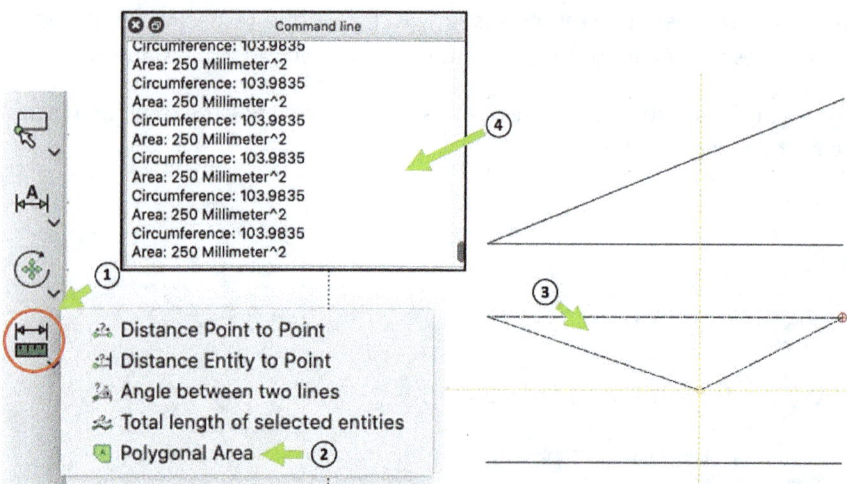

Perfect! We have now already achieved quite a lot. In the next chapter of the course, we will deal with drawing different geometries, and we will create the first two simple projects. Make sure you stick with it. The basics will soon be done!

3 Drawing Tools and Projects

3.1 Creating Simple and Complex Geometric Shapes

In this chapter, we will first familiarize ourselves with some selected drawing commands in the CAD toolbar of the program and then draw two practical examples.

Important commands in the menu "Lines":

Let's start with the category "Lines" (1), which contains all line-like geometries. Before we do this, we first open a new document by clicking on the button "New" (2).

We have already learned how to create a simple line using the command "2 Points" (3).

You can draw a horizontal line with the command "Horizontal" (4). The advantage here is that the two fields "Length" (5) and "Snap Point" (6) appear in the menu bar. At "Length" (5) you can set the desired length of the line before drawing, e.g. 10 units. If we now look at the small preview image (7) of the command in detail, we notice that a line with a small green dot is displayed here. The small green dot is the snap point, which is used to place the line on the drawing plane using the mouse cursor.

In the command settings, you can select either "Start", "Middle" or "End" for "Snap Point" (6). Depending on the selection, the point with which we set the line to the drawing layer will either be at the start of the line (left point; selection "Start"), in the middle (selection "Middle") or at the end of the line (right point; selection "End").

If you switch off the drawing grid (8) and zoom very closely into the drawing area, you can see the horizontal, black, ten-unit-long line (9) behind the yellow cursor cross. The circle (yellow here) is at the right end of the line, as the option "End" is selected at "Snap Point" (6). Set the line down with a click, then press the right mouse button and then try the options "Middle" and "Start", then you will immediately recognize the difference.

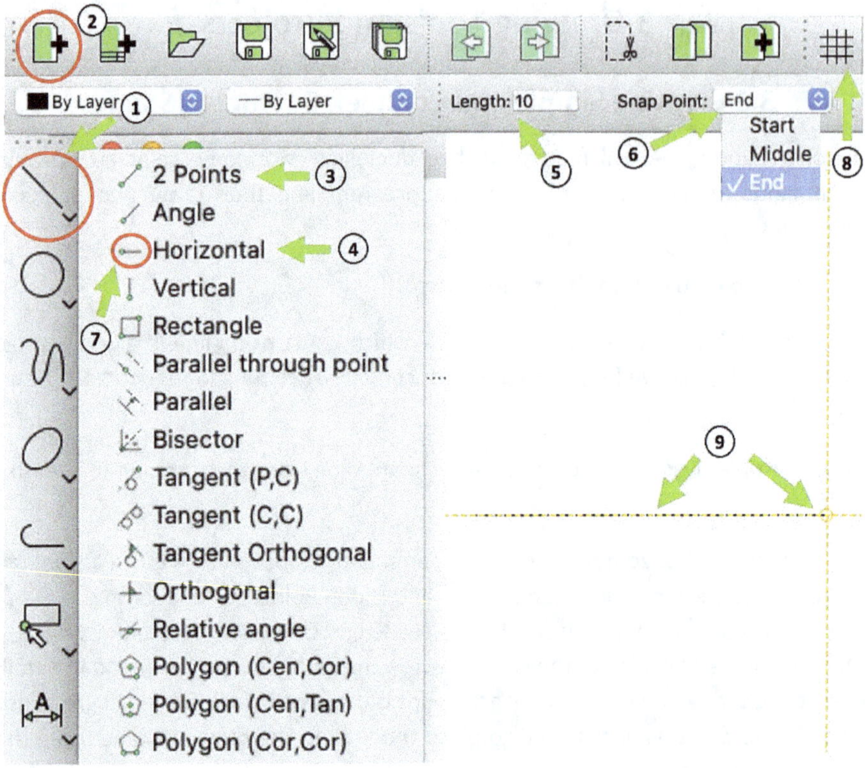

This method also applies to many other commands. For example, you can use the command "Vertical" ② to create a vertical line in the same way. Let's create a 5 mm long ③, vertical line whose snap point is set at the start of the line ④. For example, we place the line at the right end point ⑤ of the horizontal line.

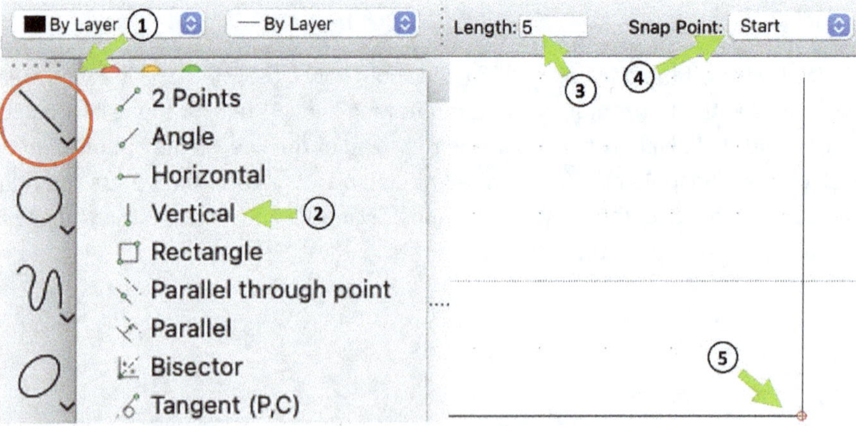

We already know how to draw a rectangle with the command "Rectangle" from the previous chapter. Next, let's take a look at the "Angle" command, which we can use to draw a line at a defined angle. If we click on the command ①, the field "Angle" ② appears in the menu bar. Here we enter the desired angle. As explained in the previous chapter, the direction of rotation is counterclockwise.

The fields "Length" ③ and "Snap Point" ④ are also available for this command. For example, we can place the line at the left end point ⑤ of the horizontal line.

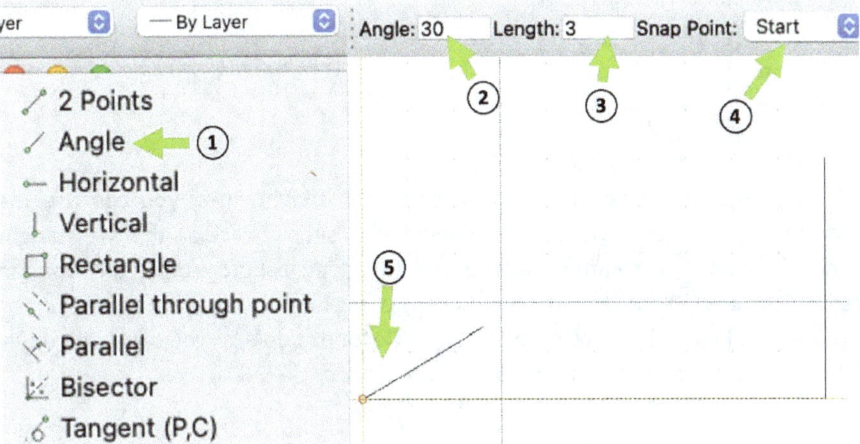

An interesting command is the "Parallel through point" command, which can be used to draw one or more parallel lines by specifying a point.

This works as follows. After selecting the command ①, the field "Number" ② appears in the menu bar, in which you enter the number of parallel lines. For example, we want to create three lines parallel to the vertical line that we drew previously. We therefore increase the number to 3 ② and then click on the vertical line ③. Now we need to define a point, which in this case specifies the distance between the parallel lines in the horizontal direction (x-axis). This can be a grid point further to the left, for example ④. This gives us three lines that are parallel and at the same distance from the vertical line ③. You are also welcome to try selecting a different distance.

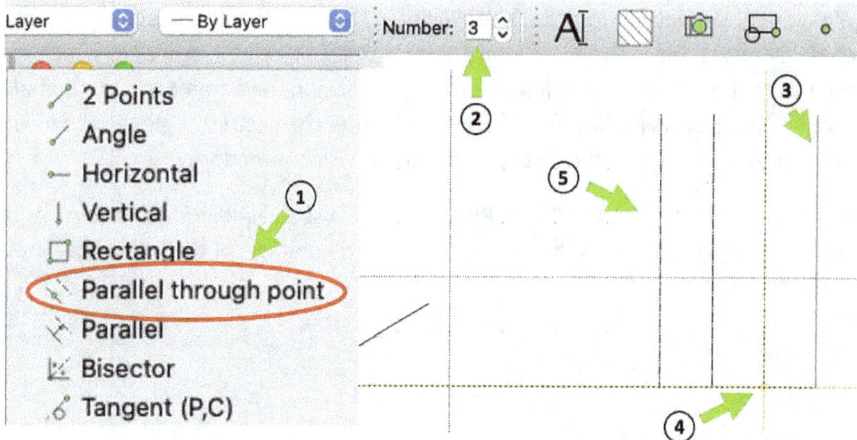

If you need the angle bisector between two straight lines, you can use the command "Bisector" ①. This command is very simple: click on the two straight lines (④ and ⑤) one after the other to form an angle. Before doing this, you can set the length ② and even the number ③ of the angle bisectors in the menu bar. This is very helpful if you want to draw a clock, for example, as you can then quickly draw the lines for hours and minutes in the clock circle (360°).

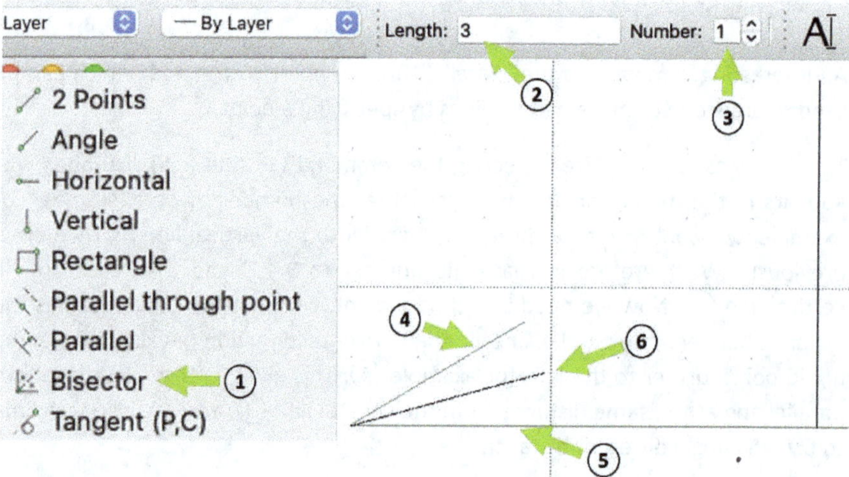

The command "Orthogonal" can be used to create a perpendicular (vertical line) on another line. To do this, after selecting the command ①, you must first specify the length ②, e.g. 2, and then define a baseline ③ and a point ④. This gives you a line that is aligned at an angle of 90° to the baseline.

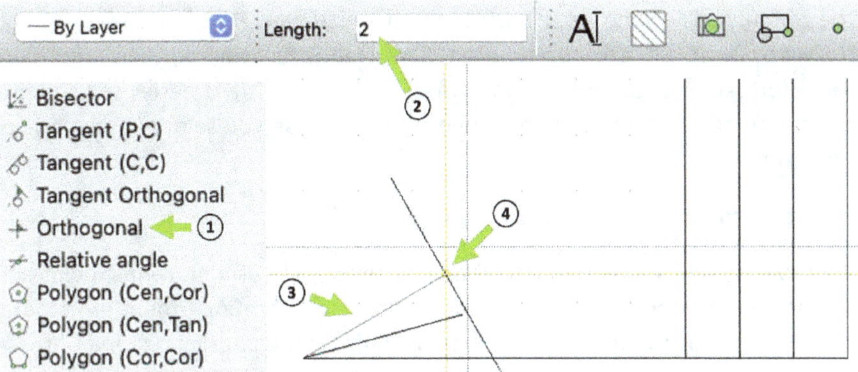

A both important and simple command is "Polygon (Cen,Cor)". Using this command, we can draw any polygon. As we already know from the previous chapter, the simplest polygon is the triangle (three corners). However, we can also draw a hexagon, for example, by increasing the number to six corners after selecting the command ① in the field "Number" ②. We then define the center of the polygon (the "Cen" in the command name is the abbreviation for "Center") by clicking anywhere in the drawing plane. Finally, we determine the point of one of the corners (the "Cor" in the name of the command stands for "Corner") and this creates the polygon. Always remember that the individual steps after selecting a command are displayed in the status bar ⑤ in the lower area of "LibreCAD" to help you.

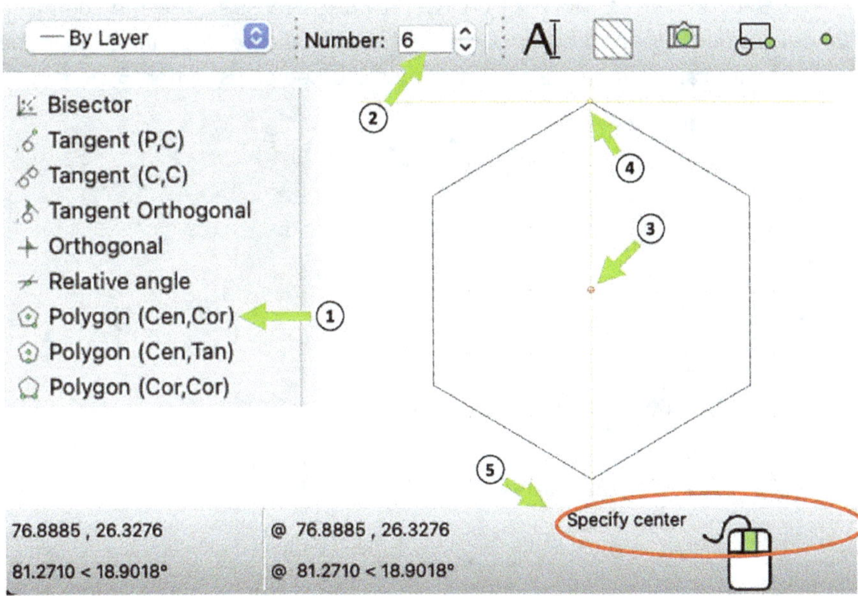

The command "Polygon" also exists in the two variants "Polygon (Cen, Tan)" and "Polygon (Cor, Cor)". The abbreviation "Tan" stands for tangent, "Cen" and "Cor" stand for center and corner. Sometimes, for example, it is easier to span the polygon using a tangent or two corners, in which case you select "(Cor, Cor)" or "(Cen, Tan)".

Important commands in the menu "Circles":

We have already learned how to draw a simple circle using a center point and another point in one of the previous chapters. In "LibreCAD" there are several other commands for drawing circles. Depending on the application, one of these commands may be most suitable. For example, try drawing two circles of the same size next to each other by using the command "2 Points" ① for the first circle ② and the command "3 Points" ③ for the second circle ④.

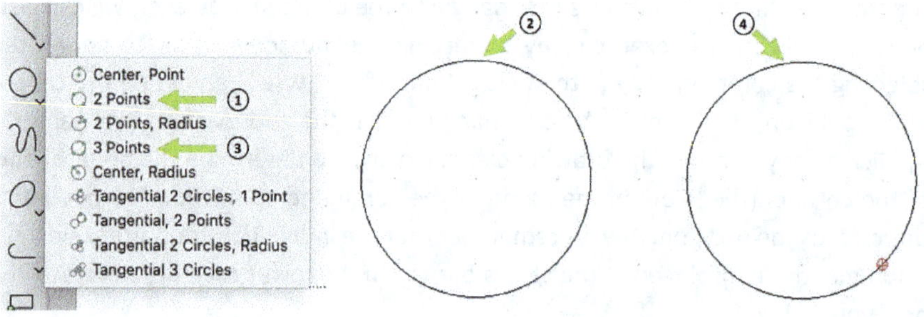

If we already know the radius of a circle, it makes sense to use the command "Center, Radius" ① for drawing. Once we have set the desired radius ② in the menu bar, we can position the circle as required based on its center ③.

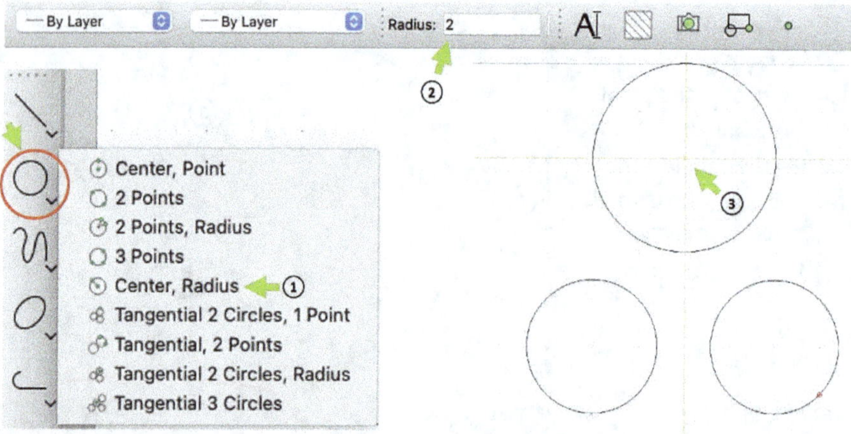

The command "Tangential 2 Circles, 1 Point" is helpful if you want to draw a circle that is tangential to two other circles. Tangential means that one geometry touches another at only one point. After selecting the command ①, simply select the two existing circles (② and ③) and then define a point ④ to define the size of the tangential circle.

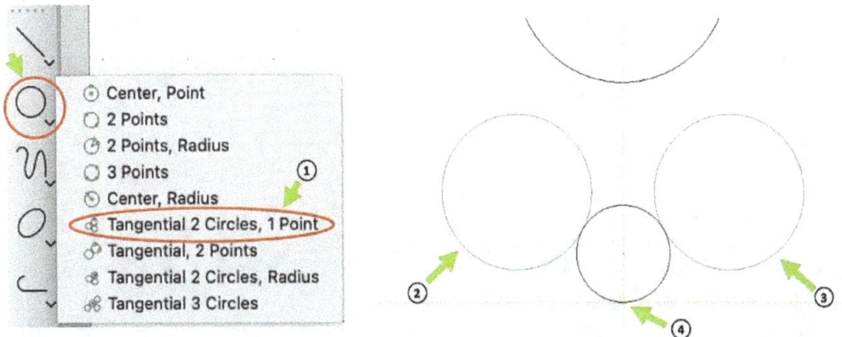

Often you also need a tangent between two circles. To do this, we need to go back to the CAD menu "Lines" ①. Here we find the commands "Tangent (P,C)" and "Tangent (C,C)". "P" stands for "Point" and "C" stands for "Circle". For the desired tangent between two circles, we use the command "Tangent (C,C)" ② and then click on the two circles (③ and ④). Depending on where we click on the circles, the tangent ⑤ is generated. There is not just one possible tangent here. Try it out by clicking on different points of the two circles. With the command "Tangent (P,C)", on the other hand, you first select a point and then a circle.

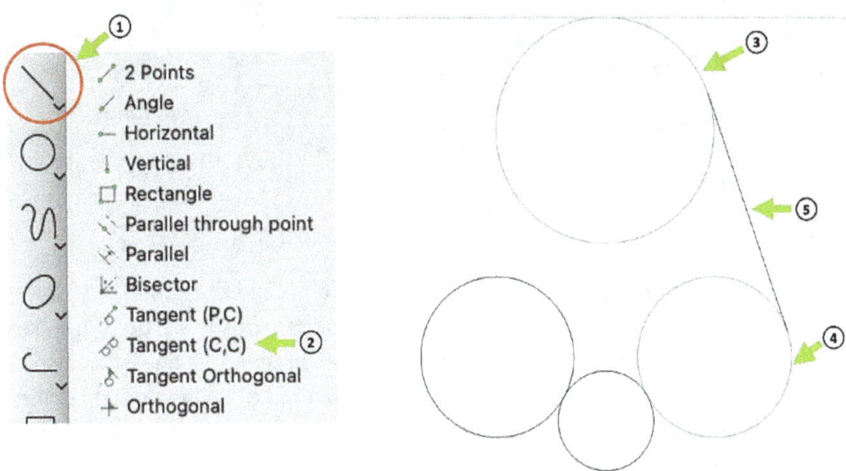

Important commands in the menu "Freehand":

An important command from this menu ① is "3 Points" ②. This allows you to draw a 3-point arc. As the name suggests, this consists of three points that are defined one after the other by clicking in the drawing plane (③ - ⑤).

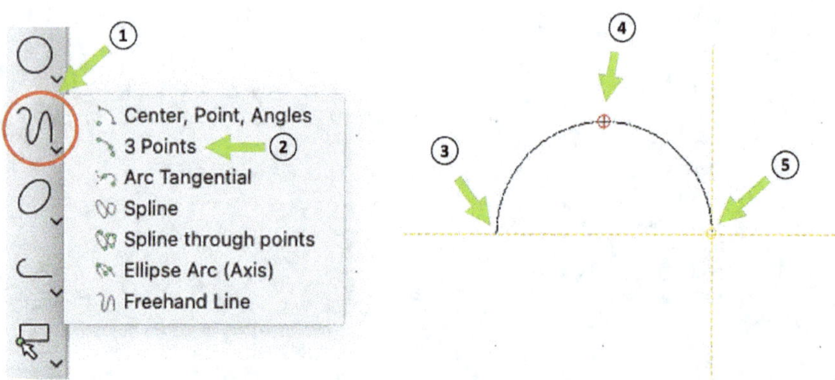

If you need a tangential arc, use "Arc Tangential". With the 3-point arc already drawn, you can use this to connect a tangential arc, for example, by first clicking on the arc, then moving the mouse cursor to the right and finally selecting an end point for the arc by clicking in the drawing plane.

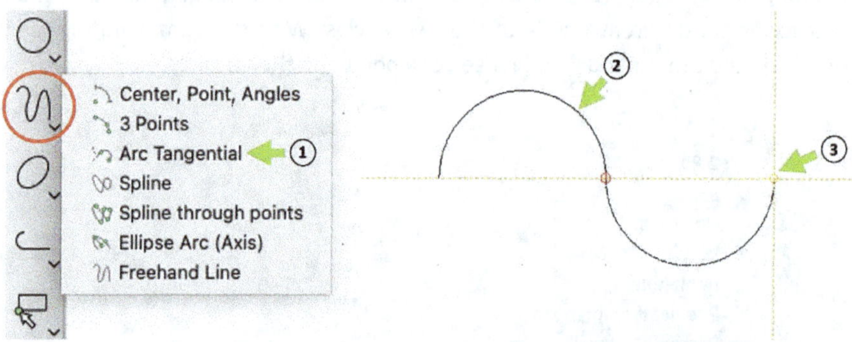

When creating more complex geometries, you often need the command "Spline" or alternatively the command "Spline through points". This is a type of freehand curve that is defined using several points. With the command "Spline", these points are set freehand during the command. With the command "Spline through points", on the other hand, you can create a curve from existing points. Let's just try this.

For the "Spline" command, we first deactivate almost all "Snap Options" ①, as otherwise we will not be able to draw freely. After selecting the command ②, we place several points in the drawing plane one after the other (③, ④, ⑤...). To create the curve, click the right mouse button after the last point. Depending on what is set in the menu bar at "Degree" ⑥, a different curvature shape will result. You can also create a closed curve here with the option "Closed" ⑦. Please try it all once.

If you would also like to try the command "Spline through points", you must first create a few points. The command for this can be found in the menu bar ⑧. Once the points have been created, it is best to activate "Snap on Endpoints" in the "Snap Options" and only then the command "Spline through points". Now you can easily select the points and create the curve.

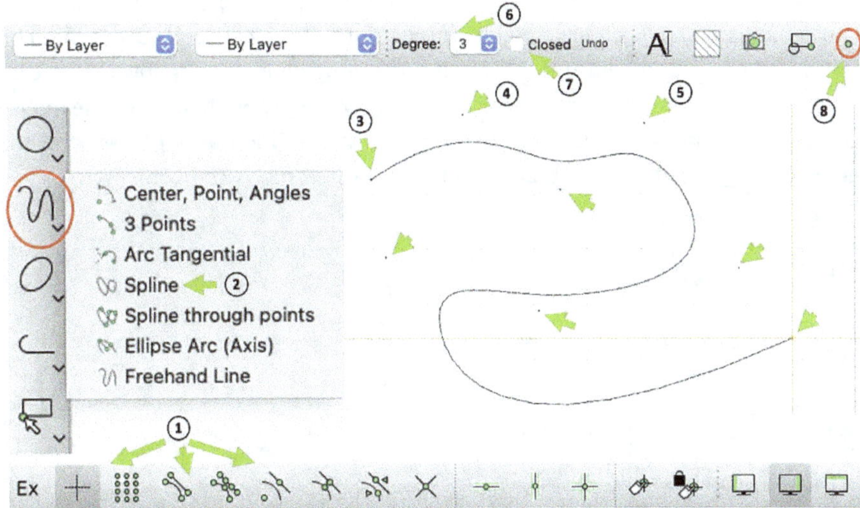

Important commands in the menu "Ellipses":

In this menu, you will find several commands that can be used to draw an ellipse in different ways. The appearance of an ellipse can be defined using a vertical and horizontal axis, a center, several points or other shapes.

For example, let's try the command "Ellipse (Axis)" ②. To do this, we must first define the center of the ellipse by clicking on the drawing plane ③. Then we move the mouse cursor to the right, for example, to define the first axis (horizontal ellipse axis) and click as soon as we have reached the desired size ④. We then move the mouse cursor upwards to define the second axis (vertical ellipse axis) and click again as soon as we have reached the desired size ⑤.

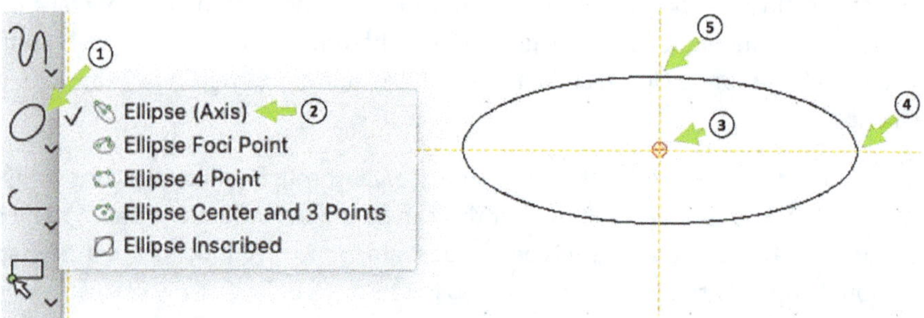

In this context, the command "Ellipse Foci Point" ② is also very helpful, with which you can create an ellipse based on its focal points. The focal points are located on the main axis of the ellipse (longer axis). The procedure is as follows: First click twice on the drawing plane at any distance (③ and ④) and then move the mouse cursor up/down ⑤ or sideways (depending on the orientation) to expand the ellipse. The geometry is created with a final click (left mouse button).

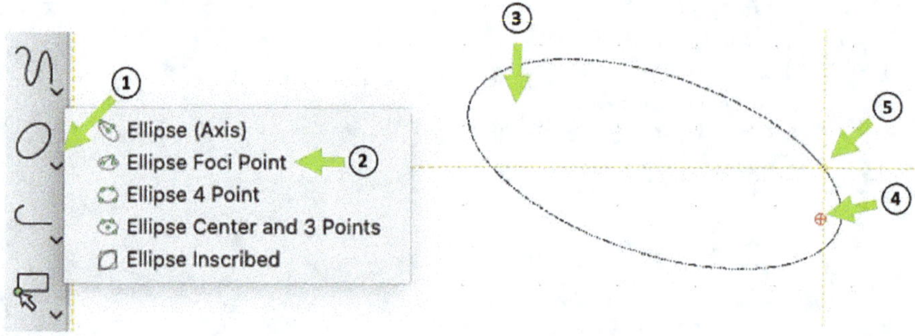

These were the most important commands for creating geometries with the CAD toolbar. We have not covered all the commands in this chapter, but the most important commands that are frequently used. Now we will draw two small projects to apply the commands we have learned.

3.2 Drawing Project 1: Floor Plan of an Apartment

The first drawing project we create is the floor plan of a student apartment. To do this, we create a new document (command "New document") and set the units of the drawing in the "Current Drawing Preferences" to "Meter". We then zoom in or out of the drawing plane until we get the status "0.1/1" ①.

First, we draw the outlines of the walls and furnishings. This will help us with the planning and later when drawing the walls and their openings. We can use red ② and dashed ③ lines for this. We start with the outer walls by drawing a rectangle ④ starting at the coordinate origin ⑤ and placing it at point ⑥.

The apartment should be three meters wide and 4 meters long, so we need three full boxes in the x-direction and four full boxes in the y-direction. For the second part of the outer walls, we create another rectangle that starts at point ⑦ and ends at point ⑧. This inner rectangle is offset by one grid point from the outer rectangle so that the walls are 10 cm thick in this case. Always remember that the "Snap Options" ⑨, especially "Snap on grid" makes drawing much easier in this case.

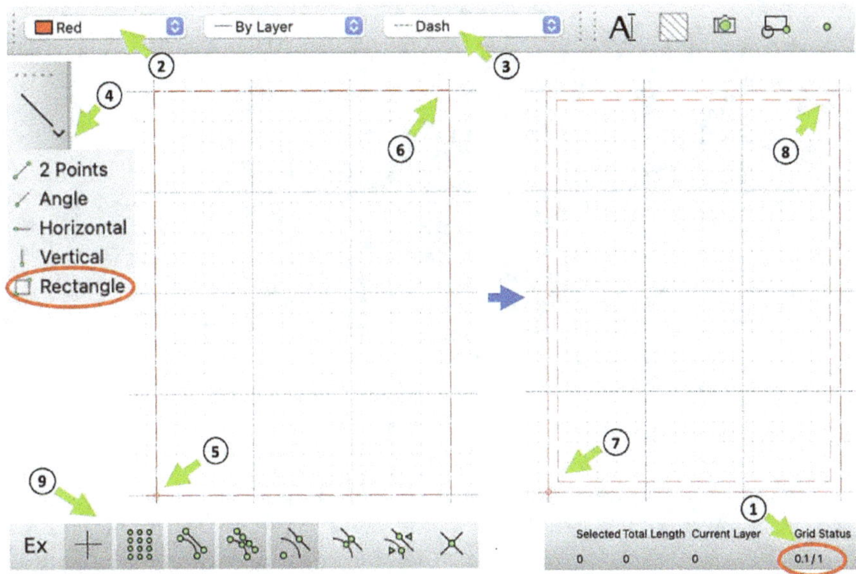

Next, we create a wall section in the lower part of the apartment to separate the kitchen area from the sleeping area, as well as a bathroom. We can also do this using rectangles.

We can stretch the rectangle for the wall section from point ① and set it down at point ②. This makes it 90 cm long and 10 cm thick. The outline of the bathroom consists of two rectangles. We start the first of these in the bottom right-hand corner of the room ③ and end it at point ④ (1.1 m wide and 1.9 m long). The second of these also starts at point ③ and ends 10 cm offset (1 grid point each) at point ⑤.

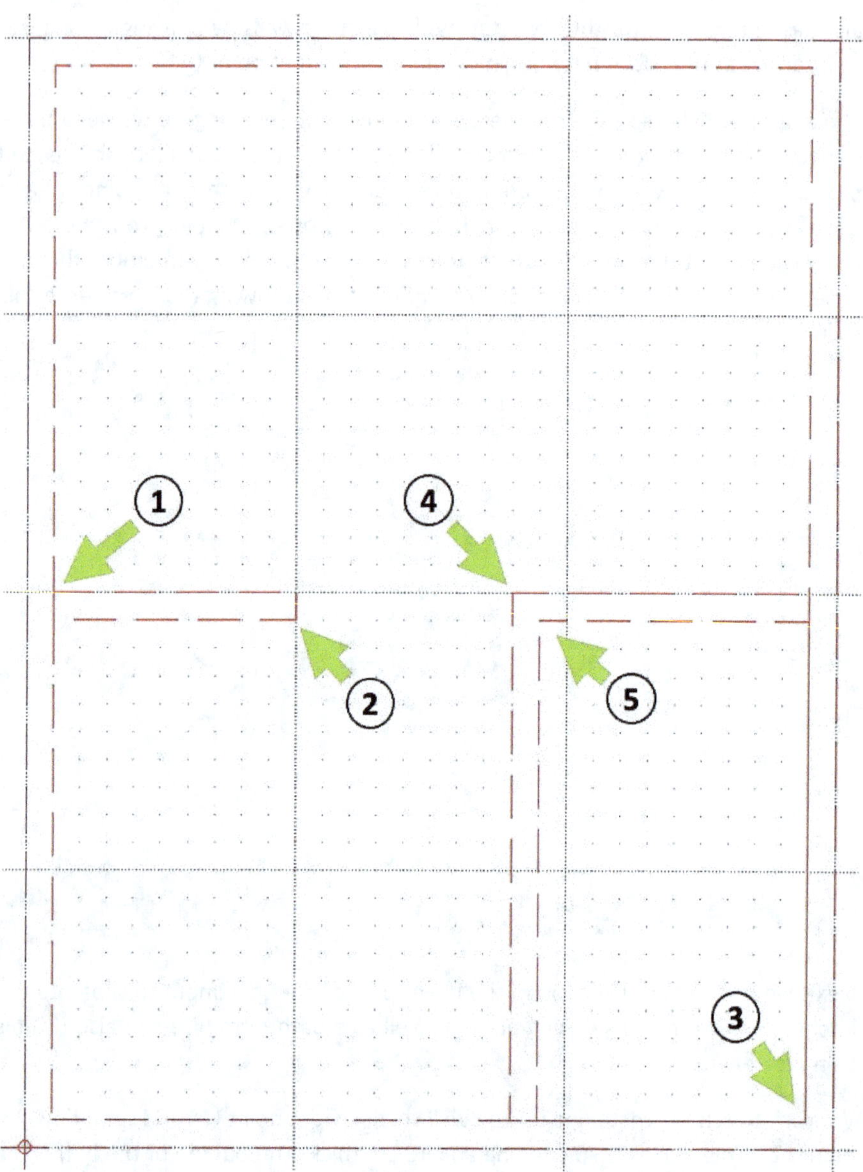

Now we can define the kitchenette and the position of the entrance door in this lower area of the apartment. We do this with lines (command "2 Points"). The kitchen unit should be 60 cm wide and extend up to the wall section. We therefore start the first line at point ② and end it at point ③. We then right-click to start the next line at a different position.

The entrance door to the apartment should start at point ④ and be 80 cm wide, so the vertical line representing the door leaf ends at point ⑤. To make it easier to draw the door later, we mark the end of the width with a short vertical line at point ⑥.

We create a door to the bathroom in a similar way. This door should be 70 cm wide, so the horizontal line (⑦ and ⑧), which will later represent the door leaf, must be seven grid points long. We mark the end of the door again with a short line ⑨.

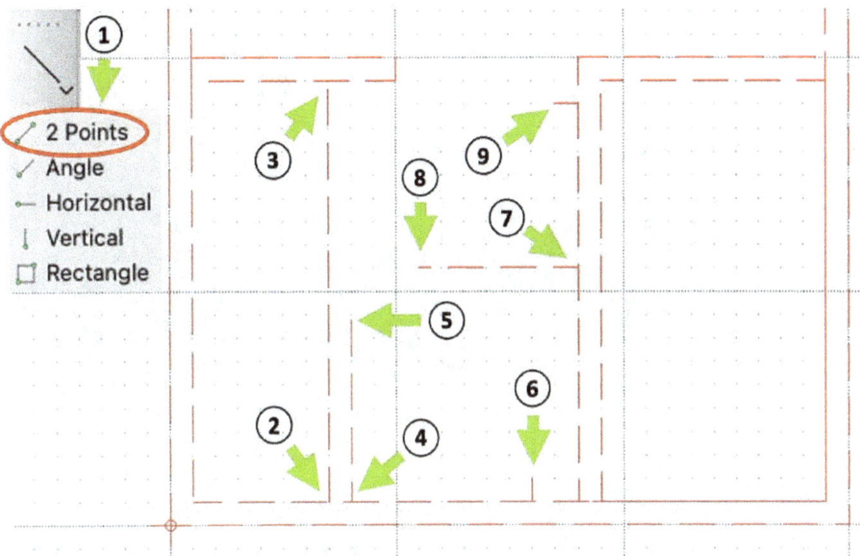

We then add the outlines of a bed, a desk, a wardrobe and a floor-to-ceiling double-sash window in the area above the wall section and the bathroom wall.

For the bed, we only need to draw a line from point ① to point ②. This makes it 90 cm wide and 1.9 m long. We can start the outline of the desk at point ③ and end it at point ④. We can use either a rectangle or two lines. This piece of furniture is then 1.1 m wide and 50 cm deep.

We proceed in the same way for the cabinet. This should be a rectangle between point ⑤ and ⑥.

Finally, we draw two vertical lines, each five grid points long, for the double-sash window. This gives it a width of 1 m (ten grid points or one box).

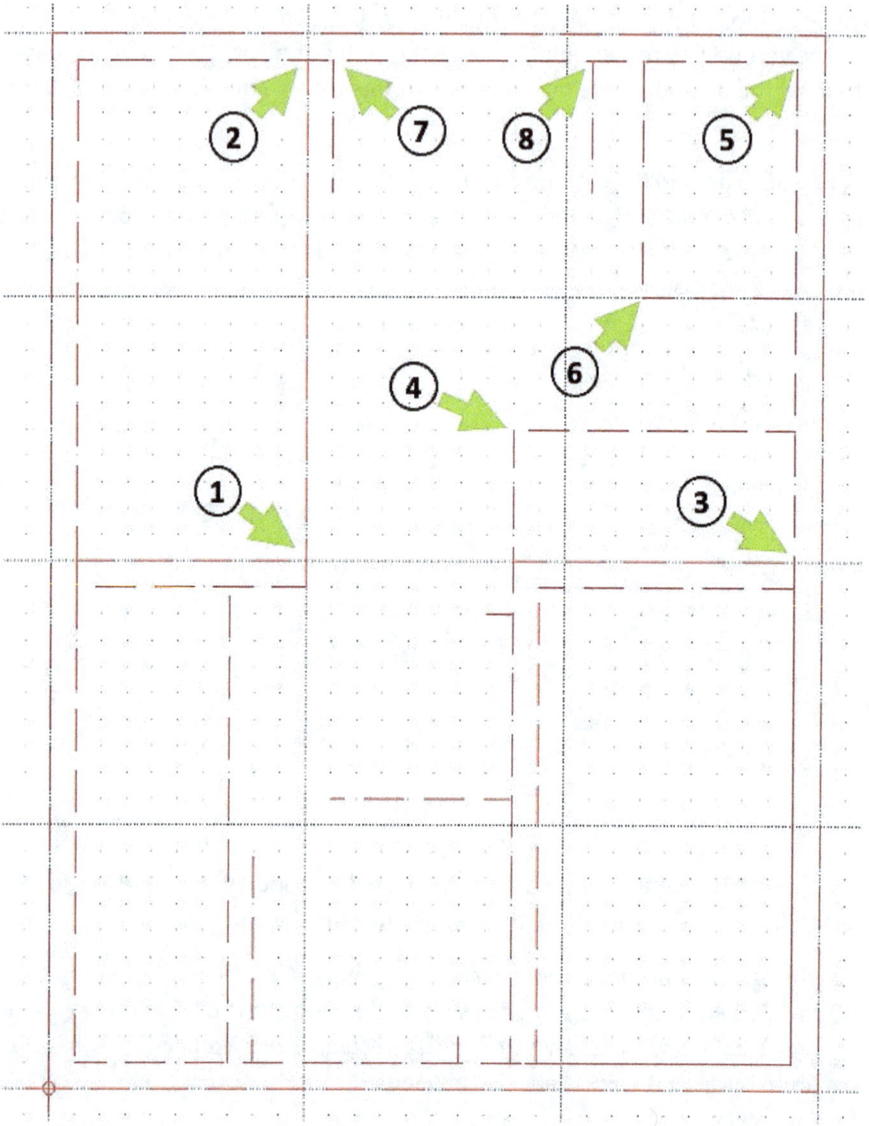

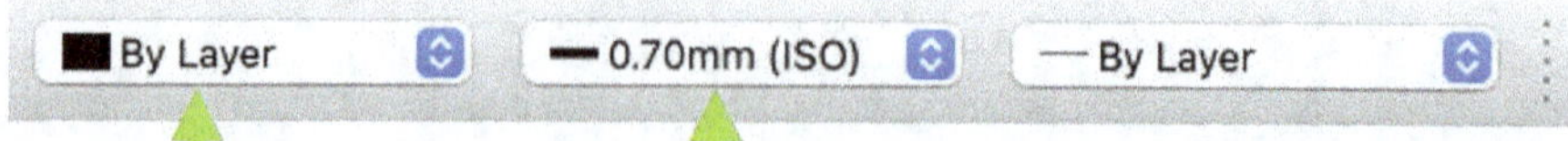

Excellent! We have now created the plan for the apartment with draft lines. Now we can draw the actual lines. To do this, we start with the walls. To make the walls stand out a little from the doors and furnishings, we first assign a slightly higher line thickness, e.g. "0.70 mm (ISO)".

<u>Important:</u> If you draw the lines straight away, you will probably notice that it looks as if the line width change has not worked. However, the line thickness actually only changes in the background and only becomes visible when you preview the drawing for printing. More on this later. For now, we just need to know that although the lines appear to have the same thickness in the drawing environment, they can have different thicknesses in the background.

Now simply draw the outline of the walls using lines from point to point directly on the red dotted lines. Check the "Snap Options" again beforehand, then the drawing will work effortlessly. When placing the lines, pay attention to the openings in the walls in the area of the doors and windows (① - ③) as well as in the area of wall connections (④, ⑤, ⑥).

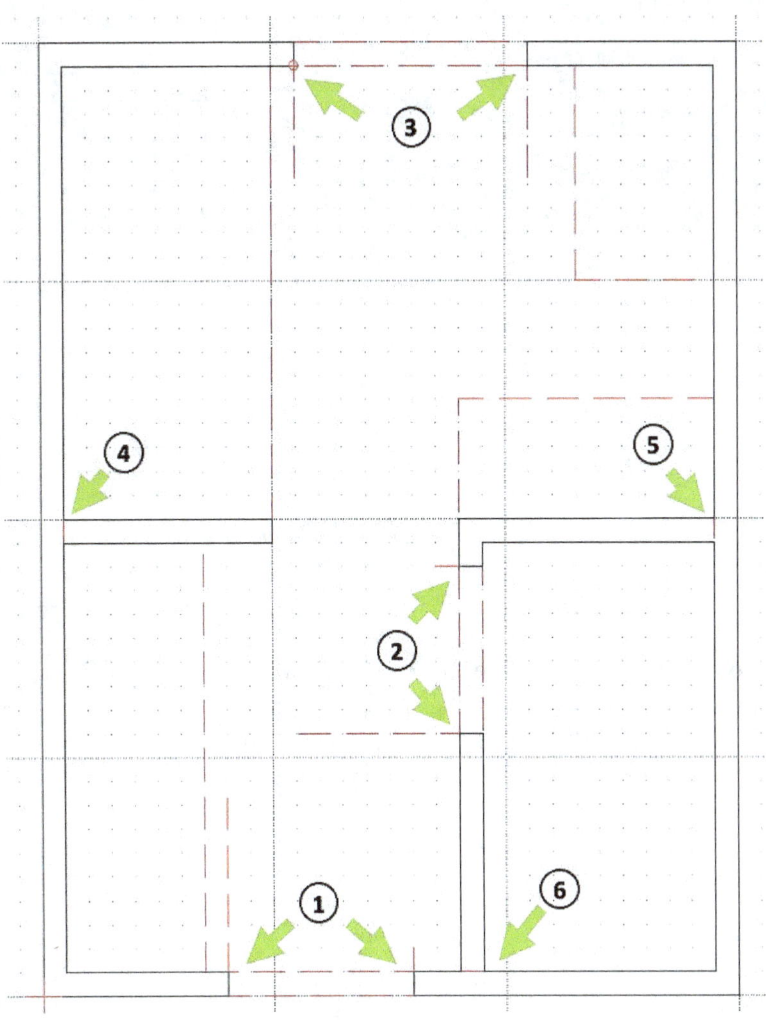

Next, we draw the doors and windows. To do this, we reduce the line thickness, e.g. to "0.50mm (ISO)".

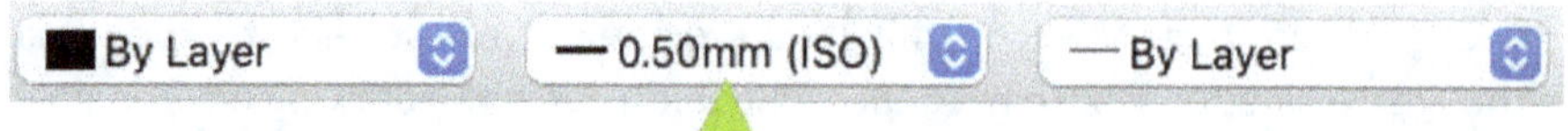

Then we first draw a line for each of the door leaves (① and ②), click the ESC key to exit the line command and then switch to the command "3 Points", with which we can create the characteristic door arch. We do this first for the entrance door by starting at point ④, then clicking in the area of point ⑤ and finally ending the arch at point ⑥. We then use the same procedure to create the door arch for the bathroom door (⑦ - ⑨).

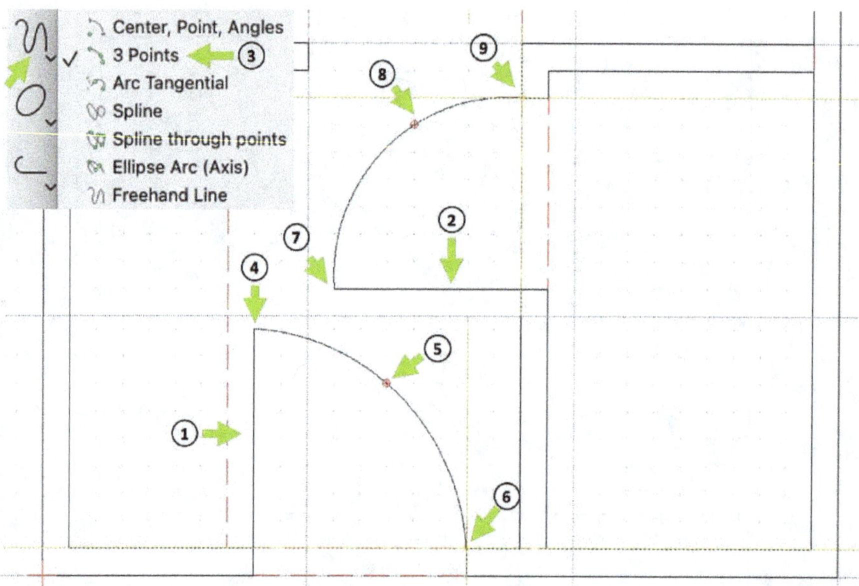

We also do this for the double-leaf balcony door, which is located in the upper area of our floor plan. First, we create the two vertical lines for the two door leaves (① and ②), then switch to the "3 Points" command and create the two arches by clicking on the points ③ to ⑤ and then ⑥ to ⑧.

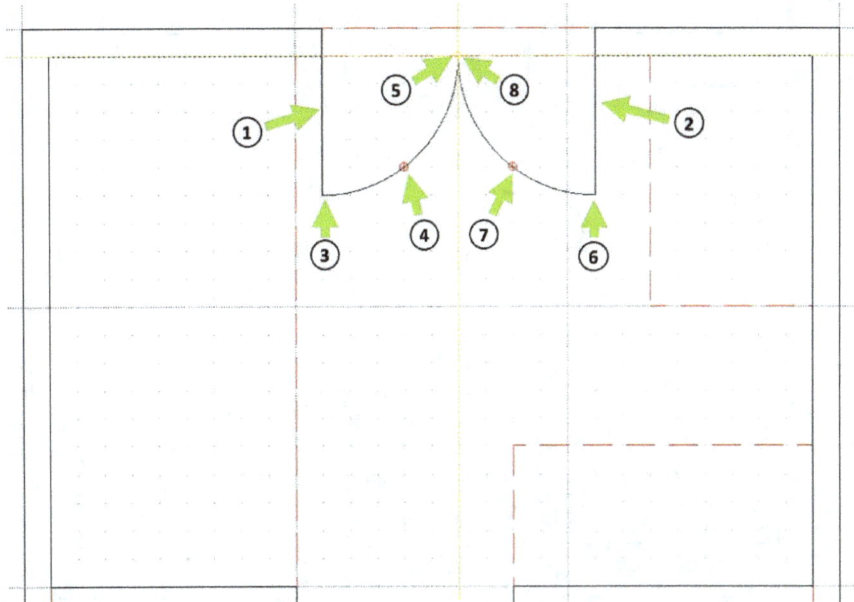

At the end of the drawing project, we can draw the furnishings. However, this is optional, and the level of detail is also up to you. For example, we use a different color ("Dark Green") and reduce the line width to e.g. "0.35mm (ISO)".

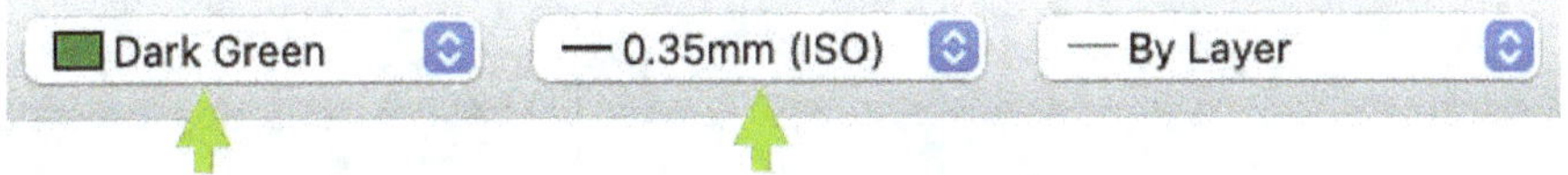

You can then draw the outline of the bed ① (with the pillow and comforter also indicated), wardrobe ② and desk ③ in the upper part of the apartment using the red lines. Simply use rectangles for this.

In the lower area of the apartment, you can add the outline of the kitchen unit ④, with a stove and sink as optional details. A shower ⑤ as well as a bathroom sink and WC ⑥ should be drawn in the bathroom. All of this can be drawn using the familiar commands (line, rectangle, circle). You can certainly do it on your own by now! The positions and shapes do not have to be exactly as illustrated, you can develop your artistic freedom here.

Finally, we delete all the visible red lines that we drew as a draft at the very beginning by clicking on them and deleting them.

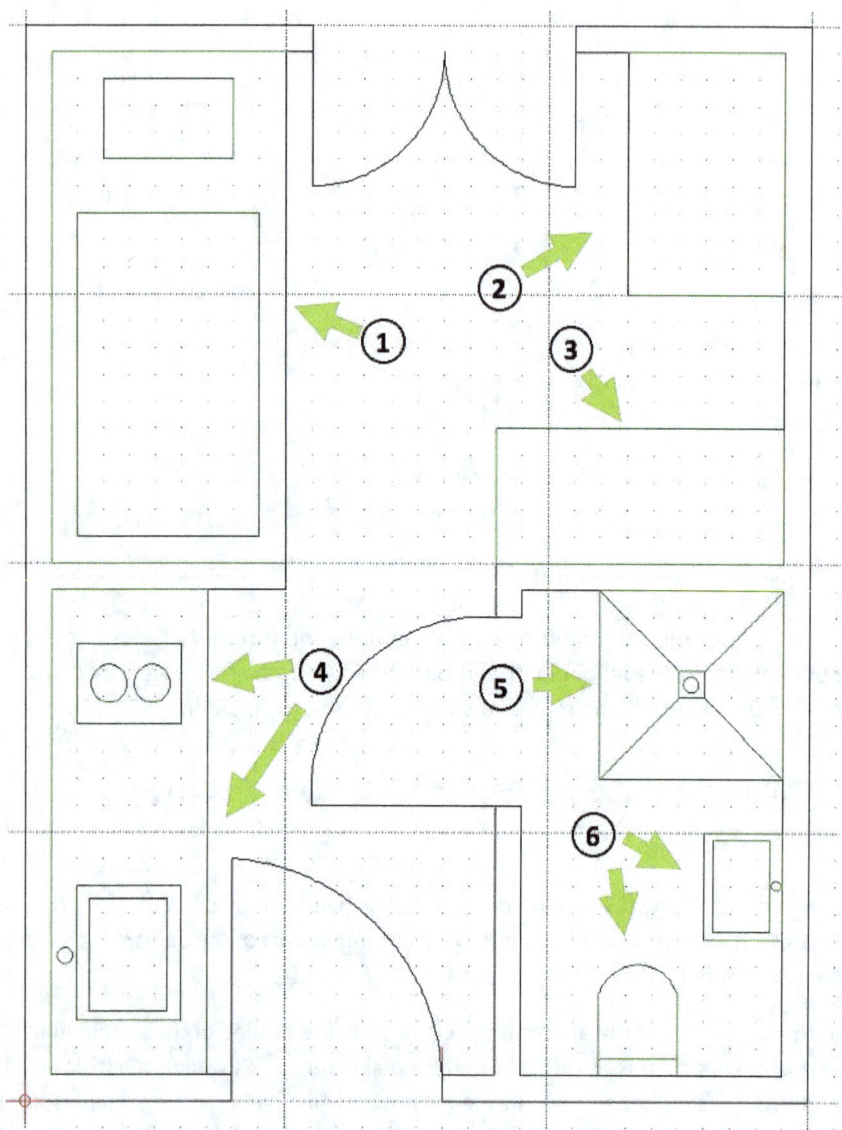

Please save this example under a name of your choice, as we will need it later in the course.

3.3 Drawing Project 2: Mechanical Component

As a second drawing project, we are creating a mechanical fastening part for a pipe. We would like to create a technical drawing (two-dimensional) for this 3D component in "LibreCAD" so that we can have the component produced.

Before we start drawing the component, let's familiarize ourselves with the so-called **three-panel projection** (also known as normal projection). This is a basic technical drawing method that is used to display all the necessary information of a 3D object in a 2D drawing.

Imagine that you place a 3D object (e.g. our component) on a table and then look at it from different angles — orthogonally (perpendicular to the plane). The viewing angles for the three-panel projection are: from the front onto the component ①, from above onto the component ② and from one side ③ onto the component.

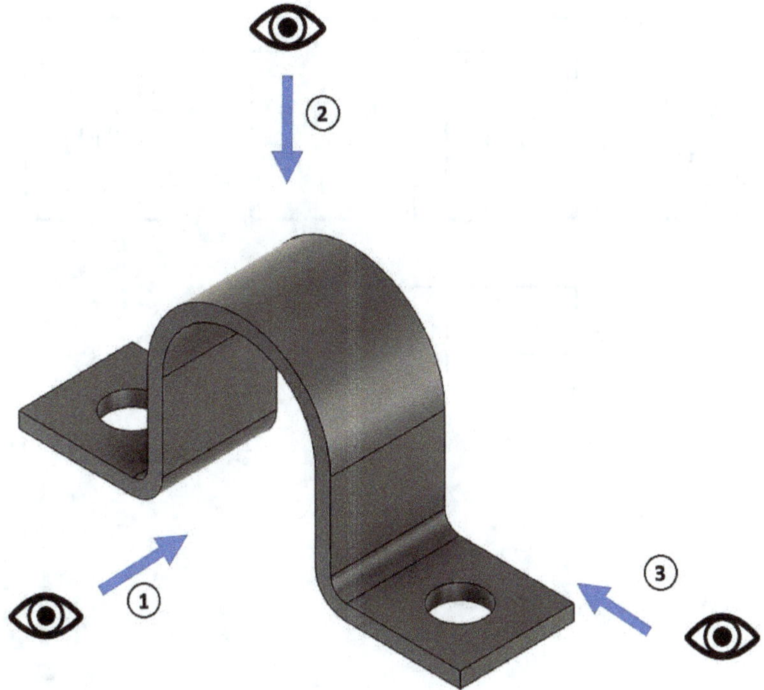

These views are arranged differently depending on the projection method. There are two projection methods (EU and US). The **front view** (also known as the main view or elevation) is positioned centrally (in the middle) in both the EU method and the US method. **The side view** of the left side (also called side elevation or cross elevation) is positioned to the right of the center in the EU and to the far left in the US. The **top view** (also called plan view or floor plan) is positioned at the bottom in the EU projection, but at the top in the US projection. The isometric view can be shown in the area of the title block of the drawing for better spatial visualization.

You can also view the 3D part from behind, below and the second side. For simple parts, however, you will not discover any new information here to describe the shape or dimensions of the part. All six views are only required for very complex parts. For simple parts, the three views mentioned are sufficient.

In Europe, the views are positioned as follows:

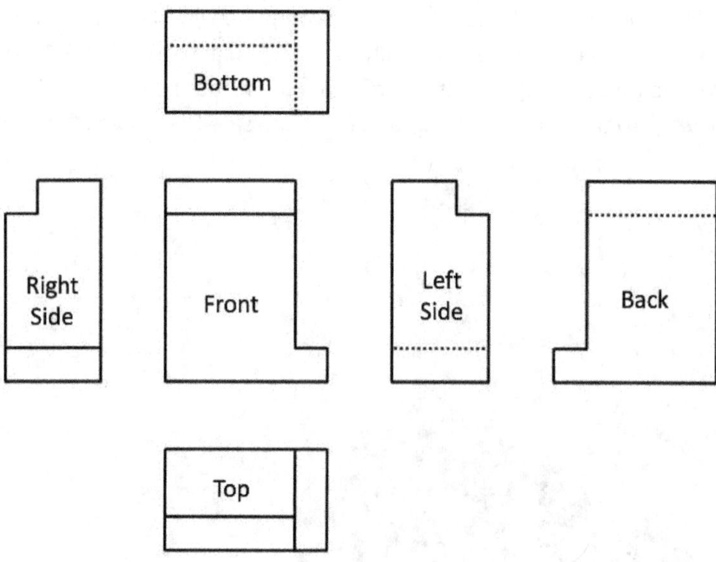

If we look at our component at the correct angle, we can see the following three views.

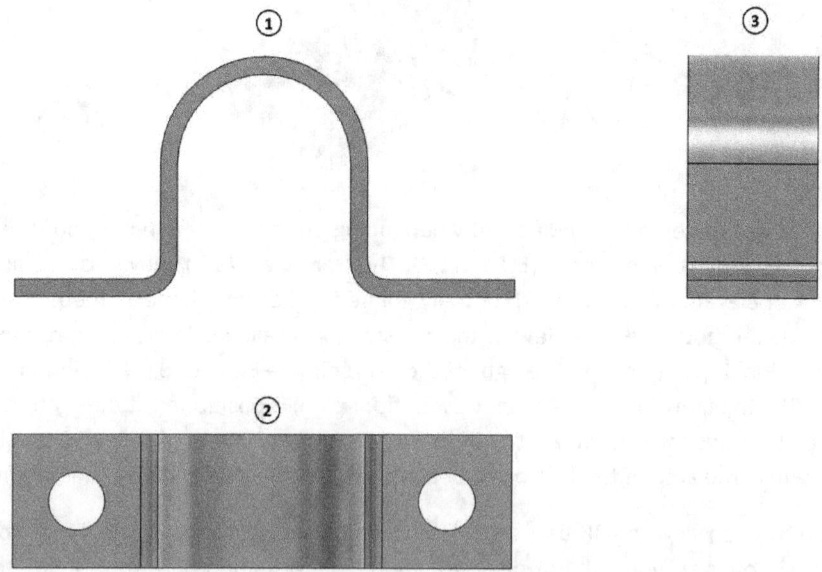

Using these three views, we can display and dimension the 3D part on a 2D drawing for the manufacturing process. In addition, in a later chapter of the course, we will also display the part in the isometric view (3D view) in "LibreCAD".

We can simply think up the necessary dimensions for the part (prototype design) or, for example, if we already have the part and want to reconstruct it (so-called reverse engineering), we would measure it with a caliper gauge. For the top view, for example, we would obtain the following dimensions:

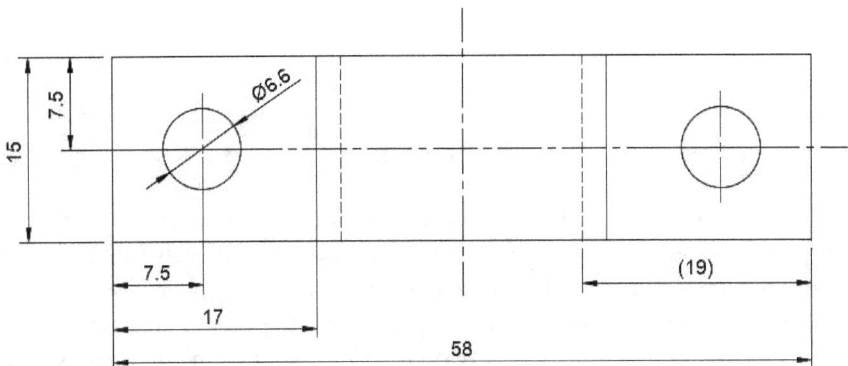

We start with the drawing by creating a new document (command "New document") and setting the units of the drawing in the "Current Drawing Preferences" to "Millimeter". This is the standard unit for drawings in mechanical engineering. We then zoom in or out of the drawing plane until we obtain the grid status "1/10" ①.

Now we can start drawing the top view of the part. To do this, we start a rectangle ① at the coordinate origin ②, count five grid boxes and eight grid points to the right (=58 mm) and one grid box and five grid points (= 15 mm) upwards and create the end point ③ of the rectangle there with a click.

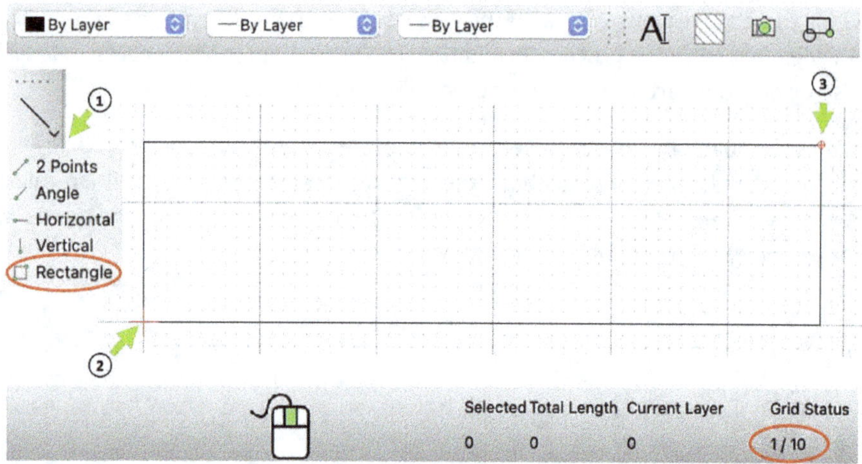

Alternatively, we could also have used the line commands "Horizontal" and "Vertical". The advantage of these two commands is that you can enter the dimension of the respective line in the menu bar. We have already learned about this in one of the previous chapters. You can also try this method to assemble the rectangle from two horizontal and two vertical lines. Counting grid points is no longer necessary.

We create the next two lines in the same way. After selecting the command "Vertical" ①, we first enter the desired length ② (15 mm) and the "Snap Point" ("Start") ③ and then place the lines 17 mm from the left and right edges of the part, i.e., at points ④ and ⑤ perpendicular to the bottom line.

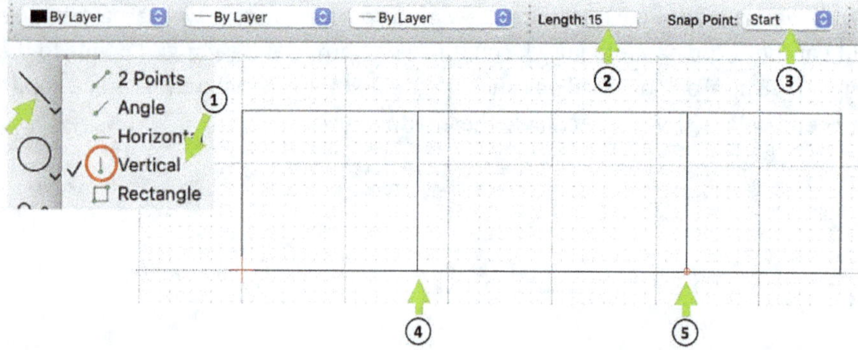

These lines are the visible edges ① and ② shown below (projected upwards; orthogonal view of the component from above). The line ③ is also shown as an edge in this isometric 3D view. However, we <u>do not</u> need to draw this, as it is only an edge for the fillet, which would <u>not be</u> visible on a real component.

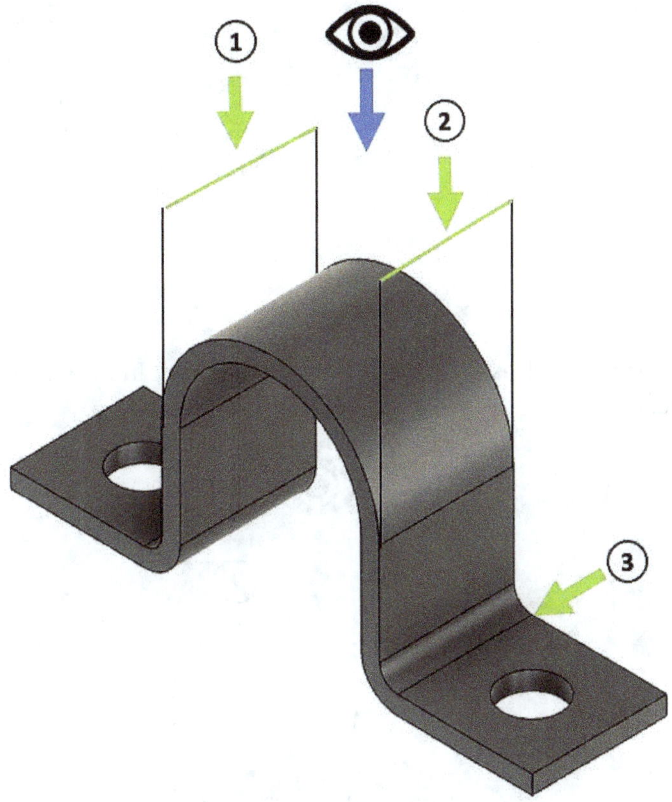

The two edges illustrated below are so-called **hidden edges**. These do not necessarily have to be displayed, but they help to visualize how the part looks in 3D. However, these edges should not be used for dimensioning. Hidden edges are drawn with dashed lines. We can either use the command "2 Points", "Vertical" or the command "Parallel through point" ① for these lines. If we decide to use this command, we first select "Dash (small)" ② as the line type, then click on one of the vertical lines ③ (anyone) and place one line (④ and ⑤) each at a distance of two grid points next to the existing vertical lines.

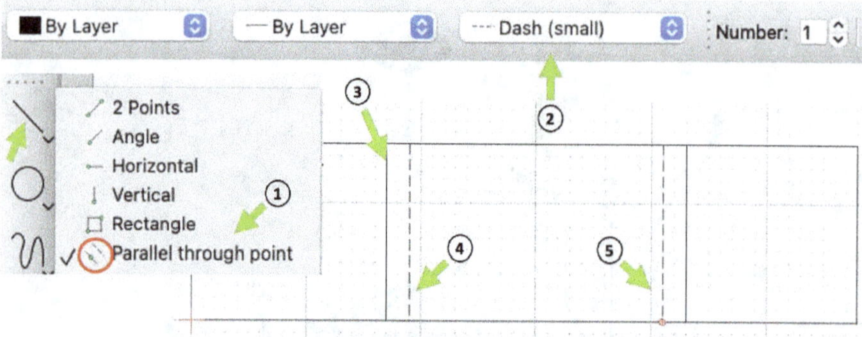

You would see these edges if you looked at the component from below instead of from above. In this case, the other two edges would be hidden.

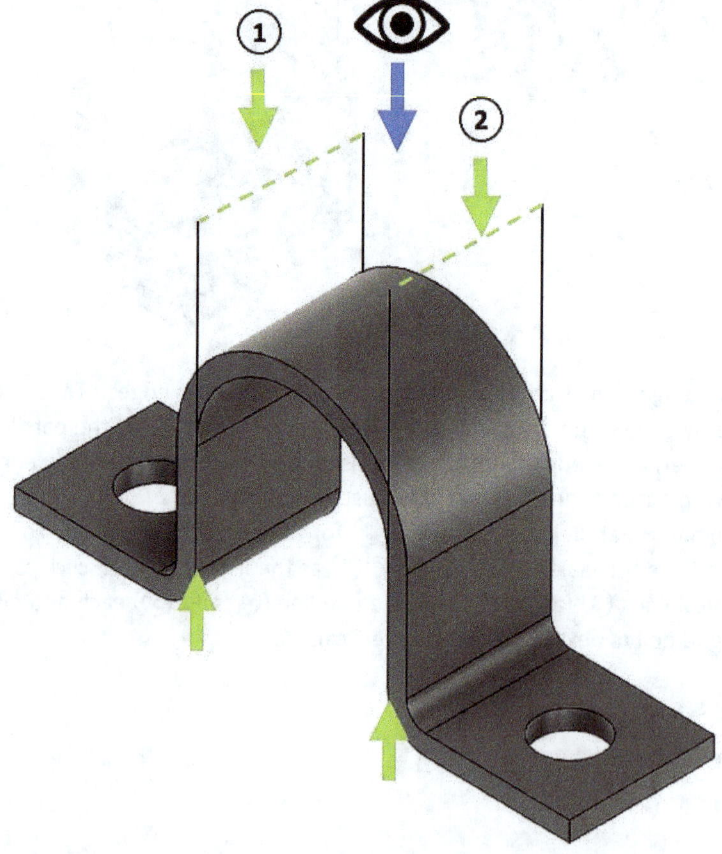

Now the two holes are still missing. As we already know the diameter and position, the easiest way to draw them is with the command "Center, Radius". The holes have a diameter of 6.6 mm. This dimension is standardized for an M8 through-hole (medium) and can be found in a mechanical engineering table book or online.

First, we set the line type ① back to the default "By Layer" and then activate the command "Center, Radius" ②. Now enter the radius (6.6/2 = 3.3) in the menu bar ③. We can then place a circle in each of the positions ④ and ⑤. According to the previous measurement diagram, we need 7.5 mm from each of the outer edges. To do this, scroll into the drawing layer until the "Grid Status" is at "0.1/1". You can then count seven grid boxes and five grid points.

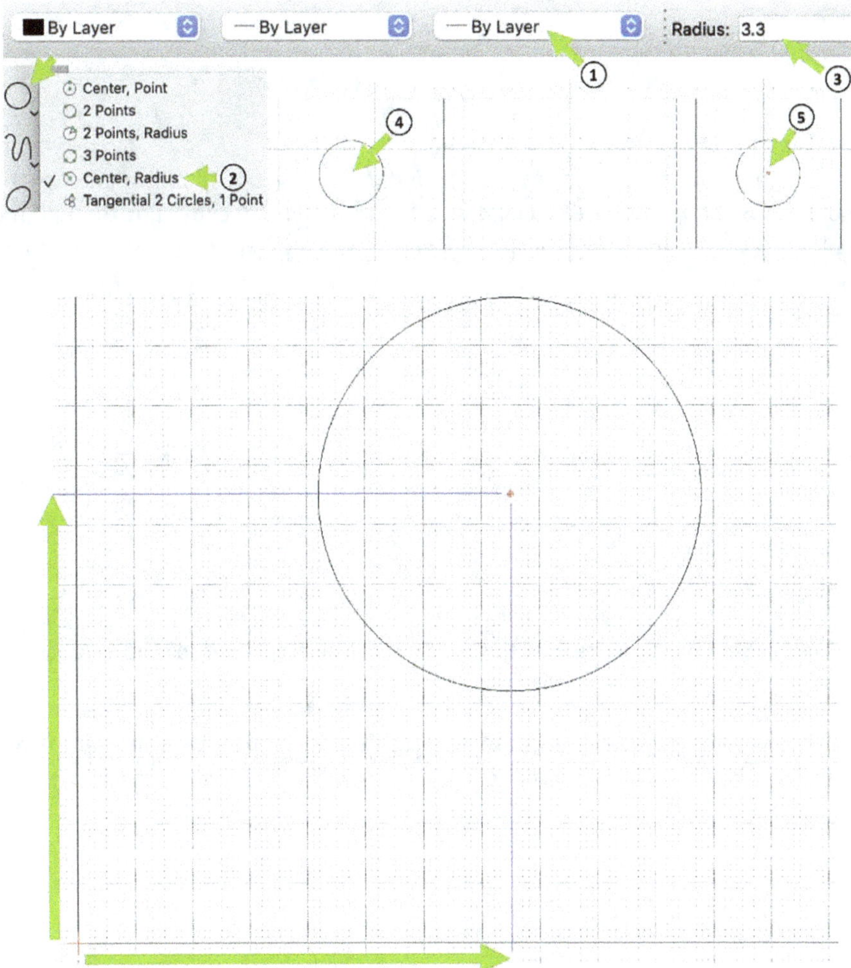

Finally, we add the so-called symmetry lines (also known as center lines) to our drawing. This part is symmetrical regarding two axes (x and y), so we need two lines of symmetry. A dash-dot line is used for such lines, e.g. "Center (small)" ①.

Draw the lines (①and ②) through the vertical and horizontal center of the part. To do this, start slightly outside the part. If necessary, zoom in to obtain the appropriate "Grid Status".

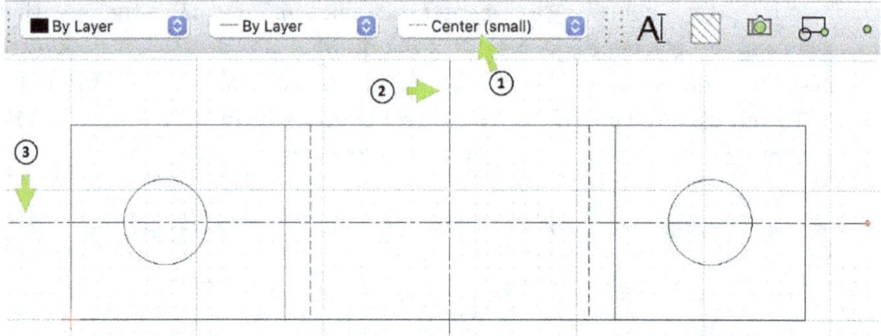

In addition, center crosses are always added to drill holes so that the center of the hole can be used for dimensioning. As a horizontal line already runs through the holes, we simply add a vertical line (① and ②) that protrudes slightly above and below the hole.

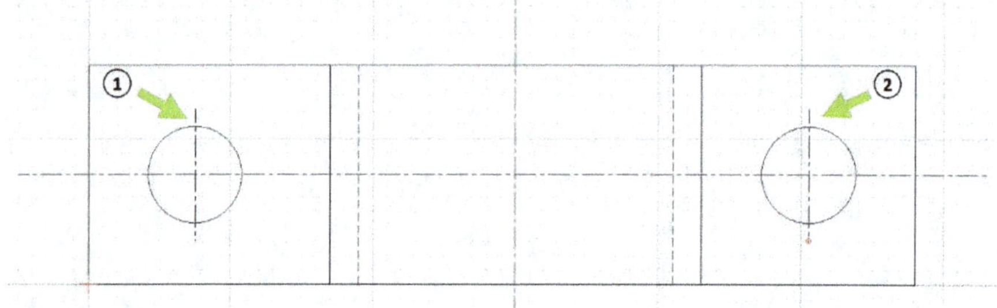

Perfect! We have now created the first projection (top view) of the three-panel view.

We now create the front view of the part. This must be positioned above the top view. For this view, we need the following dimensions in addition to the previous dimensions.

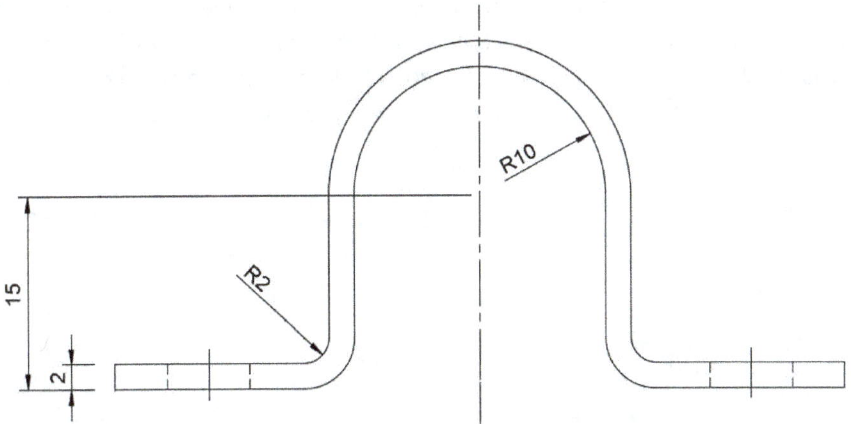

For example, we start the front view of the part four boxes above the coordinate origin ("Grid status: 1/10") with a vertical line ① that is 2 mm long ② and has the setting "Start" ③ as "Snap Point".

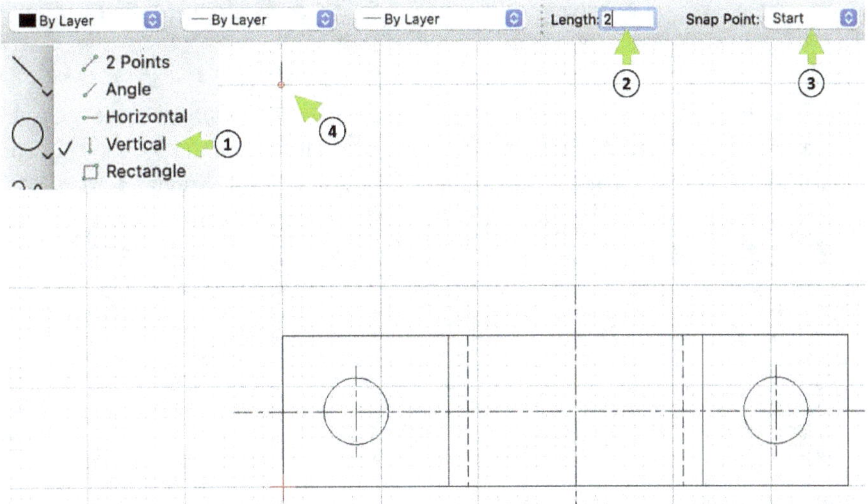

After we have set this line, we can connect a horizontal line with a length of 15 mm at the upper end point of the vertical line.

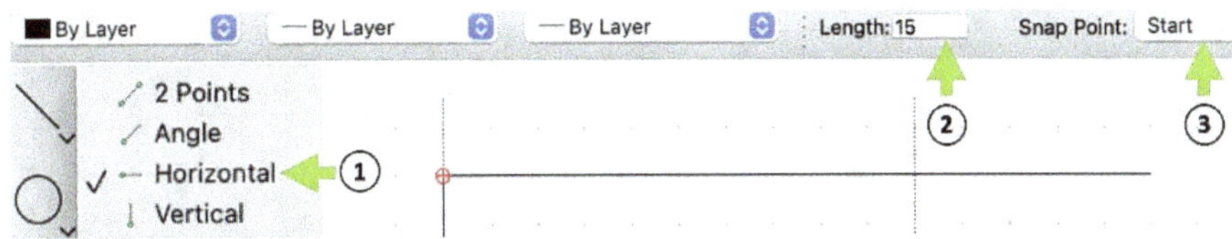

The next step would be a tangential arc. To make this as simple as possible, we first draw the 11 mm long vertical line following the arc. We set its starting point ④, measured from the end point of the horizontal line, two grid points to the top and two grid points to the right. We do this because the tangential arc has a radius of 2 mm.

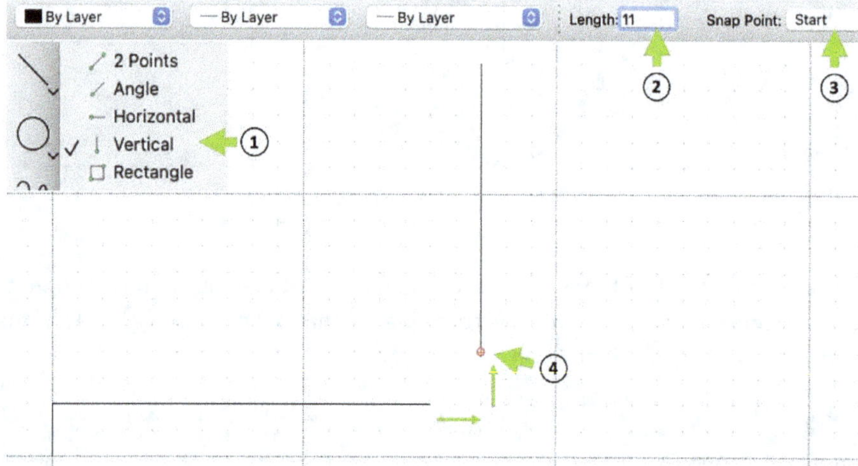

Now we can create the tangential arc by selecting the command "Arc Tangential" ①, entering the required radius of 2 mm ②, then clicking on the baseline ③ and finally selecting the starting point of the vertical line ④ as the arc end point.

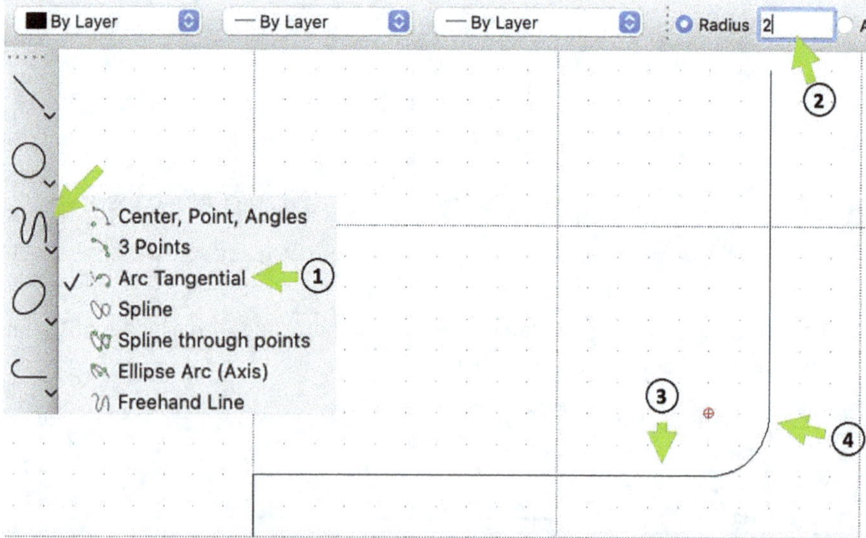

We then create a horizontal line with a length of 15 mm starting at point ① and a vertical line with a length of 11 mm starting at point ②. As the tangential arc in between has a radius of 4 mm (2 mm material thickness), we arrive at point ② by counting four grid points to the right and upwards from the end of the horizontal line. Also add the tangential arc ③ with a radius of 4 mm.

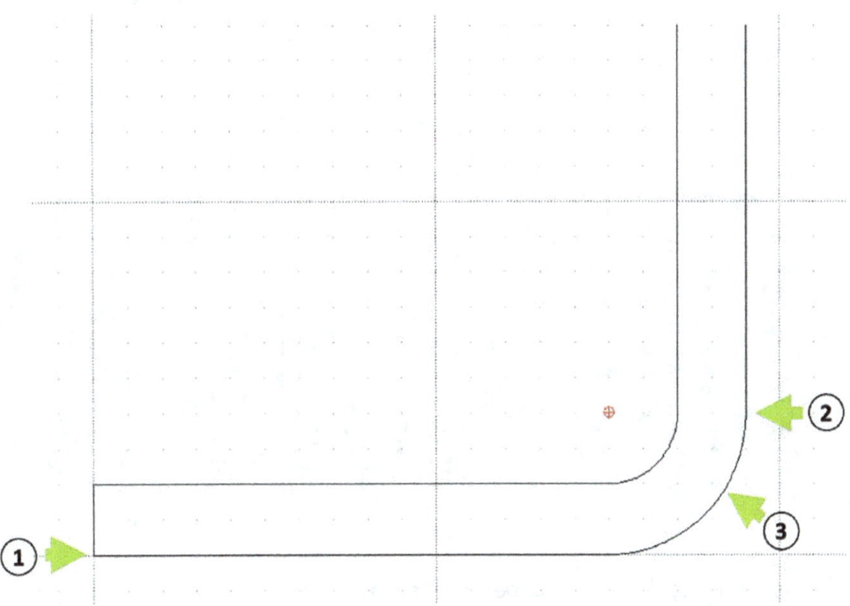

Next, we draw the symmetry line of the part. To do this, we switch the line type to "Center (small)" ①. As the part has a total length of 58 mm, we need to draw this line at a distance of 29 mm from the point ②. To do this, we count two grid boxes and nine grid points from ③. We set the starting point ④ approx. five grid points below the horizontal starting line and the end point in the area ⑤. We can move this to the final position later.

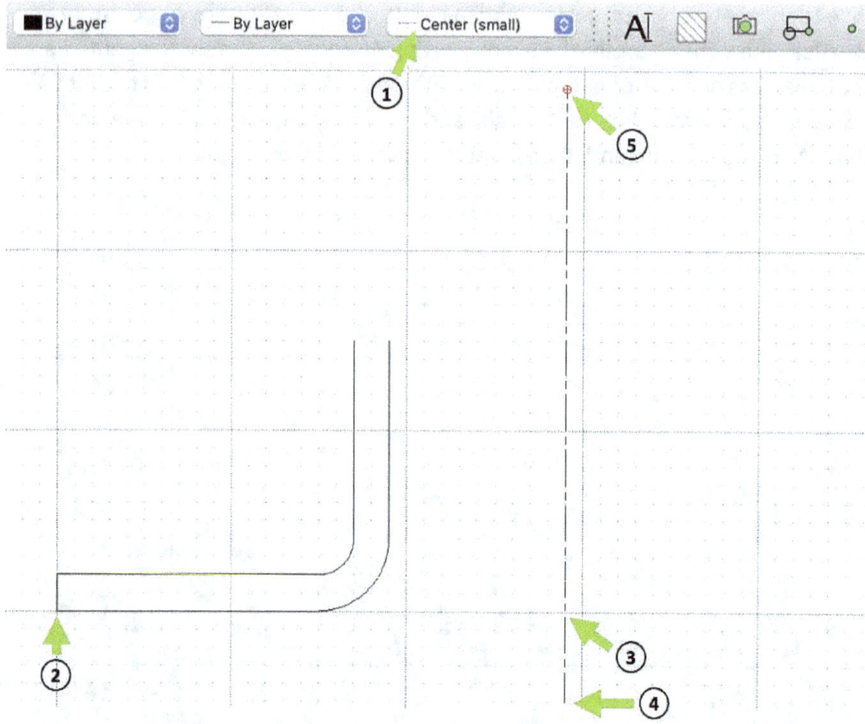

It makes sense to design the upper two arcs of the part as tangential arcs again. To be able to do this, we next draw the right side of the view. As the right side is the mirror image of the left side, the procedure for creating it is the same as before, but from right to left instead of left to right. There is also a special command for this in "LibreCAD", which creates the mirror image of a geometry. However, we will get to know this later. Please create the right-hand side independently with lines and tangential arcs, this is a good exercise! Start, for example, at point ②, which is 58 mm (five grid boxes and 8 grid points) away from point ①. Alternatively, you can also count from the center line. Remember to change the line type back to the setting "By Layer".

We can then add the two tangential arcs. For the inner arc, we need a radius of 10 mm ②, the baseline ③ and the end point ④. We create the outer arc with a radius of 12 mm ⑤ (2 mm material thickness) as well as the baseline ⑥ and the end point ⑦.

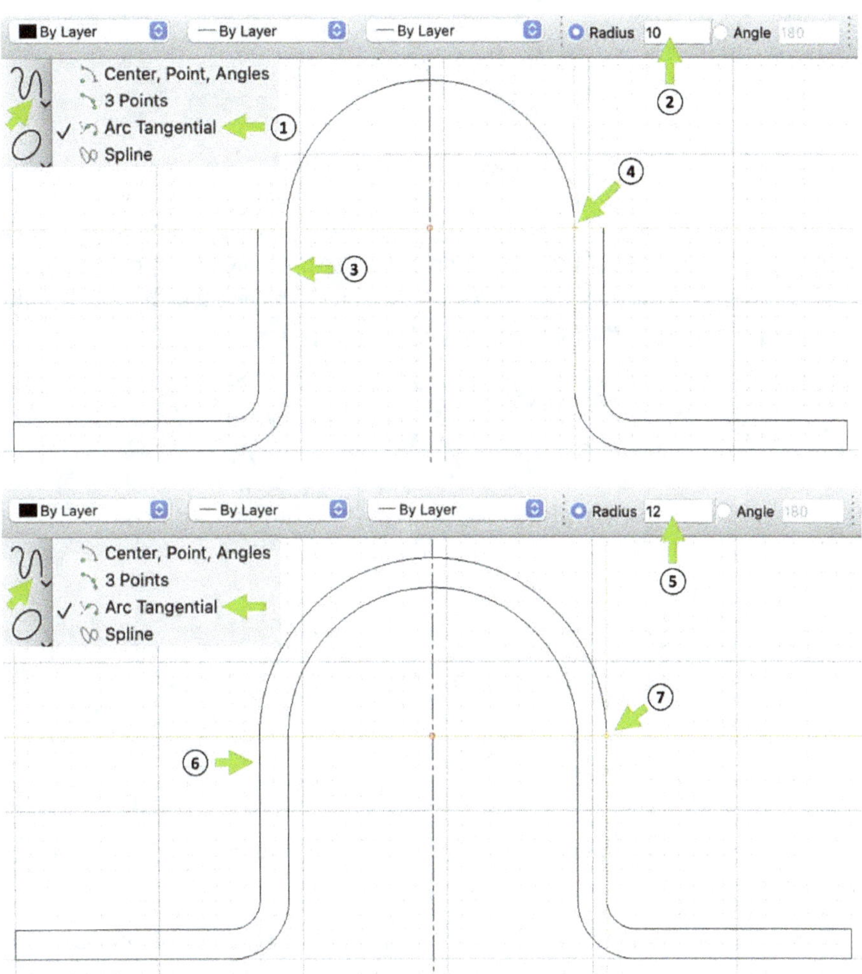

The hidden edges for the two holes are still missing. To do this, we select the line type "Dash (small)" and count a distance of 4.2 mm ② from point ① for the first vertical line. For the second vertical line, we need a distance of 10.8 mm ③ from the point ①. This works best if we first zoom into the "Grid status: 0.1/1".

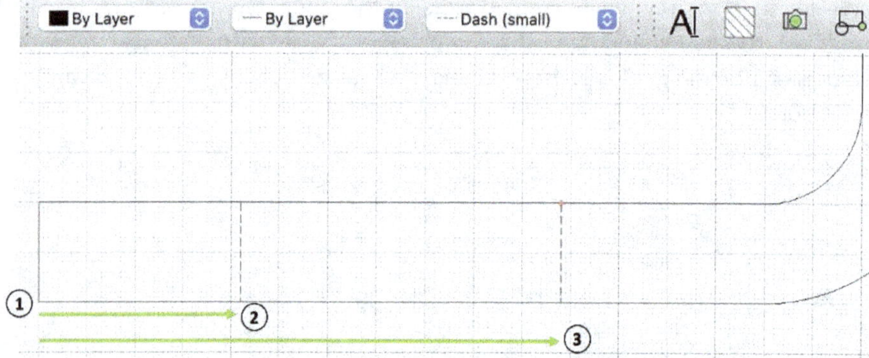

We then do the same on the other side of the part. Finally, we also draw center lines (① and ②) for these holes. To do this, change the line type back to "Center (small)" and place a vertical line in the middle of each hole.

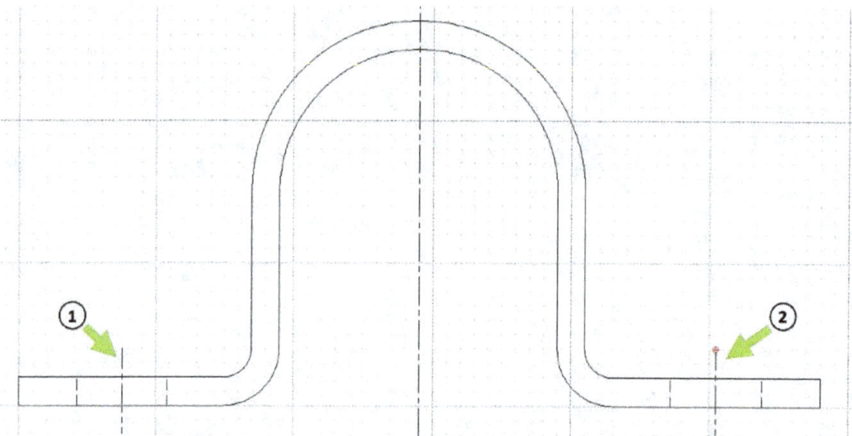

Perfect! This view is now also finished, and we can create the last view — the side view.

We can still see the height of the component from the side view; otherwise, all dimensions are already given. In technical drawings, each dimension should only be entered once if possible. Double dimensions or auxiliary dimensions can be bracketed. We will take a closer look at how to dimension the part correctly in the next chapter.

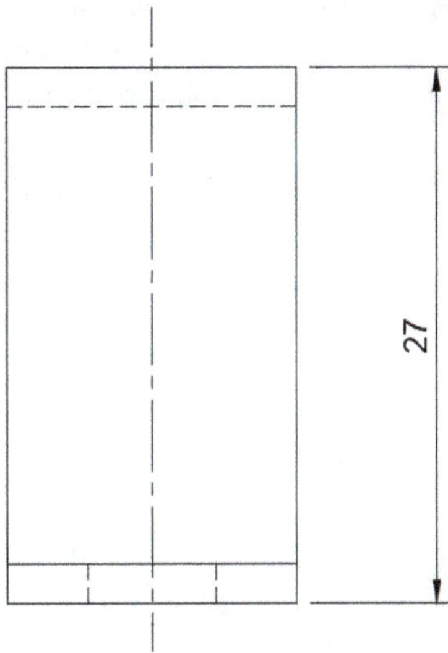

We start this side view approx. two boxes next to the front view by drawing a rectangle ①, which starts approximately in the area ② and ends 15 mm further to the right and 27 mm further up at point ③. Make sure that this side view is at the same height as the front view.

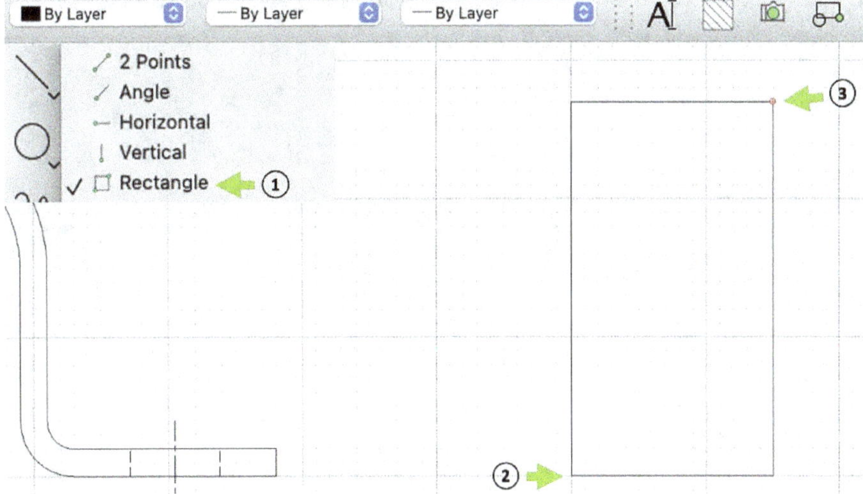

We can then draw the visible edge ① in the lower area and the concealed edge ② in the upper area of the view. The distance to the outer edge is 2 mm in each case (material thickness of the part). For the hidden edge, we again use the line type "Dash (small)". We can then add a symmetry line ③ ("Center (small)"). To do this, it is best to zoom back into the drawing environment "0.1/1" to be able to count the 7.5 mm distance to one of the vertical outer edges. Finally, we add the concealed edges of the hole ("Dash (small)") with a distance of 3.3 mm (6.6 mm / 2) each from the symmetry line. Also use "Grid Status: 0.1/1" here.

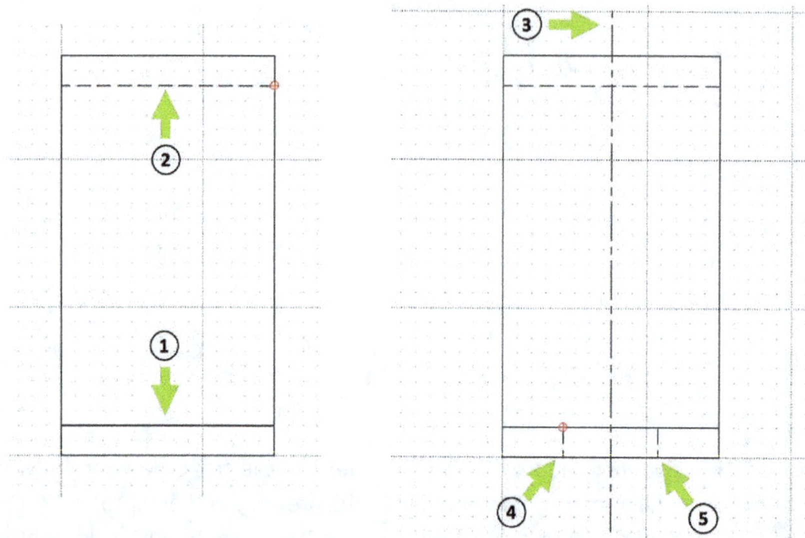

Flawless! We have now created the three-panel projection of the component. The dimensions are still missing for a correct technical drawing. Be sure to save the drawing, as we will need it again later.

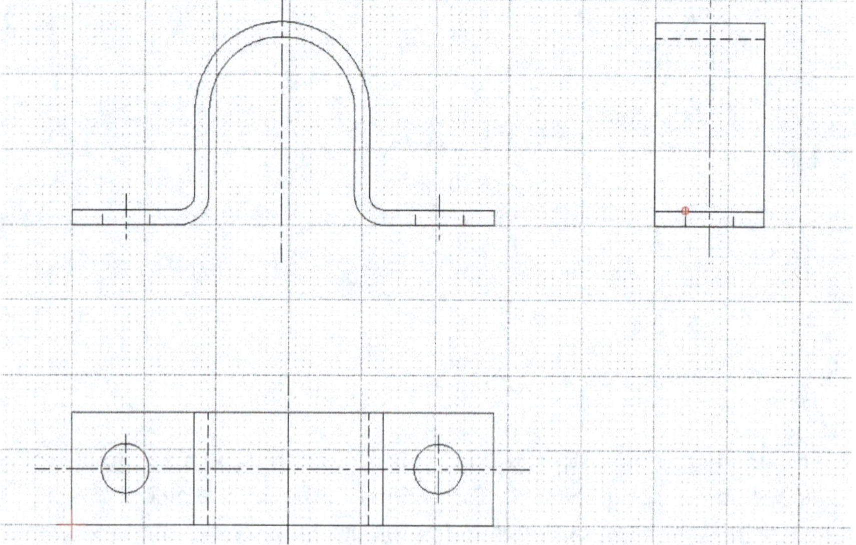

3.4 Creating Dimensions

In this chapter, we will look at how to create dimensions. In addition to the menu "Measure", which we have already covered in one of the previous chapters, there is the menu "Dimensions". This can also be found in the CAD toolbar on the left-hand side of "LibreCAD". In the following, we will use the commands in this menu to dimension our technical component. Afterward, we are going to dimension the floor plan of the student apartment that we had previously drawn.

First, we dimension the top view of the mounting part. Here we can specify the basic dimensions such as the length and width of the part. Let's try this with the command "Linear" (1). We always use this command (1) when we want to dimension a horizontal or vertical distance between two points of a geometry (e.g. line). Horizontal dimensioning is the default setting for this command. This can be recognized by the fact that the value 0 is entered in the menu bar at "Angle" (2). You can switch between horizontal and vertical dimensioning using the two symbols (3) in the menu bar. For vertical dimensioning, "Angle" (2) has the value 90.

To create the dimensioning, we then click on the point (4) and then on the point (5) of the line or geometry that we want to dimension. The dimensioning (6) then appears. We then define its distance to the geometry with another click (7). This creates the final dimensioning.

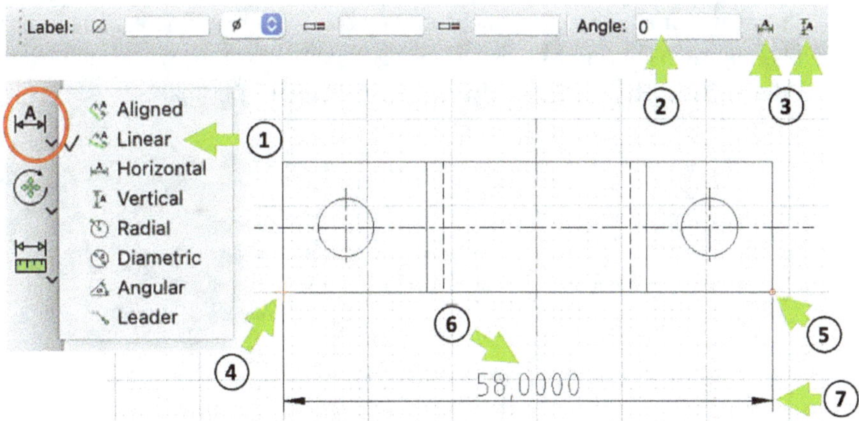

When dimensioning, it is noticeable that many zeros are displayed as decimal places. To change this, we need to call up the already known "Current Drawing Preferences" (1) and change some settings in the area (3) in the "Dimensions" (2) tab.

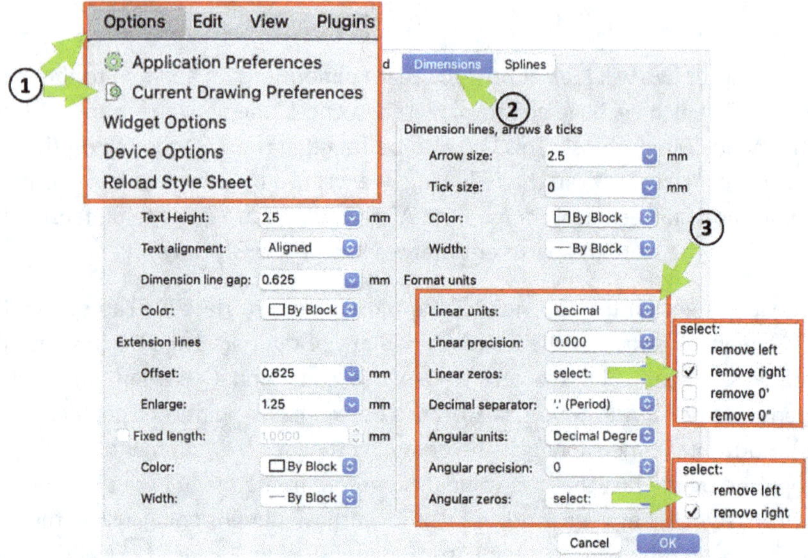

To remove only the superfluous zeros after the decimal point, we can check the option "Linear zeros" and set "remove right". If we do not want a comma but a point as a decimal separator, we can set this at "Decimal separator". For the dimensioning of angles, we can also remove the zeros after the decimal point at "Angular zeros". With "Linear precision" and "Angular precision" you can set the accuracy using the decimal places. If you would like to use the imperial measurement system (USA), i.e., measure in inches, you would select the option "Engineering" at "Linear units" instead of "Decimal". However, we would like to retain the metric system in the following, i.e., the option "Decimal".

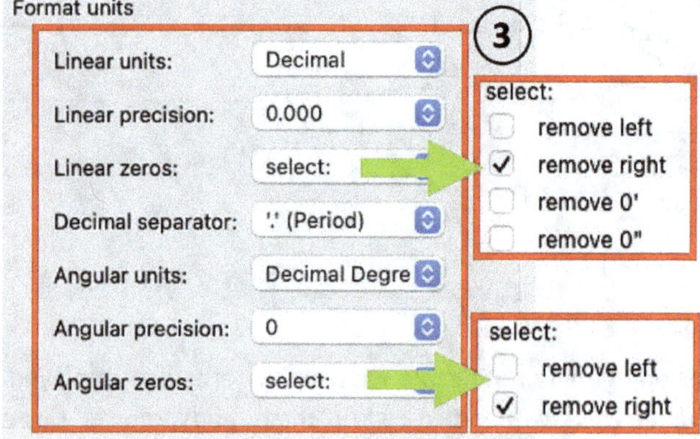

Once we have confirmed the parameters with "OK", the dimensioning should be displayed correctly.

Next, we can dimension the length of the component. To do this, we can use the command "Linear" again and then — as explained earlier — switch to vertical dimensioning in the menu bar. Alternatively, we can also use the command "Vertical" ①. This command can only be used to create vertical dimensions between two points of a geometry. The counterpart "Horizontal" for horizontal dimensions is also available as a separate command.

To create the dimension, we select the two end points (② and ③) of the line and position the distance of the dimension to the geometry with another click ④.

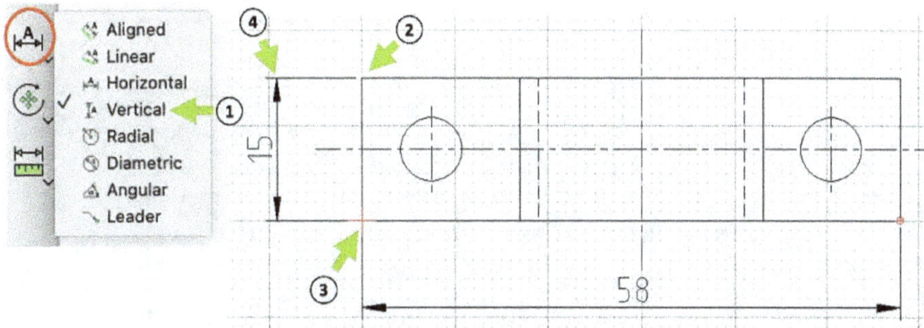

Once you have created a dimension, you can move it by first clicking on the dimension and then dragging the small blue dot ①. Such a dot ② also appears for the dimension.

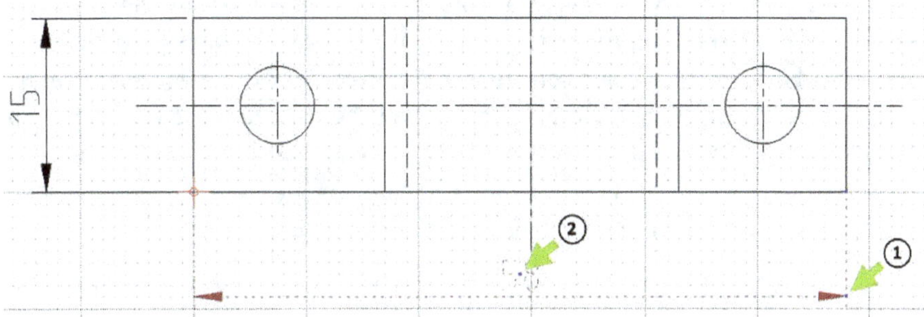

In this view, we can create three more length measurements. As this is a symmetrical part, we can use the center lines as dimension reference lines.

For example, we first create a horizontal dimension (command "Horizontal" or "Linear") between the centers of the two holes ① and ② to define the distance between the holes. For better selection, zoom into the drawing plane if necessary. The distance should be 43 mm. We also specify a tolerance here as an example. We can do this in "LibreCAD" after selecting the dimensioning command in the menu bar. In the selection field ③ we can, for example, select the +/- symbol for a symmetrical tolerance specification. The dimension is then replaced by the symbol. We then enter the dimension (43 mm) manually in the field ④ in front of the +/- symbol. Then enter the tolerance, e.g. 0.3 mm. The dimension ⑤ should then look as shown. If you need an upper and lower tolerance value, you can do this in area ⑥.

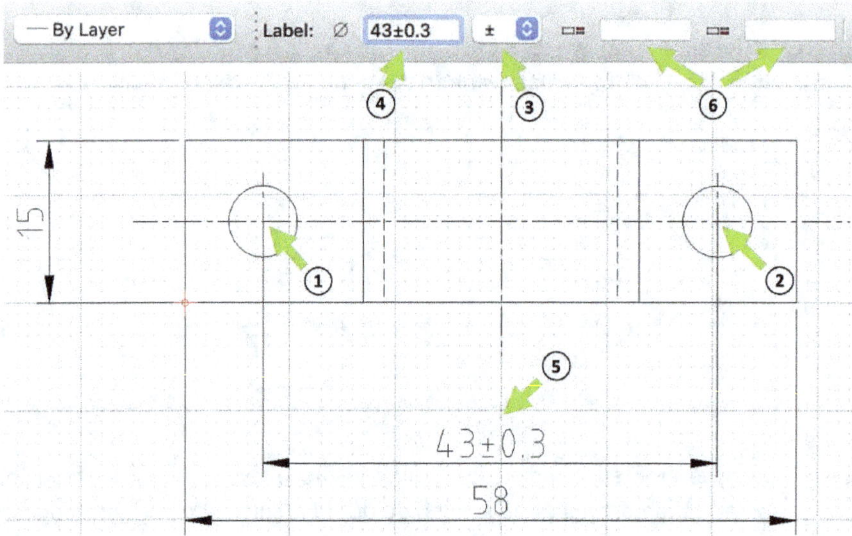

As already mentioned, you should refrain from specifying duplicate dimensions. If you still want to specify a redundant dimension — e.g. for simpler production — you should bracket the dimension. Such a dimension would be, for example, the vertical position of the horizontal center line of the part, on which the holes are also located. This dimension is half of the component width and can therefore be calculated. We can create a vertical dimension between ① and ② and bracket it by entering "(7.5)" in the field "Label" ③ in the menu bar.

We then create a horizontal dimension (26 mm) between the points ④ and ⑤ to dimension the two visible edges.

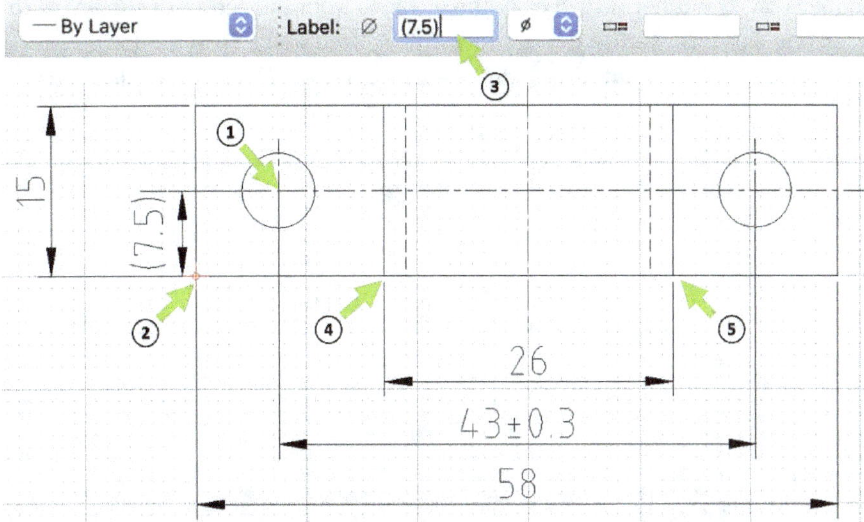

The last dimension we create in this view is the diameter of the two holes. As the holes are symmetrical and the same size, we only need to dimension one hole. The diameter of a circle is dimensioned with the command "Diametric" ①. After selecting the command, simply click on the desired circle ② and the dimension appears. For circles, a diameter symbol is also placed in front of the dimension, which we can select in the area ③. We then have to enter the dimension manually in the field ④ behind the symbol. Finally, you can position the dimension so that it is easy to read.

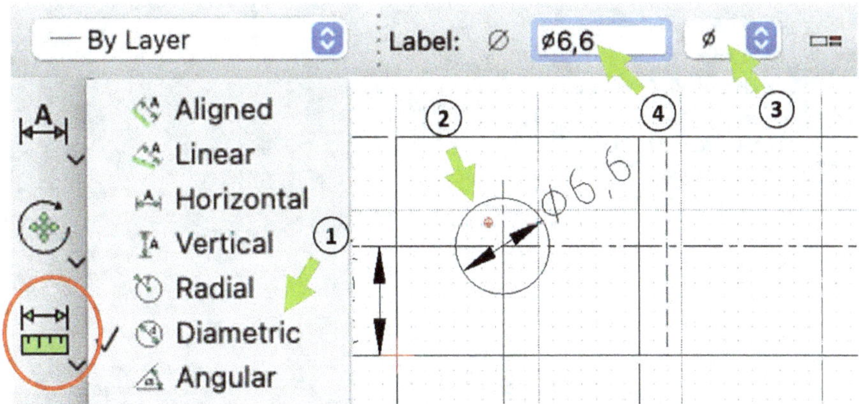

Excellent. Now we dimensioned the front view of the part.

In this view, we first set two vertical dimensions ①. One of these is to define the material thickness of the part, so we use the corner points (② and ③) for this dimension. The other is to specify the distance from the center of the arc to the baseline. For this, we use the center point ④ (the easiest way to do this is with "Snap Option: Snap Center" ⑤) and the corner point ③ of the baseline.

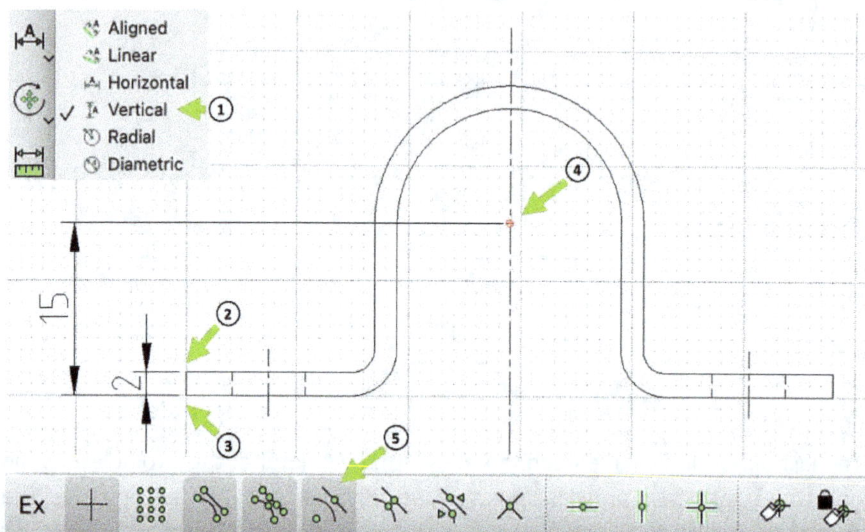

As we have already set many dimensions in the plan view and the part is also symmetrical, only two dimensions are missing in this view. These dimensions should indicate the radius of the bends. For sheet metal parts, you should always dimension the respective inner radius of the bend. This is done with the command "Radial" ① and by clicking on the respective arc (② and ③).

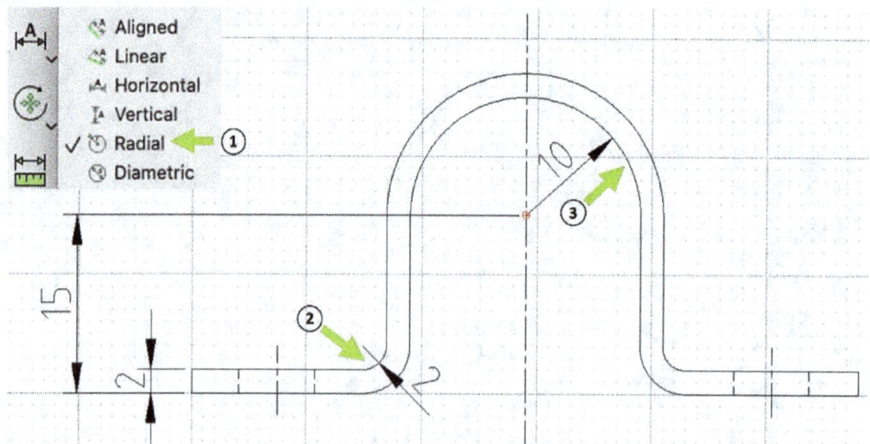

We do not need any further dimensions in this view. As already mentioned, dimensions should not be entered twice. All other dimensions can be calculated from the existing dimensions.

Before we dimension the side view, let's take a look at the two commands "Aligned" and "Angular". The "Aligned" command can be used to create a dimension that is parallel to the dimensioned points or a line. And with the command "Angular" you can dimension angles.

For example, we could click on the two points ② and ③ (end points of the arc) in the front view after selecting "Aligned" ①. This creates a dimension that is parallel to the imaginary line between these two points. If, on the other hand, we were to select these two points with the commands "Linear" or "Horizontal" or "Vertical", the horizontal or vertical distance would be dimensioned. Try it and you will see the difference immediately. However, this dimension makes no sense in this drawing, so we will delete it again.

To dimension an angle, select the command "Angular" ④ and then simply click on two lines (⑤ and ⑥) one after the other whose angle you want to dimension. Although the angle of 90 degrees is obvious in this drawing and the specification is therefore redundant, you could leave the dimension as it is.

We do not need the command "Leader" ⑦, which can be used to create an arrow using several points. However, there are no dimensions on it.

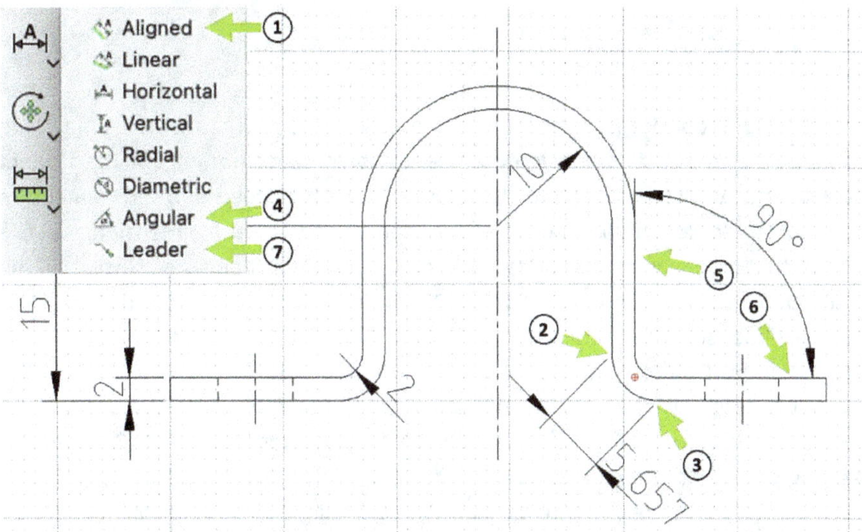

Now we come to the dimensioning of the side view. However, we no longer need any dimensions for this view, as we have already drawn in all the necessary dimensions in the other views. We could only specify the total height of the part. We bracket the dimension, as the total height can also be calculated from the dimensions of the front view.

After activating the command "Vertical", we can set the dimension between the two corner points ① and ② and specify the bracketed dimension at "Label" ③.

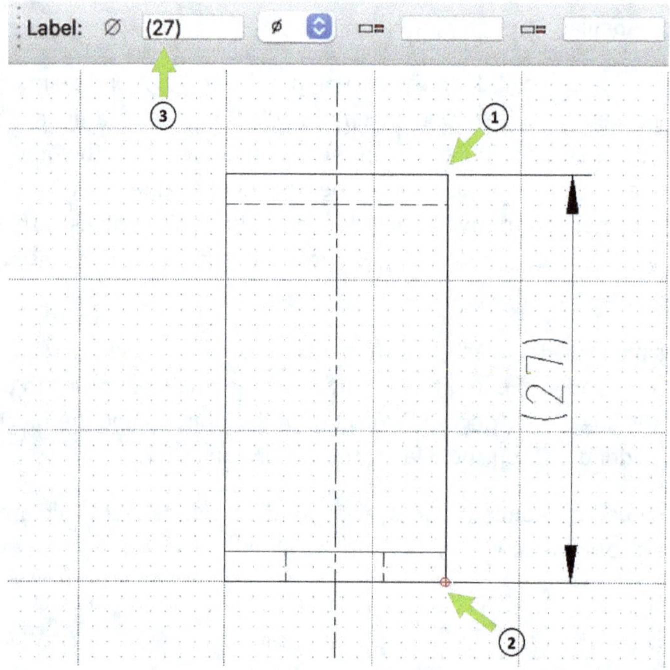

Perfect. Our mounting part is now fully dimensioned. Be sure to save the file. Next, we would also like to dimension the previously created floor plan of the student apartment. As this is an architectural project, we first need different dimension arrows. In addition, if you open the floor plan and try to set a dimension, you will notice that it appears much too large. We therefore first change the settings in the "Current Drawing Preferences" in the "Dimensions" tab ①, as we did at the start of the dimensions for the fastening part. As we set the unit to meters at the beginning of this drawing, the dimensions are also in meters. To ensure that the size of the dimensions matches the drawing, we set the scaling factor "General Scale" to the value "0.05" ②. We then set the value for "Tick size" ③ to 1. This setting changes the dimension guides from arrows to crosses, which is typical in architecture. We also need to activate the dimensioning style typical for architecture. We can do this at "Linear units" ④ by selecting "Architectural (metric)". If you want to enter the data in feet and inches (USA), i.e., in the imperial measurement system, you would alternatively select "Architectural" here.

However, we do <u>not</u> do this. Finally, we change the accuracy to two decimal places at "Linear precision" by selecting the value "0.00" at ⑤. We also need to check "Fixed length" so that the dimension lines have a fixed length, as is typical in architecture, and <u>do not</u> extend to the geometry.

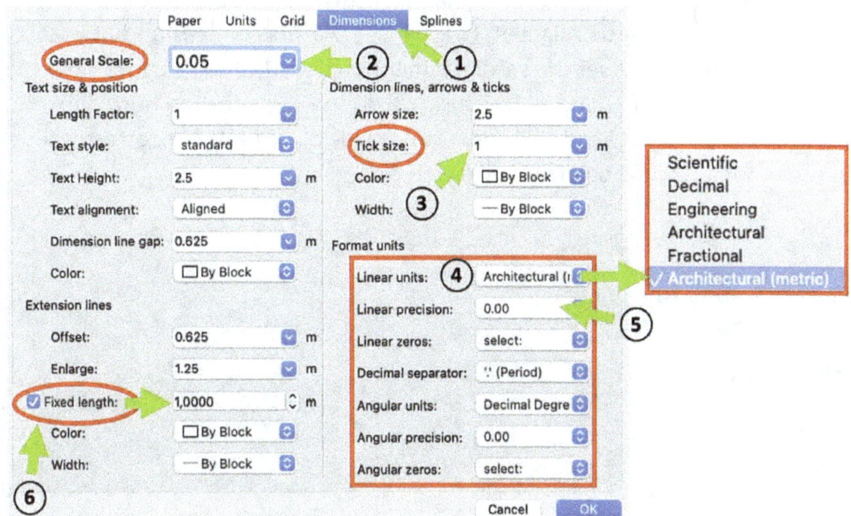

There are differences in the dimensioning of architecture compared to the dimensioning of technical components. In architecture, all dimensions that are in meters are given as decimal dimensions (separated by a point). For example, if a wall is 8.75 m long, the dimension is given as "8.75". If the wall is 5 m long, it is given as "5.00". The decimal places (zeros) remain so that it is clear that the unit is meters. All dimensions less than one meter, on the other hand, are given as centimeters and without a point. For example, if a wall is 24.00 cm thick, the measurement is given as "24". Unlike in mechanical engineering, in architecture two different units (meters and centimeters) are combined in a drawing. The only difference here is the point with the decimal places in meters. If, however, a centimeter measurement has a decimal place, which is the case, for example, if a wall is 11.5 cm thick, then the decimal place will be superscripted. In this case, the specification is "11^5".

The commands for creating dimensions work in the same way as before. In general, it is most convenient to use the command "Aligned". As we already know, this command creates a parallel dimension to two points. This also means that the command "Aligned" will also create a horizontal dimension if the points are in a horizontal alignment. And if the points lie in a vertical alignment, the command will also create a vertical dimension. This means that we <u>do not</u> have to switch between vertical and horizontal, which would be the case with the "Linear" command.

Dimensional chains are used in architecture. However, this would <u>not be</u> done in mechanical engineering due to the tolerances. In addition, several dimension chains are used in architecture. In the first dimension chain, openings (windows and doors) and pillars are dimensioned. This dimension chain is closest to the building and is therefore created first. Let's take a look at our example. After selecting the command "Aligned" ①, we set the first dimension between the points ② and ③. We set the second dimension directly after the first dimension between the points ③ and ④. Finally, we do the same for the third dimension between the points ④ and ⑤. If you have made all the settings correctly above, the dimensions should be displayed as follows.

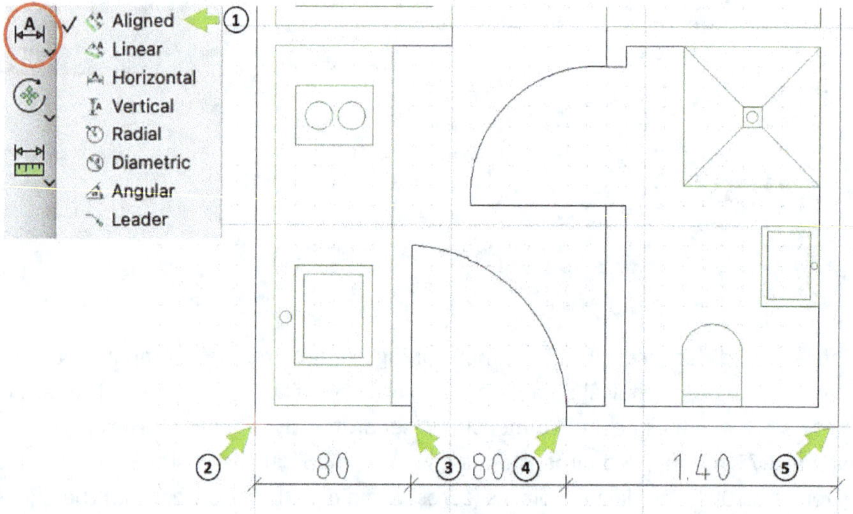

For windows and doors, the opening height is usually specified in addition to the opening width. This is set below the dimension line. We have to create this dimension manually in "LibreCAD". We can do this with the command "Mtext" ①. After clicking on it, a settings window opens. Here we can enter the dimension at "Text" ②, e.g. 2.01 m, i.e., "2.01". We then have to adjust the height of the font to our other dimensions. The value "0.11" ③ would fit here, for example. Then confirm with "OK" and place the dimension ④.

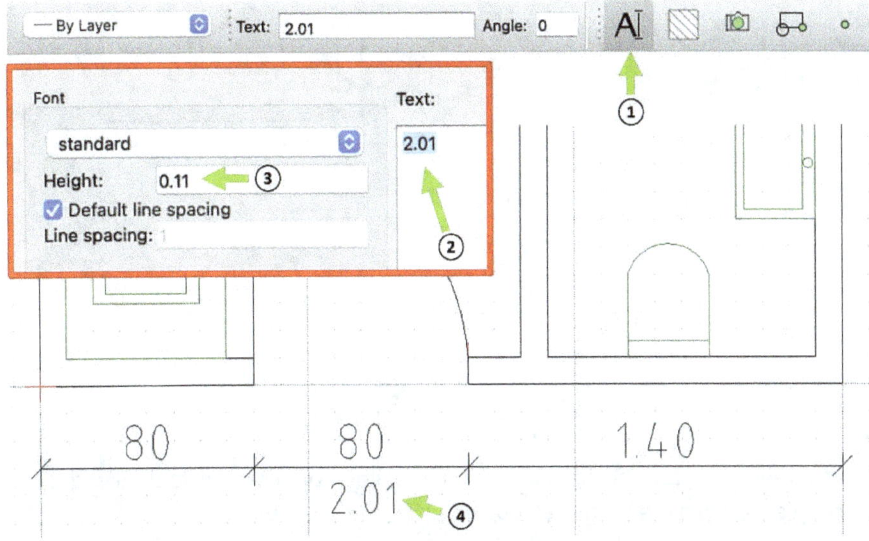

In the second dimension chain, enter the wall thicknesses and the internal dimensions of the room. To do this, activate "Snap on Grid" ① and create the dimensions between the points ② and ③, ④ and ⑤ as well as ⑥ and ⑦. If the dimensions (e.g. for the walls) do not fit between the dimension crosses, you can place the dimensions next to or above them (⑧ and ⑨) after creating them by clicking and dragging.

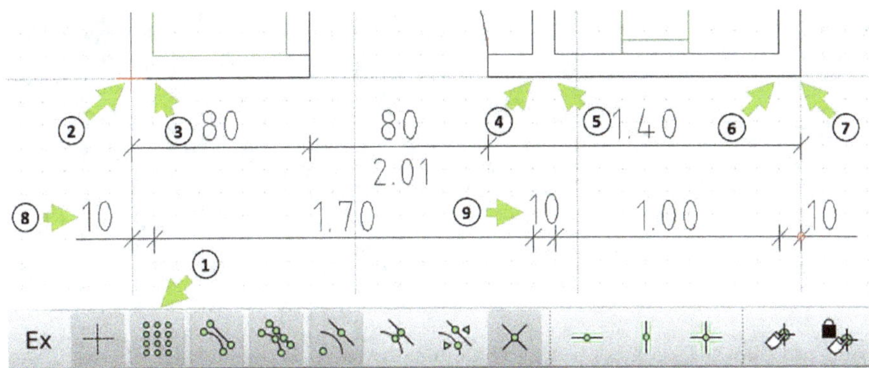

In the last dimension chain (on the very outside), you enter the external dimensions of the building. In our case, this is only one dimension, namely the dimension between the points ① and ②.

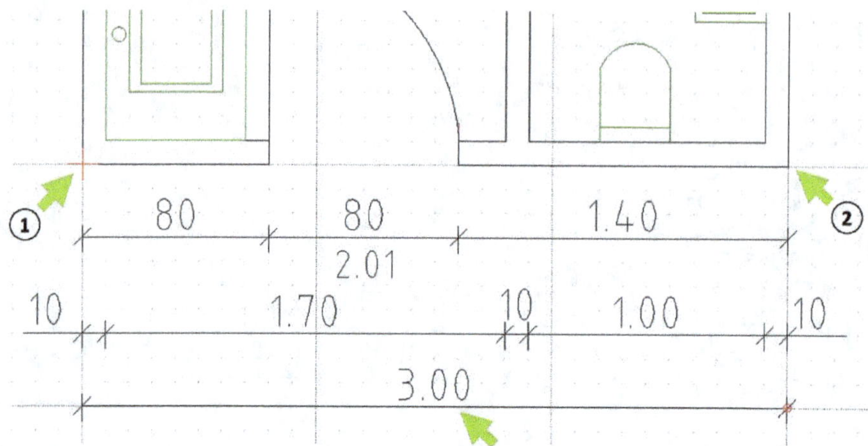

The dimensions for the upper area of the floor plan would look like this, for example. You can create these yourself using the same procedure.

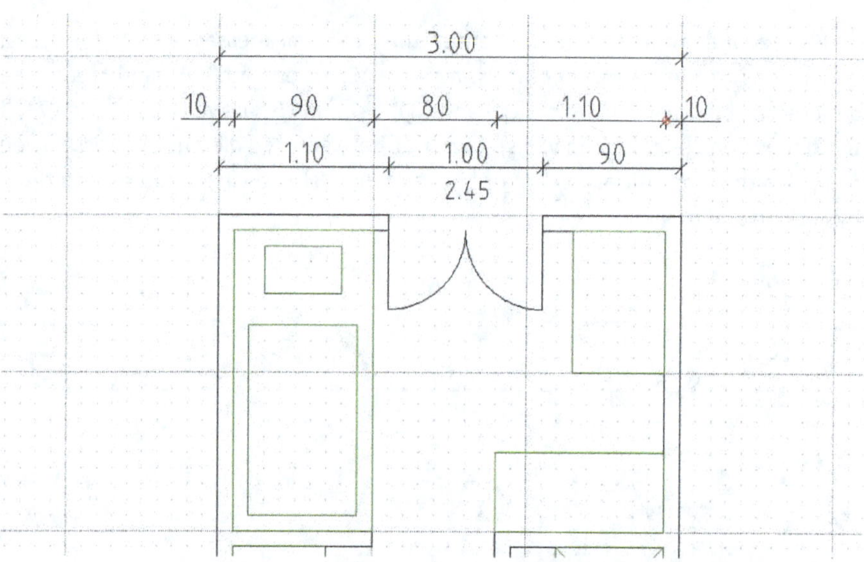

And the dimensioning on the right-hand side would look like this. We no longer need the dimensioning on the left-hand side, as no new information would be visible here.

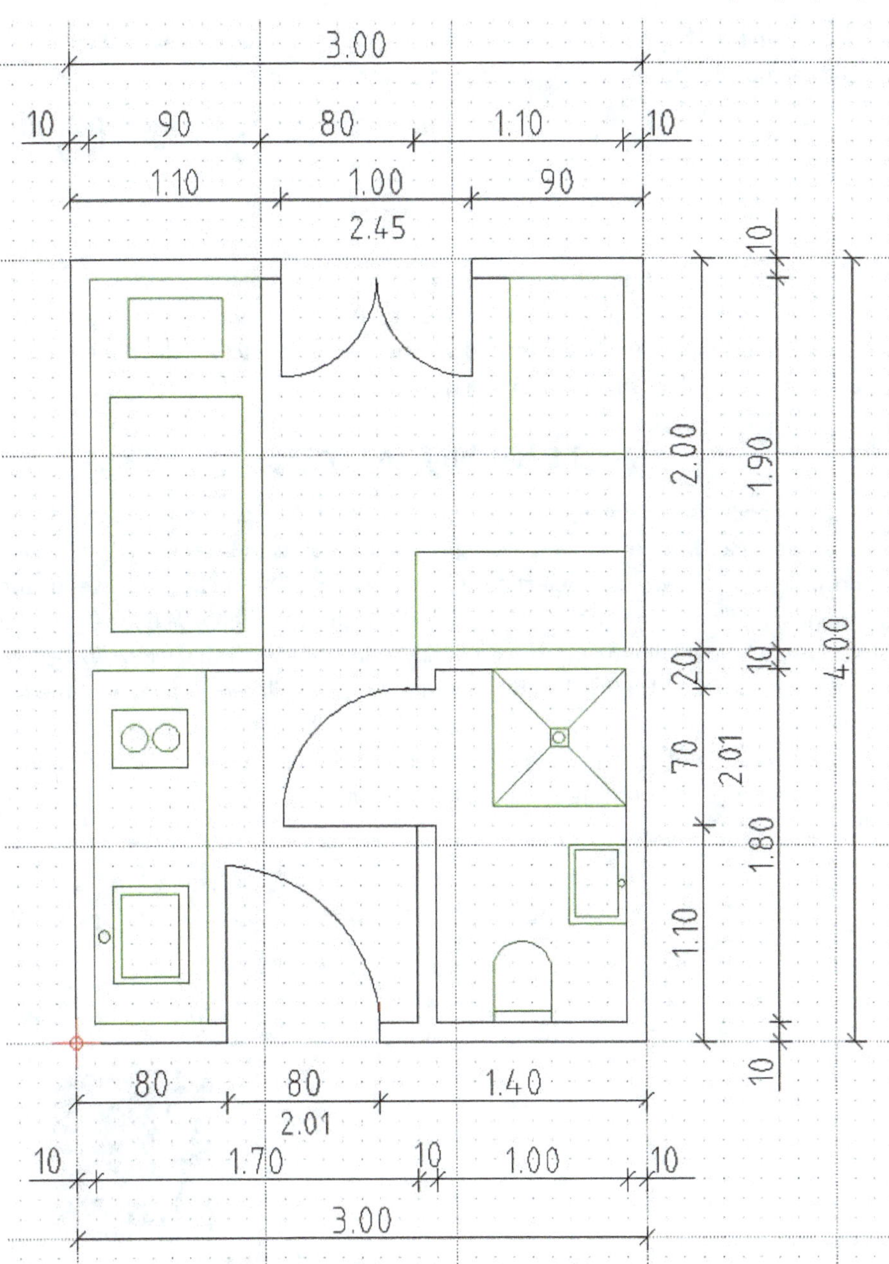

<u>Note:</u> The dimensioning for the door height on the right-hand side must be rotated by 90 degrees. To do this, first create a text with the command "MText" ①, enter the relevant parameters in the settings window — as shown above — and then confirm with "OK". <u>Before</u> placing the text, you can then enter an angle of 90

degrees in the "Angle" ② field in the menu bar. This rotates the text by 90 degrees and can now be positioned in the drawing layer with a click.

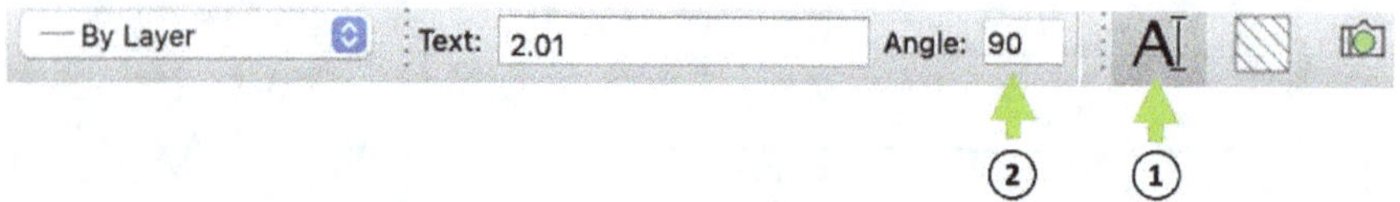

Excellent! Now we know how to correctly and easily dimension technical mechanical engineering components and architectural floor plans in "LibreCAD". Using the examples, we have learned in a clear way how to use the dimensioning commands in "LibreCAD" with confidence.

3.5 Hatching and Filling

Hatches and fills can be created in "LibreCAD" with the command "Hatch". To do this, we first draw a simple rectangle of two points (① and ②) in a new document, which we then select by clicking on it ③. This rectangle serves as the boundary of the fill or hatching. Then click on the command "Hatch" ④ and a settings window will appear. If we check "Solid Fill" ⑤ in this window, we can create a fill. If we also tick "Enable Preview" ⑥, we will see a preview of the fill. The color of the fill is black, as the option "By Layer" is set in the menu bar for the setting "Line Color" ⑦. If we want a different color for the fill, we would set this here before clicking on the command. The command is executed by clicking on "OK".

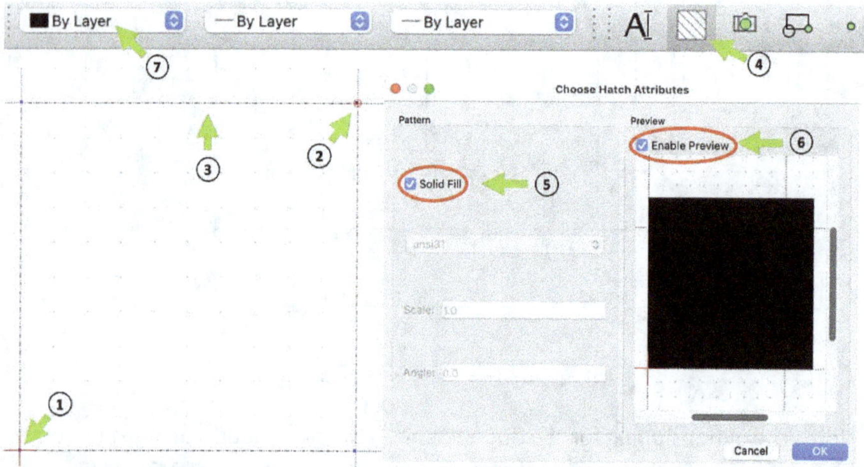

As an alternative to a solid fill, we can also create hatchings. To do this, we undo the filling process, click on the rectangle again and then select the command

"Hatch" again. In the settings window, we uncheck "Solid Fill" ①. This allows us to select from a variety of hatchings in the field below using a drop-down menu ②. For example, we can select the hatching "ansi31", which consists of evenly spaced lines parallel to each other and aligned at an angle of 45° to the baseline. This hatching is generally used for sectional areas (representation of cross-sections). We can use the fields ③ and ④ to scale the hatching and change the angle of the hatching. You are welcome to try this out. You can see the effects of changes in the preview image.

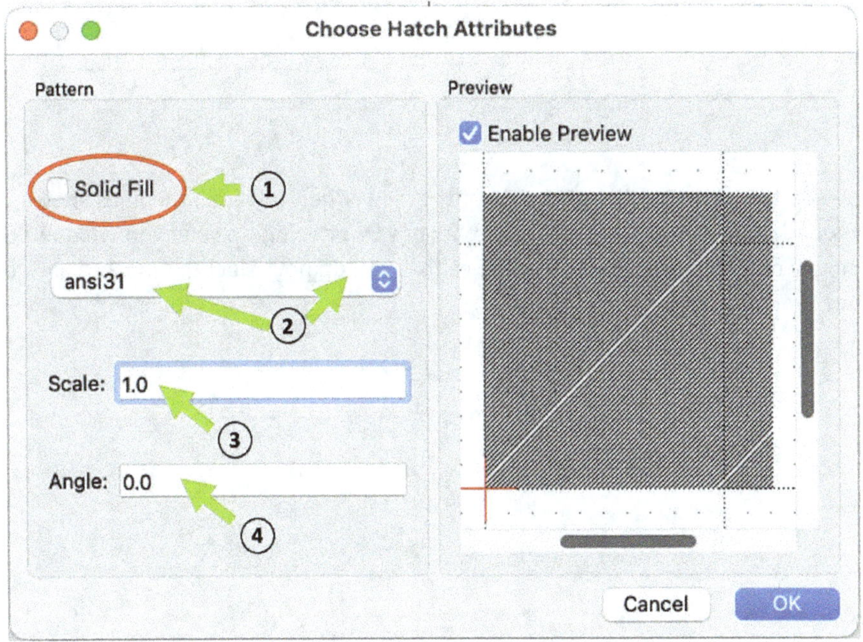

As you could already see when selecting "ansi31", the list of possible hatchings is very long. The best thing to do here is to try some or even all the possibilities. For architecture, for example, hatchings such as "ar-b816" (bricks) and "ar-conc" or "concrete" (concrete) or "ar-parq1" (parquet) are interesting. For furniture construction, for example, the hatchings "gost_wood" (wood) or "gost_glass" (glass) are useful.

Let's try this out using our two examples. If, for example, we want to transform the front view of the fastening component into a sectional view, we can do this relatively easily. The outer contours are identical in this case. It is important that the holes are not hatched. Why? Assuming we cut exactly through the middle of the component (in the plan view from top to bottom in the longitudinal direction), the holes will only be pierced in the center line at the cut edges. The cylindrical inner surfaces of the holes remain untouched. In this case, the concealed edges become visible edges in the sectional view. In order to create the hatching correctly, we need to define the individual partial surfaces correctly. Hatching or filling always requires a closed area. Therefore, we redraw the areas near the holes into the partial areas ① and ② and then add the two lines ③ and ④.

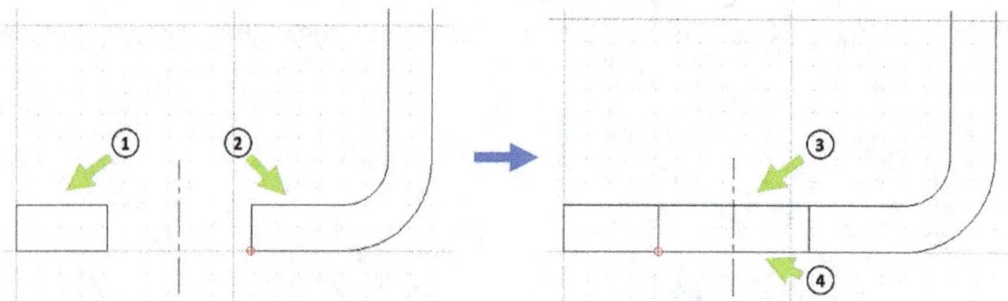

We do the same on the other side of the view. Then select all the lines shown in dashed lines below <u>without</u> arrow markings by drawing up selection windows or simply clicking on the lines. Make sure that you <u>do not</u> select the marked lines or the symmetry lines (arrows)!

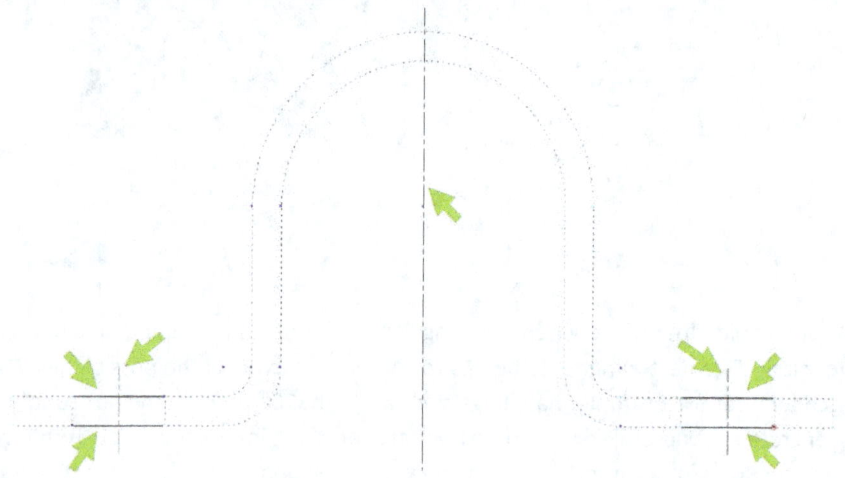

After the selection, we can execute the command "Hatch" with "ansi31".

If all areas have been delimited correctly and all lines have been selected correctly, you should receive the following result, which shows the sectional view of the part. You can see here that the holes have not been hatched.

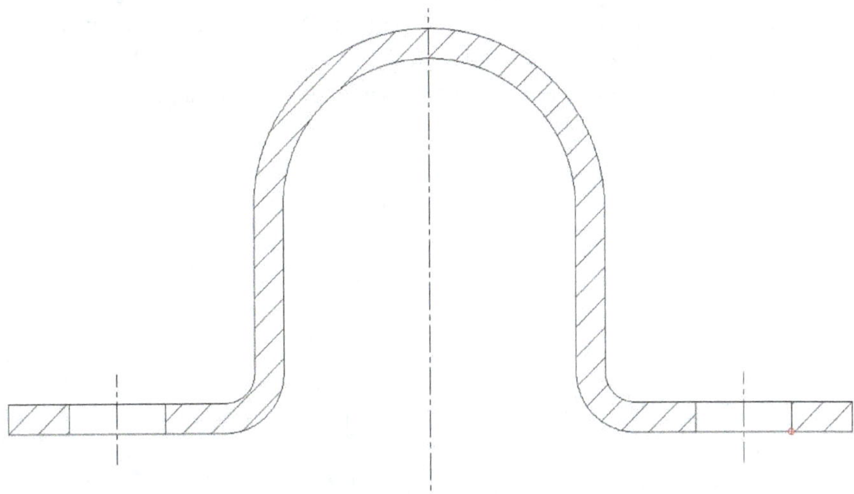

The floor plan of the student apartment works in the same way. Here, we only need to select a different scale for the hatching, as it would otherwise be much too large — just like the dimensions before. When we arrive at the hatching settings, we therefore select the value "0.05" ① at "Scale", for example. The preview then turns black, as the lines in this view are so close together that it looks like a solid fill.

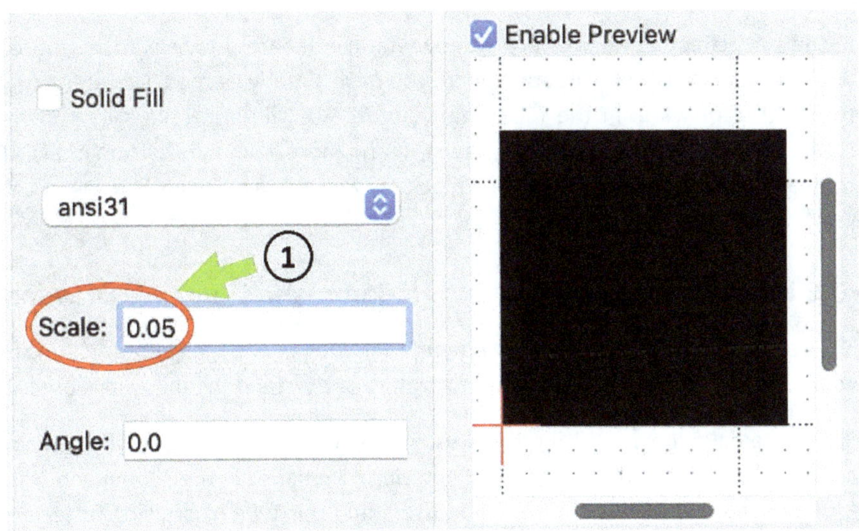

Before we get to these settings, however, it makes sense to trace the outlines of the walls of the floor plan again with lines in order to obtain completely closed surfaces. Normally, you would create the hatching directly after drawing the walls. This step would then be omitted. Adding the hatching afterward is more difficult because you have to select the correct lines (closed areas). This can lead to problems. Try hatching the left-hand area ① of the apartment first and then the right-hand area ②. Remember the previously mentioned scaling!

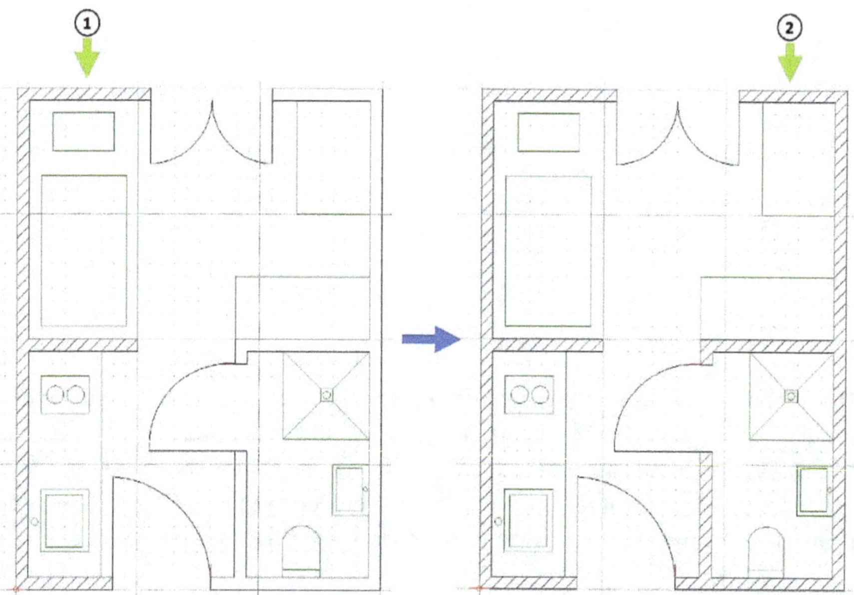

In the next chapter, we will look at how you can create drawings in an entirely different way in "LibreCAD". Stay tuned, you have already learned a lot about how to use the software. In the following chapters, we will also take a look at the creation of isometric views (3D views), learn more commands from the CAD toolbar, how to work with layers and blocks as well as file output and true-to-scale printing, among other things.

3.6 Using Keyboard Commands ("Command Line") for Drawing

To prepare for this chapter, I recommend that you go through *chapter 2.2* of the course again. This will make it easier for you to understand the following content.

So far, we have drawn in "LibreCAD" using the PC mouse. However, you can also create geometries in this program by entering commands in the "Command Line" — completely without a mouse. Some users find this type of drawing faster and more precise, others prefer to draw with the PC mouse. In addition, the command variant allows you to enter several commands at once and also use the command line as a calculator. It is a matter of taste and also depends on the application whether you can draw better or worse with the PC mouse or the command line.

We enter the commands in the "Command line" window (bottom right by default; *see chapter 1.3*). If you cannot find this window, you should check whether it is activated. This is done at "Dock Widgets" ② in the menu "Widgets" ①.

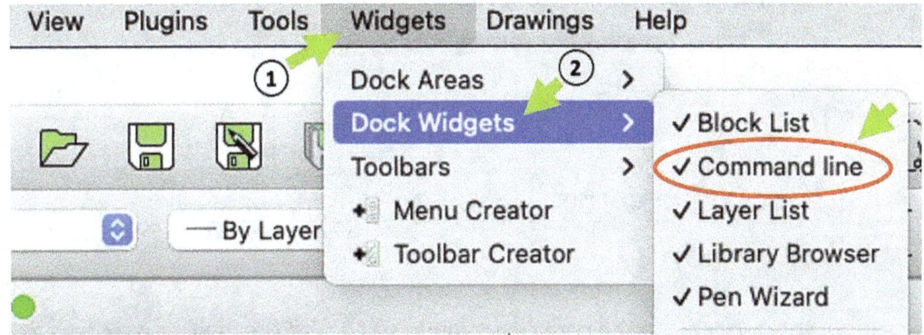

To draw a geometry using command inputs, you need the name of the command on the one hand and the coordinates of the desired geometry on the other. For example, we would like to draw a rectangle 10 units wide and 12 units high. For the rectangle we need the command "rectangle", the abbreviations "rect" or "rec" also work. Enter one of these commands in the command line and press the Enter key.

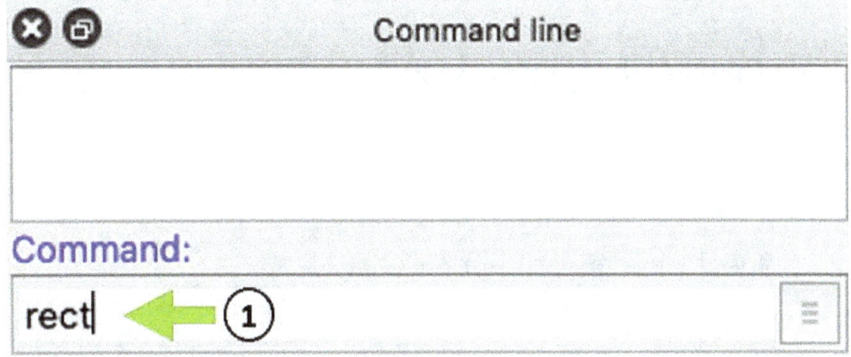

The command is then active and "Command: rect (rectangle)" should appear in the command line as confirmation ①. A note ② appears above the input line, indicating what to do next. In this case, we need to specify the first point of the rectangle, which is why "Specify first corner" appears. The specification is now made using coordinates. If we want to start the rectangle at the coordinate origin, for example, we enter the value "0,0" ③ for the first point and confirm the entry again with the Enter button.

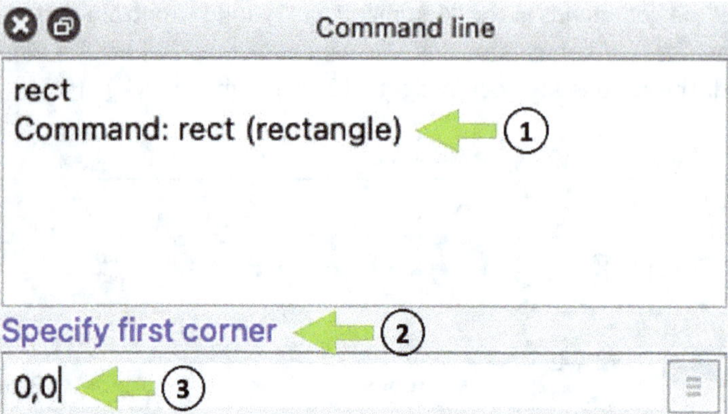

The input then appears in the command window ①, and the next step is displayed above the input line ②. For the rectangle command, we must define the second corner point ("Specify second corner"). The coordinates of the second corner point are "10,12", as the width (x-coordinate) of the rectangle should be ten units and the height (y-coordinate) twelve units. After confirming with the Enter key, the rectangle is created.

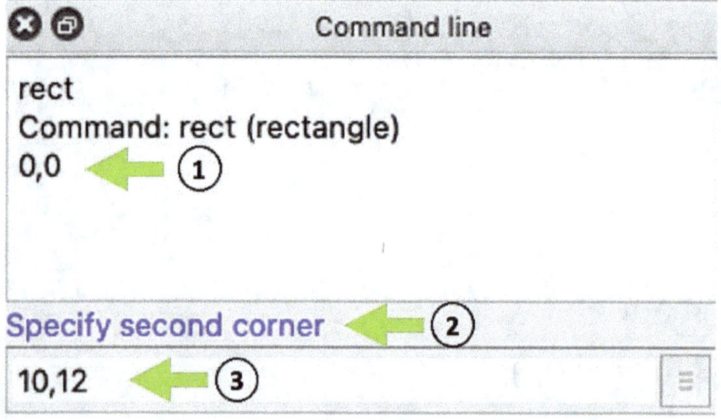

"Specify first corner" ① then appears again above the input line, as the rectangle command is still active. You can therefore draw the next rectangle straight away. Let's assume we need another rectangle of identical size, but with a distance of ten units (x-direction) from the previous rectangle. Up to now we have entered absolute coordinates, in this case we can enter relative coordinates. This provides the advantage that we can continue drawing directly from the point at which we are currently located (top-right corner of the first rectangle; coordinates "10,12"; last input) ②. Relative coordinates are specified in "LibreCAD" with a preceding @ symbol. As an alternative to the @ symbol, you can also specify relative coordinates with two points between the numbers. As we want a distance of ten units from the top right-hand corner of the first rectangle to the second rectangle, the specification for the first corner of the new rectangle is "@10,0" ③ (alternatively: "10..0"). This defines the top-left corner ④ of the new rectangle. Why 0? Because we are only moving by ten units in the x-direction — we are <u>not</u> moving in the y-direction. We remain in horizontal alignment with the last corner ② of the first rectangle.

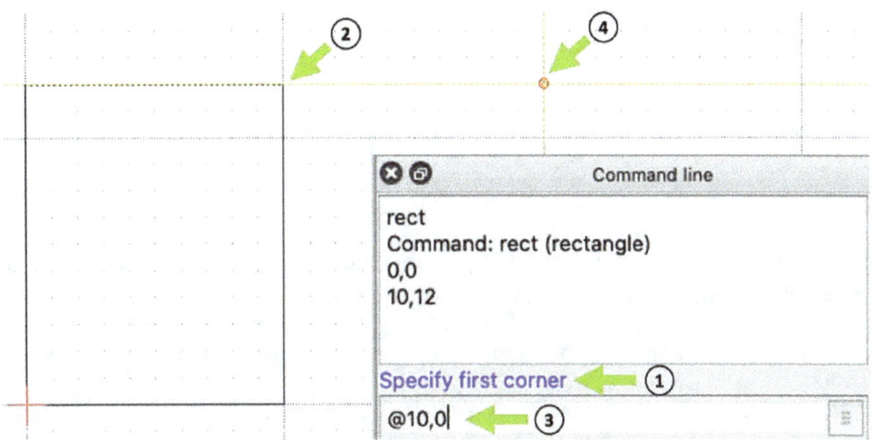

In absolute coordinates, we should have specified this corner as "20,12". Remember the coordinate display in the status bar of "LibreCAD" (*chapter 2.2*). If you move your mouse over the drawing plane, you can easily see the coordinates. Relative coordinates are therefore always helpful when we know the distance between two geometries or the size of a geometry. In this case, we <u>do not</u> need to calculate the absolute coordinates. Now, please try to draw the second corner of the rectangle on your own. Enter the corner point in relative coordinates. You know that the rectangle should be 10 units wide and 12 units high. The rectangle should also be at the same height as the first rectangle. What is the input? The solution will follow shortly.

Solution: We must move ten units to the right in the positive x-axis direction (+10) and twelve units downwards in the negative y-axis direction (-12) from the previously defined corner point ①. The coordinates for the second corner point ② are therefore "@10,-12" ③ (alternative: "10..-12").

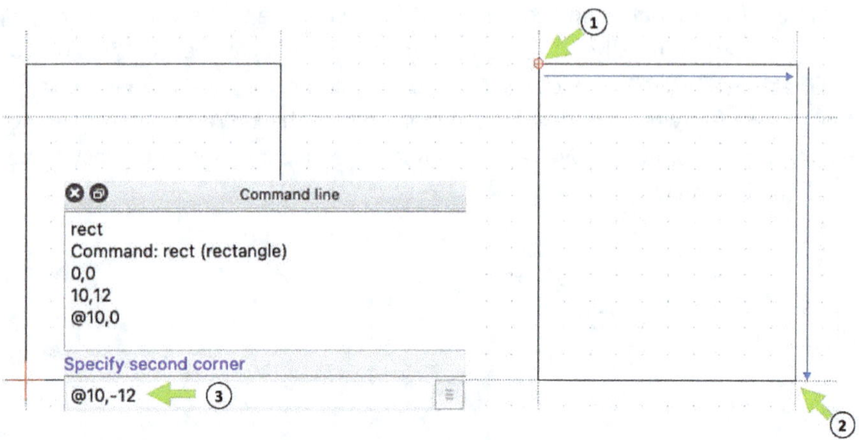

Now, we could draw the next rectangle straight away, but we would rather not do that. We therefore end the command with the ESC key.

The respective commands for relevant geometries are listed below.

- 2-point line ("2 points"): Command "l", "li" or "line"
- Horizontal line ("horizontal"): Command "hor" or "horizontal"
- Vertical line ("vertical"): Command "ver" or "vertical"
- Rectangle ("rectangle"): Command "rec", "rect" or "rectangle"
- Parallel line through point ("Parallel through point"): Command "pp" or "ptp"
- Tangent with point and center ("Tangent (P,C)"): Command "tangpc" or "tangentpc"
- Circle through center and point ("Centre, Point"): Command "ci" or "circle"

A table with all available commands can be found at:

https://docs.librecad.org/en/latest/ref/tools.html

But let's get back to drawing with the mouse. In the next chapter, we will learn how to use the 2D software "LibreCAD" to create a 3D view (isometric view) of 3D components. Such views look very professional, so don't miss out!

3.7 Displaying 3D parts in "LibreCAD" (Isometric View)

In this chapter, we will learn how to display objects in three dimensions in "LibreCAD". To create a 3D view, we can create the so-called isometric view of a part.

The isometric representation is a projection through which a three-dimensional object can be represented on a 2D environment (drawing paper, PC screen). The three-dimensional impression is created by the fact that in this projection the angle between two of the three axes (length, width, height) of the part on the drawing paper is 120 degrees. It is important that the dimensions along each axis in the isometric drawing ("iso" = equal; "metric" = dimension) are drawn to the same scale. In addition, lines that are parallel in space are also parallel in the projection. However, this results in a distortion of angles and circular geometries. For example, circles appear as ellipses.

Let's now take a look at an example of how isometric drawing works. For example, we have the three-panel projection of the following part and want to create a 3D view for this part.

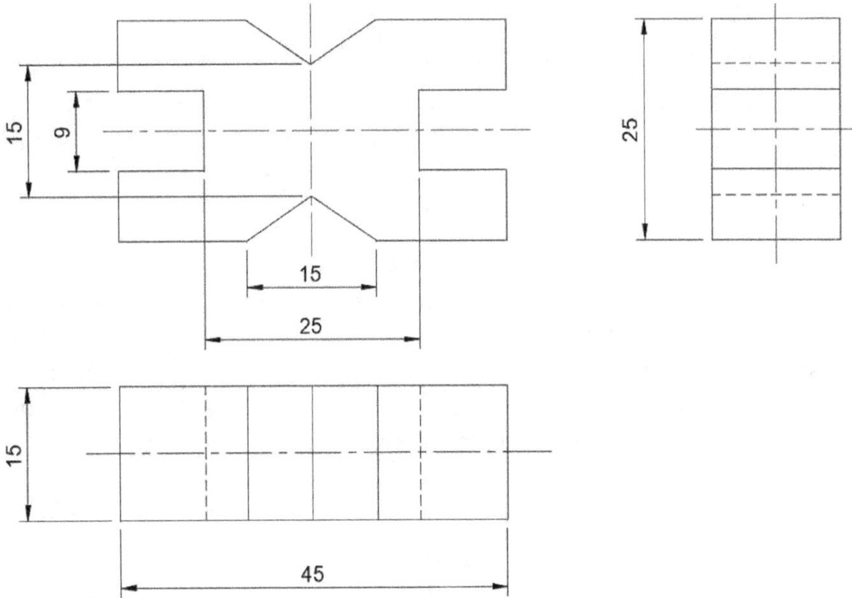

You need a good spatial imagination if you want to visualize a part in 3D based on the three-panel projection, especially for more complex parts. The isometric view we want to create will look like this.

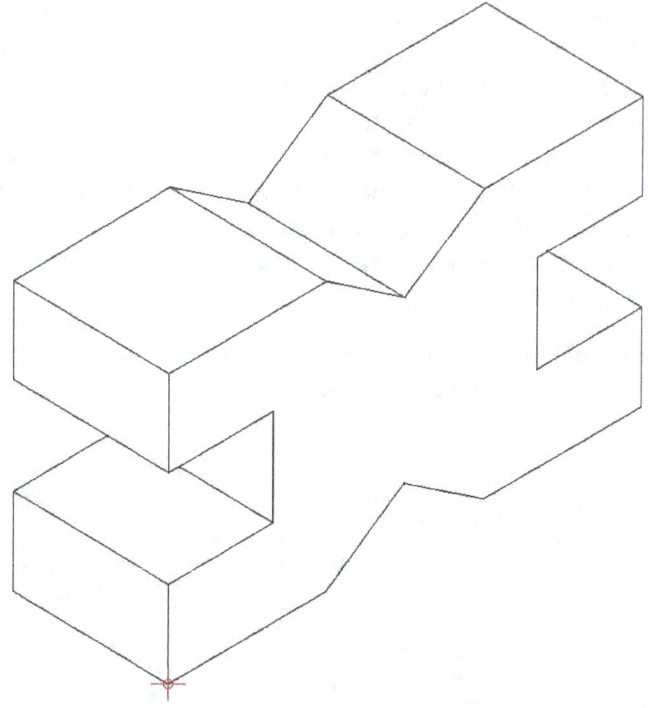

Until now, we had a drawing grid in "LibreCAD" that consisted of horizontal and vertical lines (x-axis and y-axis). To draw an isometric view, we need a drawing grid that represents three axes (x, y, z) — with an angle of 120 degrees between two axes. Fortunately, in "LibreCAD" there is the possibility to activate such a drawing grid. Switching to this grid is done in the tab "Grid" ② at "Current Drawing Preferences" ①. Here we have to activate "Isometric Grid" ③ instead of "Orthogonal Grid".

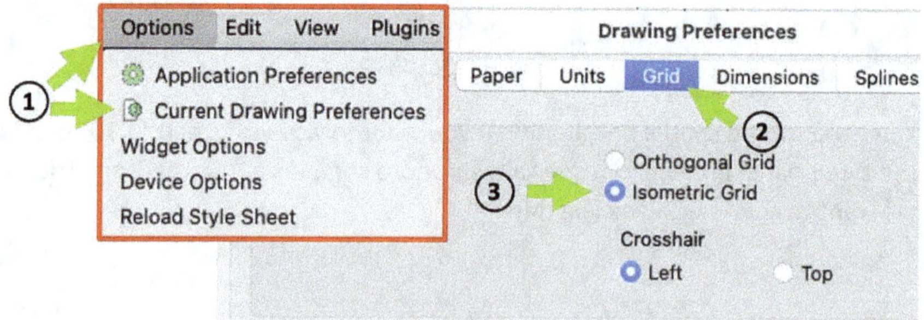

If we have confirmed the setting with "OK", the drawing grid then changes to the following display (without arrows and text in the software).

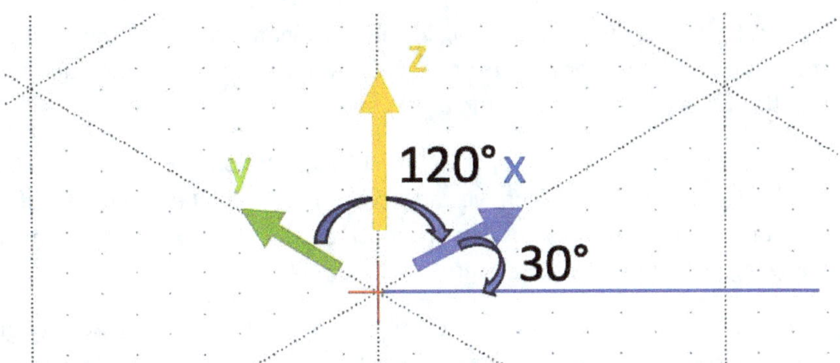

Let's imagine that we also had the 3D part physically on our desk in reality. Then we would only have to place the component at a slight angle in front of us and look at it from the right angle so that we can recognize the isometric view. Try this out with any object you like. Next, we would measure the physical component with a caliper using all corners. We can then draw these corners in "LibreCAD" and then just have to connect them with lines. This is how easy it is to create the isometric view. Alternatively, we can also take the dimensions from the three-panel projection and calculate them. This requires a little more imagination.

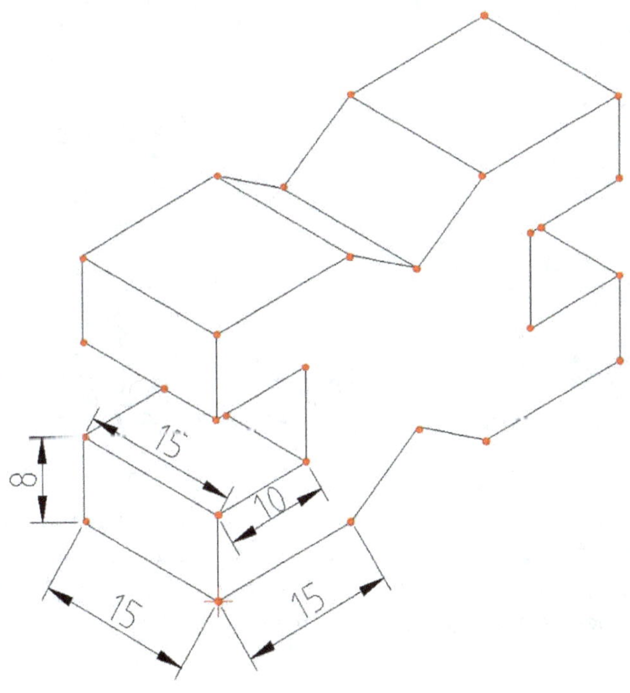

The easiest way is to start the drawing at the coordinate origin, i.e., the front and bottom corner of the part. Here we can draw the first two corner points or alternatively the first two lines of the part.

To do this, we first check whether the correct "Snap Options", in particular "Snap on Grid" ①, are activated. Then we can simply slide along the grid points of the axes when drawing, which makes drawing much easier. We also need to zoom into the drawing plane until the "Grid Status" is set to "1/10" ②.

Similar to when drawing the three-panel projection, the distance between two grid points is now one unit and a grid box has exactly ten units each. The grid box is now a parallelogram ② with sides of equal length instead of a rectangle. Therefore, we can draw the first line ③ by moving from the coordinate origin, one grid box and five grid points, along the positive x-axis direction. The second line must also run 15 units, but along the positive y-axis direction ④.

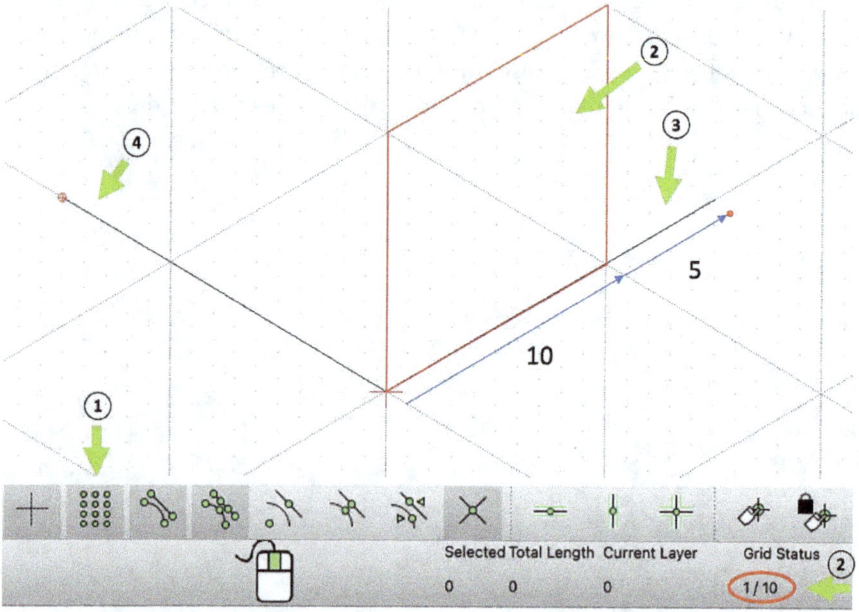

Now we simply continue in this way. Always remember to consider the parallelism of lines, then drawing is easier. So next we draw two vertical lines, each with a length of eight grid points (① and ②). Then a connecting line ③ and another line ④ with a length of ten grid points. As mentioned, please note the parallelism.

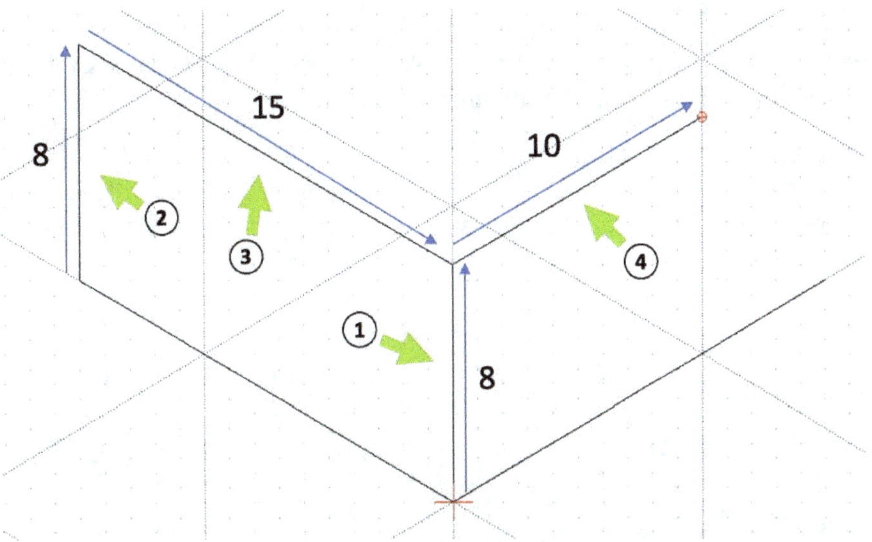

Now we have drawn the front corner of the part. Then we would simply continue to measure the part and draw the next lines.

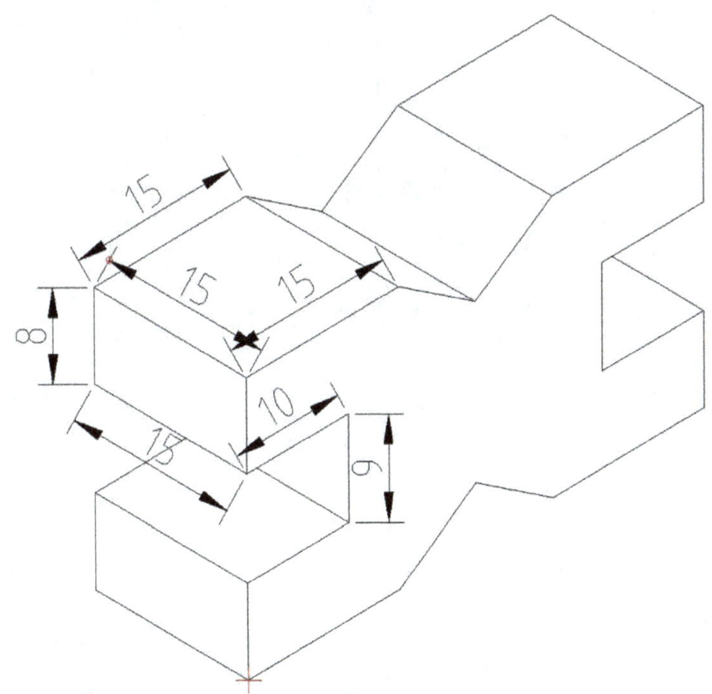

For example, we can take the following path and from ① to ⑥ we can place line to line. Again, pay attention to the parallelism of the lines when counting the grid points. Then we also draw the lines from ⑦ to ⑨.

The two lines ⑩ are hidden by the component in the last piece in the isometric view. The easiest way to place these lines is to only have "Snap on Grid" and "Snap Intersections" active. This allows us to count the grid points and select the intersection with the component at the end of the line.

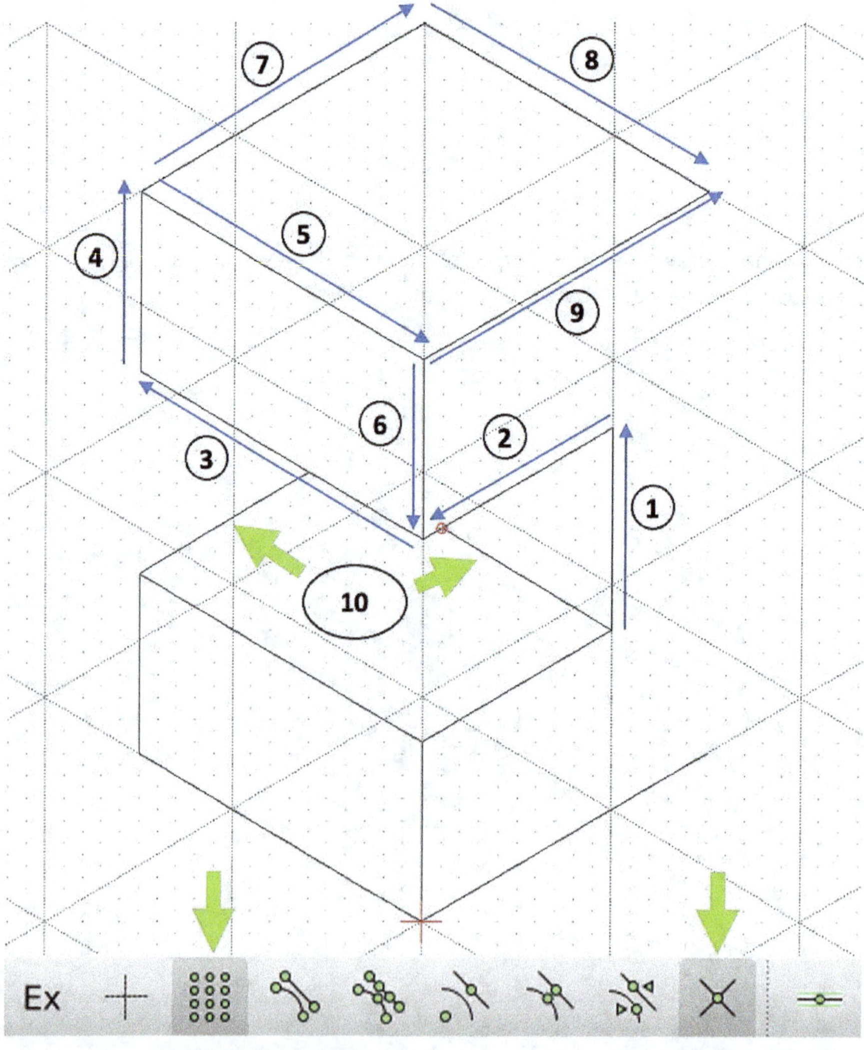

Then it continues with the middle section, which has a triangular notch at the top and bottom. This is 15 mm wide and 5 mm deep.

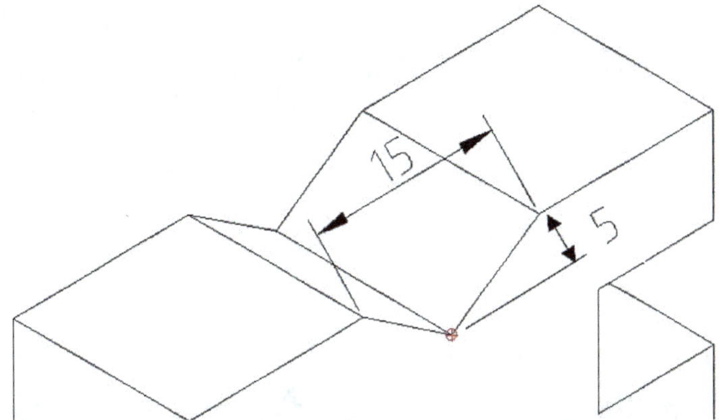

We can create a rectangular auxiliary geometry (① and ②) in red for each. These rectangles must be 15 mm wide and 5 mm high. Then, we only activate "Snap Middle" to be able to select the center point ④ of the line. Then also "Snap on grid" to be able to select the end point ⑤. We repeat this for the other points and lines, and also create a connecting line ⑥.

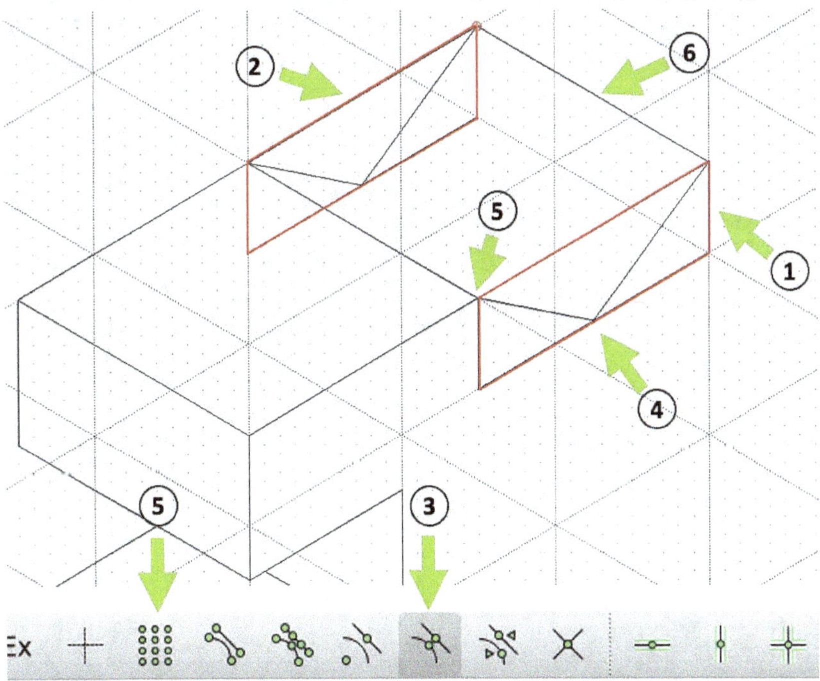

After deleting the red auxiliary lines and applying the same procedure to the lower area, we obtain the following intermediate result.

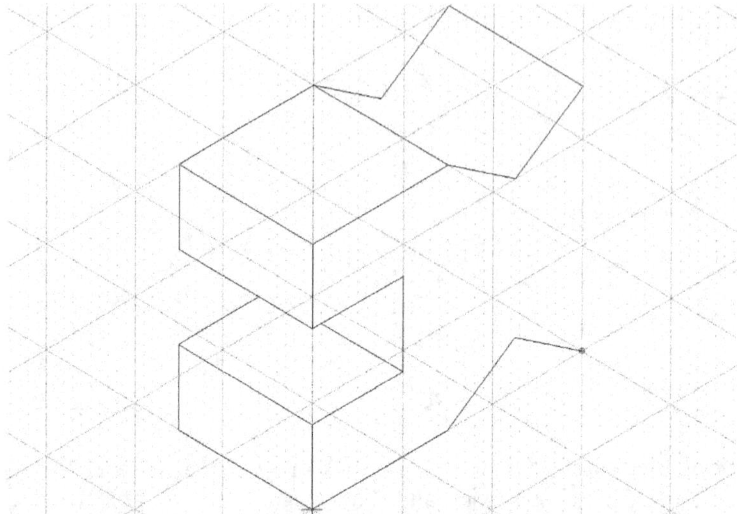

As the part is symmetrical, we know all the other dimensions for the rest of the part. To make the example clearer, the dimensions are shown again below. Please try to complete the part on your own.

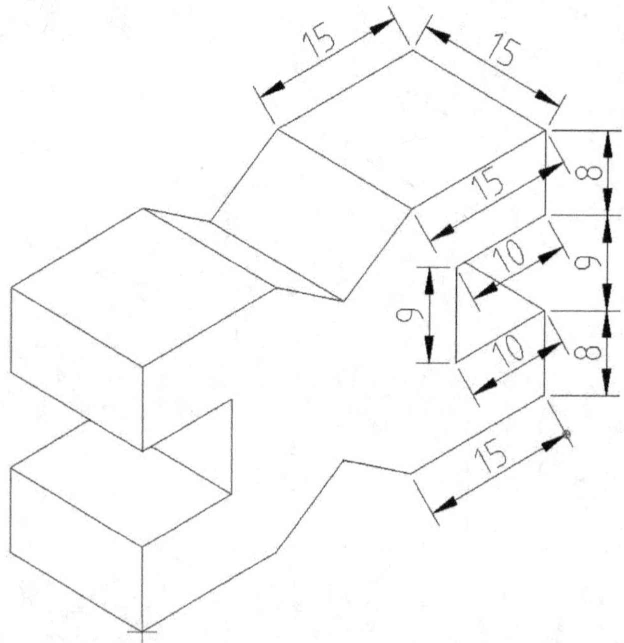

Solution: The following procedure would be possible, for example. Of course, other ways also work!

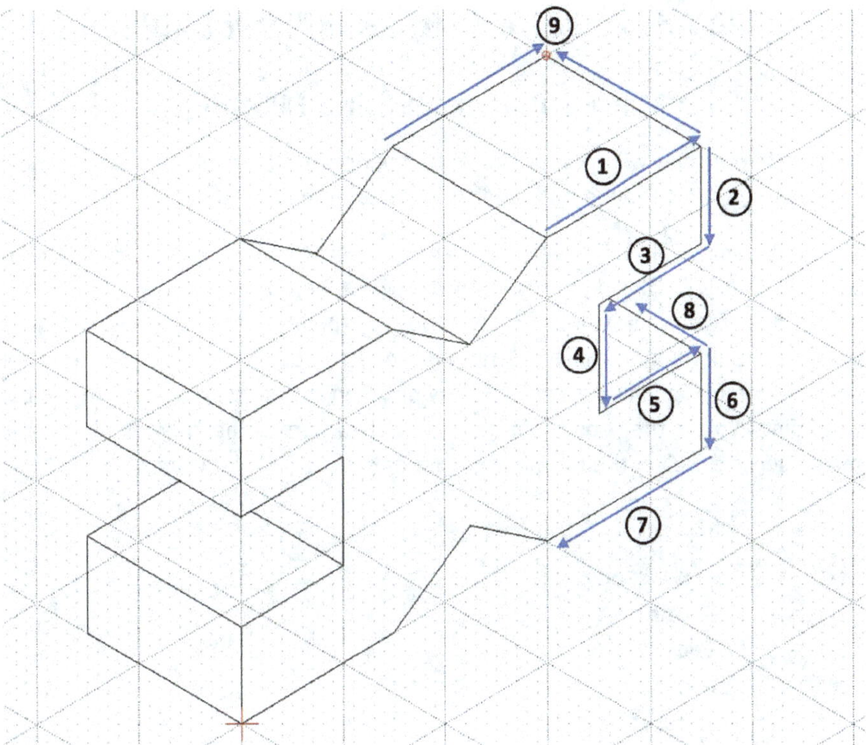

Perfect, that's how easy isometric drawing works in "LibreCAD". Now we can also create 3D views of components.

Unfortunately, it is not possible to create rotatable 3D models in "LibreCAD" because — as mentioned at the beginning — it is a 2D drawing program. If you are interested in rotatable and manipulable 3D models that can also be printed with a 3D printer, for example, then you will need 3D CAD software such as "FreeCAD" or "Fusion360". Further information can be found at the end of the course.

4 Advanced Techniques in "LibreCAD"

4.1 Moving, Rotating, Scaling, Mirroring ...

In this chapter, we will look at the most important commands of the "Modify" menu, which can be found on the left-hand side of the CAD toolbar.

The first command is "Move/Copy" and is used to move or copy a drawing geometry. Let's try this on our isometric drawing. Before we select the command (② and ③), we select all the drawn lines ① (pull up the selection window or click on the lines individually). Then we need to specify a reference point for copying or moving. This point can be any point on the drawing plane. We will use this point to place the copy of the geometry elsewhere in the drawing plane, so it makes sense to select the foremost corner of the part ④, for example.

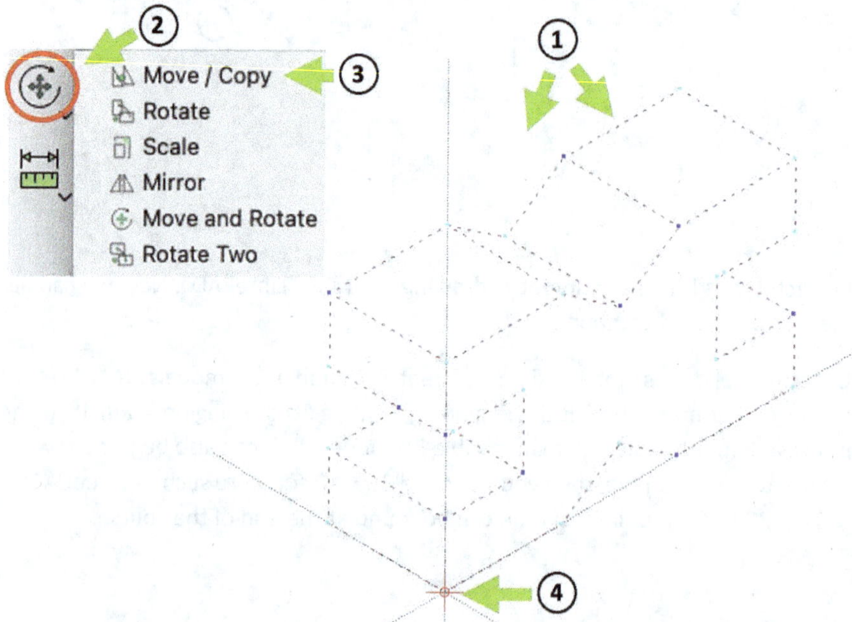

After selecting the point, a duplicate of the geometry appears, which we can place in the drawing plane by clicking on the selected reference point, e.g. a little further to the right of the original. A settings window appears, in which we can specify whether we want to create a copy ("Keep Original") or simply move the geometry ("Delete Original"). We can also create multiple copies ("Multiple Copies"). For example, we select "Keep Original" as we want to duplicate the part.

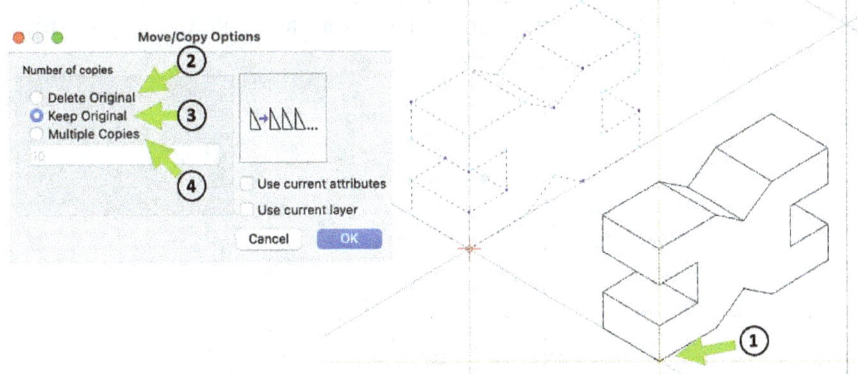

After selecting the geometry, you can also use the shortcut CTRL+C to copy a geometry and CTRL+X to move it. The copy or the cut original can then be pasted in both cases with CTRL+V. The specification of the reference point remains identical. The shortcut CTRL+Z, which undoes the previous action, is also helpful here.

The "Rotate" command can be used to rotate a selected geometry. First select the original geometry ① and then the command ②. Next, enter a point ③ for the center of rotation. The geometry will later rotate around this point, which should be in the middle of the geometry, for example. Then, as before, you must specify a reference point ④. The part for the rotation is gripped at this point. Finally, we place the point ⑤ — depending on the rotation — in the drawing plane.

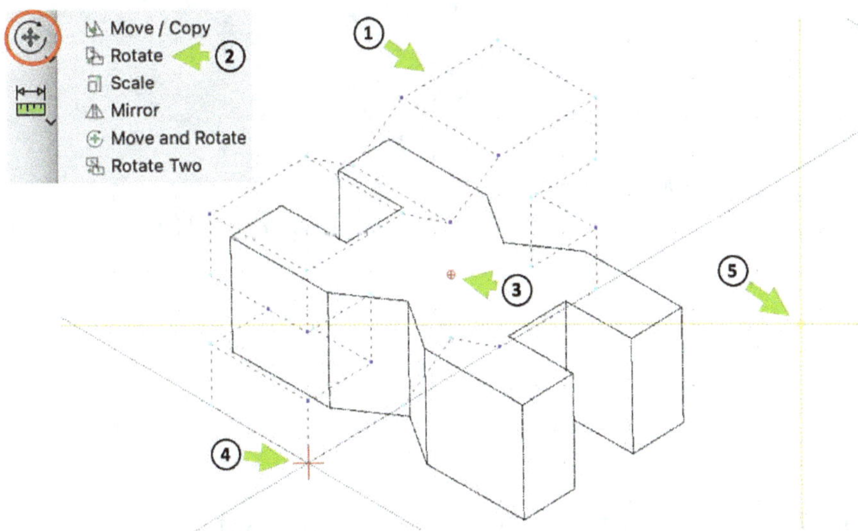

A settings window appears, in which we can enter the exact angle of the rotation (120° in this case) and determine whether we want to delete the original (rotate only) ② or keep it (create a rotated copy).

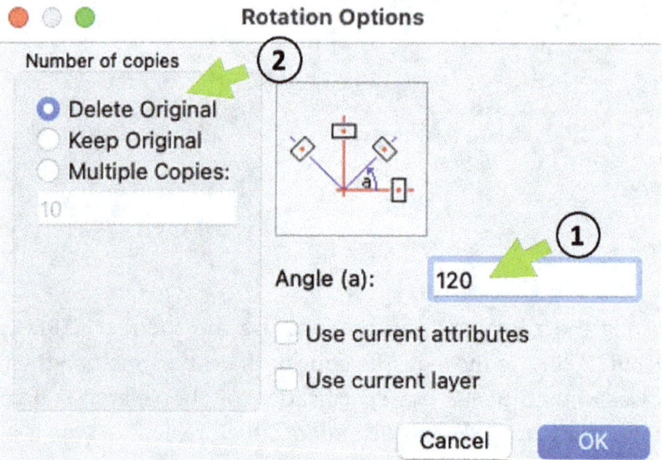

The command "Scale" (to be found below "Rotate") works in the same way as the command "Move/Copy". Only the settings window is different. Here, we can specify the scaling factor ① in the x and y direction. If the option "Isotropic Scaling" ② is active, all x and y dimensions are scaled equally. This means there is no distortion. With a positive scaling factor, the geometry is enlarged, with a negative factor it is reduced.

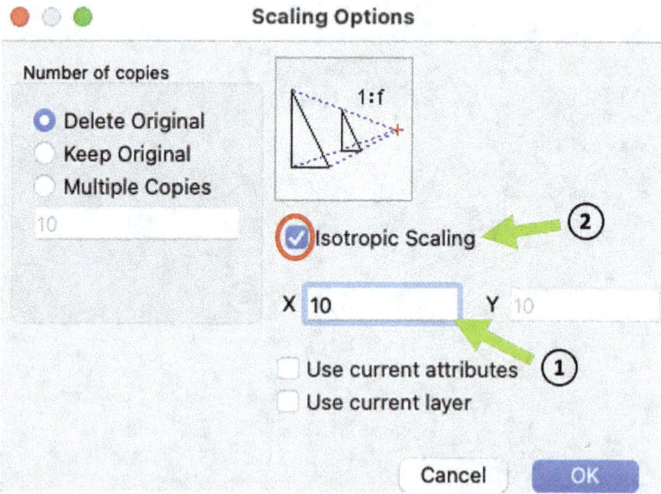

The "Mirror" command is very important, as it can be used to mirror geometries using a line of symmetry. This often speeds up and simplifies the drawing process considerably and works as follows. First, select the geometries that you want to mirror. Then select the command. Now you have to define two points on the drawing plane one after the other, which define the symmetry line. Finally, a settings window appears with the options "Delete Original" or "Keep Original" (select). After confirming with OK, the mirrored object appears.

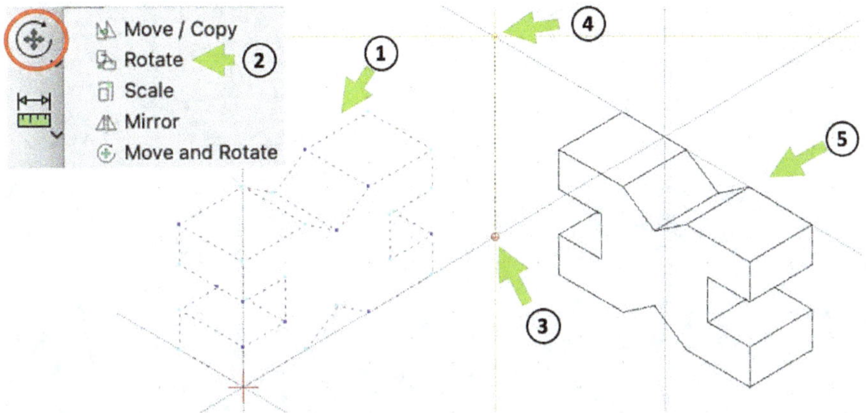

For the next commands, we switch to a new document with an orthogonal drawing grid (*see chapter 3.7*). Let's assume we have the following circle and line.

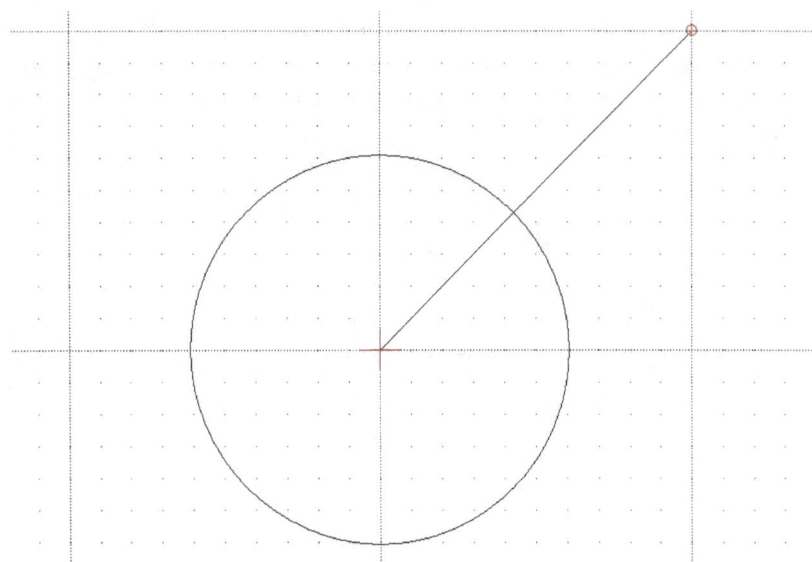

We now want to remove the part of the line that lies outside the circle, i.e., cut off the line at the point of intersection with the circle. To do this, we can select the command "Trim" ①. With this command, you first specify the bounding geometry, in this case the circle ②. Next comes the geometry to be trimmed, in this case the line ③. Make sure that you click on the line within the circle. You must always click on the part that you want to keep. For example, if we want to keep the outer part of the line, we click on the line outside the circle. Please try both.

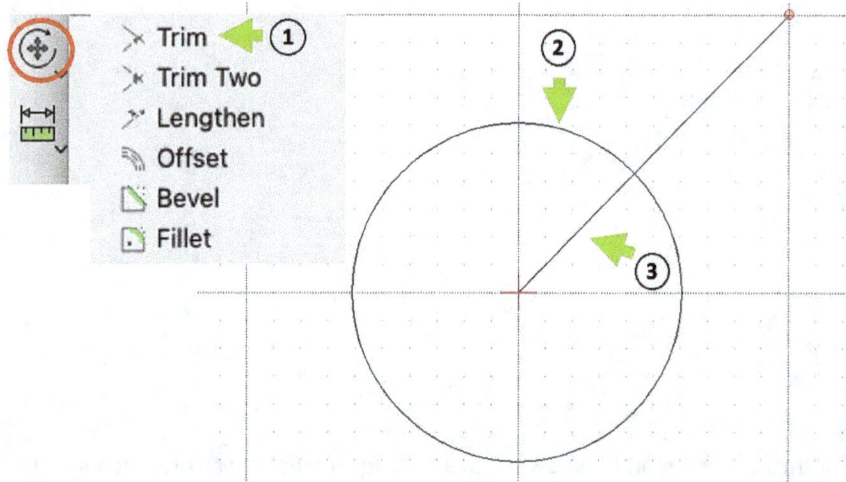

Another useful command — especially when drawing sheet metal or other thin-walled parts — is "Offset". This command can be used to duplicate a geometry at an even distance. Let's take a look at the front view of our fastening part from one of the previous chapters. The following geometry would have sufficed to quickly create this view.

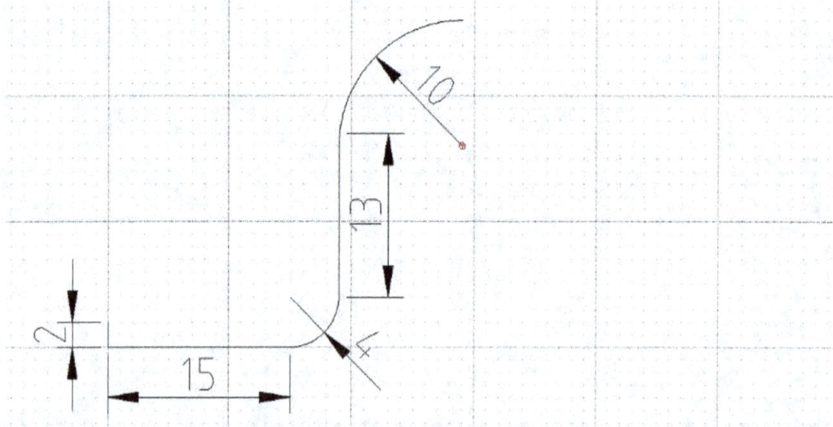

We can now edit this initial geometry with the command "Offset" by selecting all lines and arcs ① — <u>except</u> the vertical 2 mm line — (dimensions removed) and then clicking on the command ②. We must then enter the desired distance in the field ③ in the menu bar. In this case, this is 2 mm (material thickness). We can then specify the direction of the command by moving our mouse back and forth. Finally, move and click approximately in the area ④. The correctly aligned duplicate is then created (already shown here).

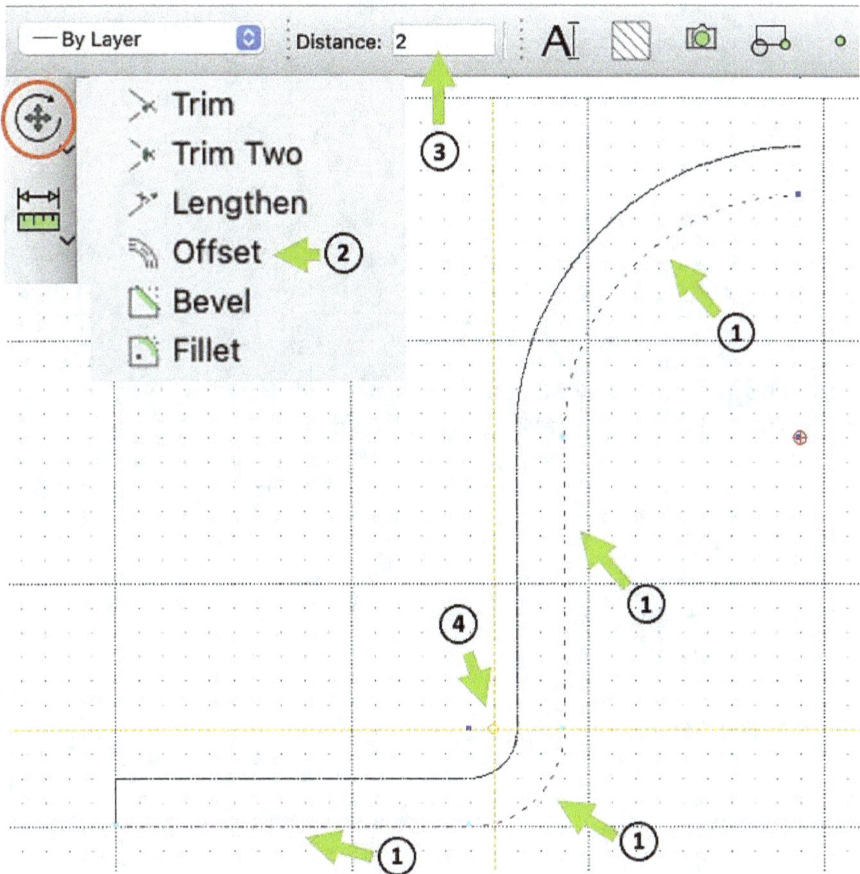

Now we already have half of the front view. As the part is symmetrical, you could create the other half quickly and easily using the already familiar "Mirror" command. You are welcome to try this out. This works in the same way as shown earlier for the isometric view.

The next two helpful commands in this menu are "Bevel" and "Fillet". These commands can be used to chamfer ("Bevel") or round ("Fillet") a corner. Let's assume we have a rectangle of any size whose edges we want to modify. Then we do this by selecting one of the two commands — e.g. "Bevel" — and then entering the desired dimension (②) and (③)) of the bend and then selecting two lines (④) and (⑤)) that form an edge (command already executed here).

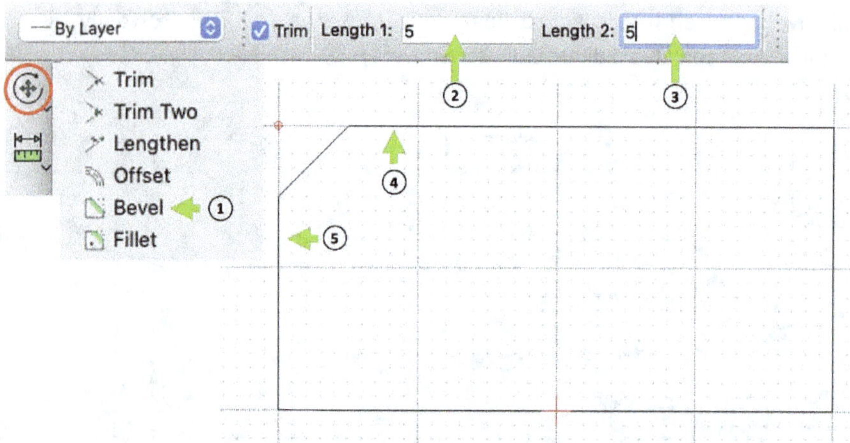

This works in a similar way with the command "Fillet". Here, however, we have to enter a radius in the menu bar instead of a length.

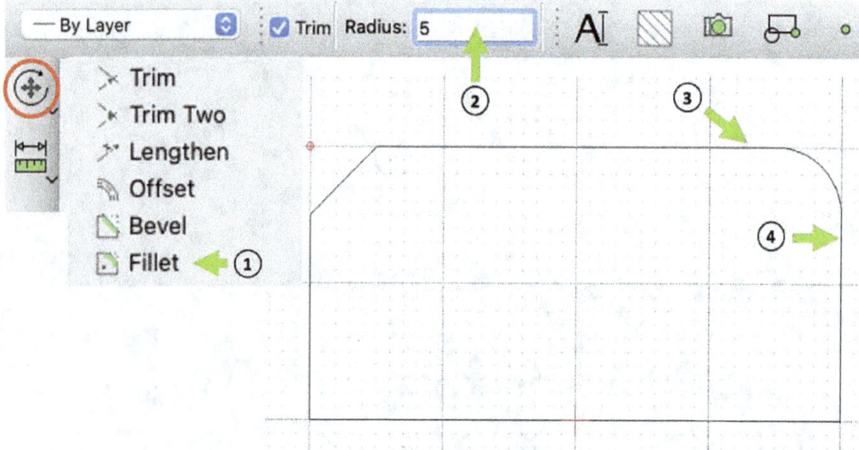

Perfect! These were the most important commands in the "Modify" menu. In the next two chapters, we will deal with layers and blocks.

4.2 Working with Layers — "Layer List"

As already mentioned in previous chapters, you can imagine layers in "LibreCAD" as transparent foils that lie on top of each other and on which you can draw independently of each other. This offers the advantage of separating different categories from each other easily and quickly. In architecture / construction, for example, you can draw a floor plan on several layers. The first layer could, for example, consist of the exterior walls, the second layer of the interior walls, the third layer of the windows and doors, the fourth of the interior fittings and so on.

The menu window "Layer List", which is located in the middle of the right-hand window bar by default, is relevant for creating and managing layers (*see chapter 1.3*). If you cannot find this window, you should check whether it is activated. You can do this at "Dock Widgets" ② in the menu "Widgets" ①.

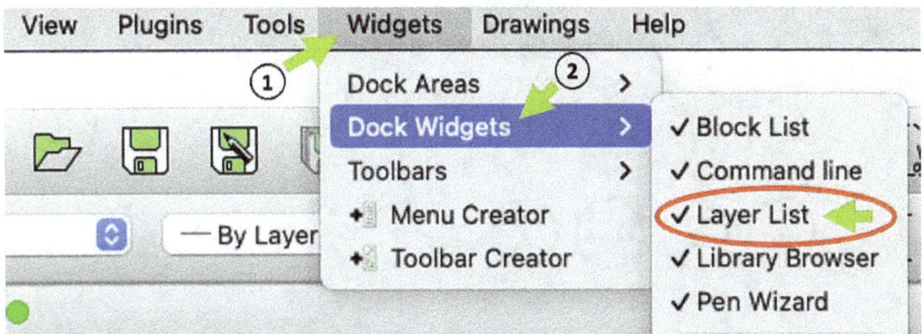

This window ① is divided into three tabs by default in the program, and is therefore combined with "Block List" and "Library Browser". As the name suggests, the levels in this window are shown as lines in a list. By default, there is a first level with the designation "0" ②. Each layer has identical setting options, which are represented by icons. By clicking on the eye symbol ③, you can hide or show a layer, and by clicking on the padlock symbol ④, you can lock or unlock the layer. Locking means that you cannot make any changes (e.g. delete or move) to the existing geometries or dimensions. This is helpful if geometries of the layer are to be protected from unintentional modification during the drawing process. By clicking on the printer icon ⑤, you can select whether the layer should be displayed when printing or not. We will deal with file output and printing in one of the next chapters. The # symbol ⑥ can turn all geometries of a line into construction geometries. All lines are then infinitely long and are <u>not</u> displayed in the printout by default. The rectangle ⑦ shows the current color of the layer. To change these and other attributes of a layer, select the layer and then click on "Modify layer attributes/rename" ⑧.

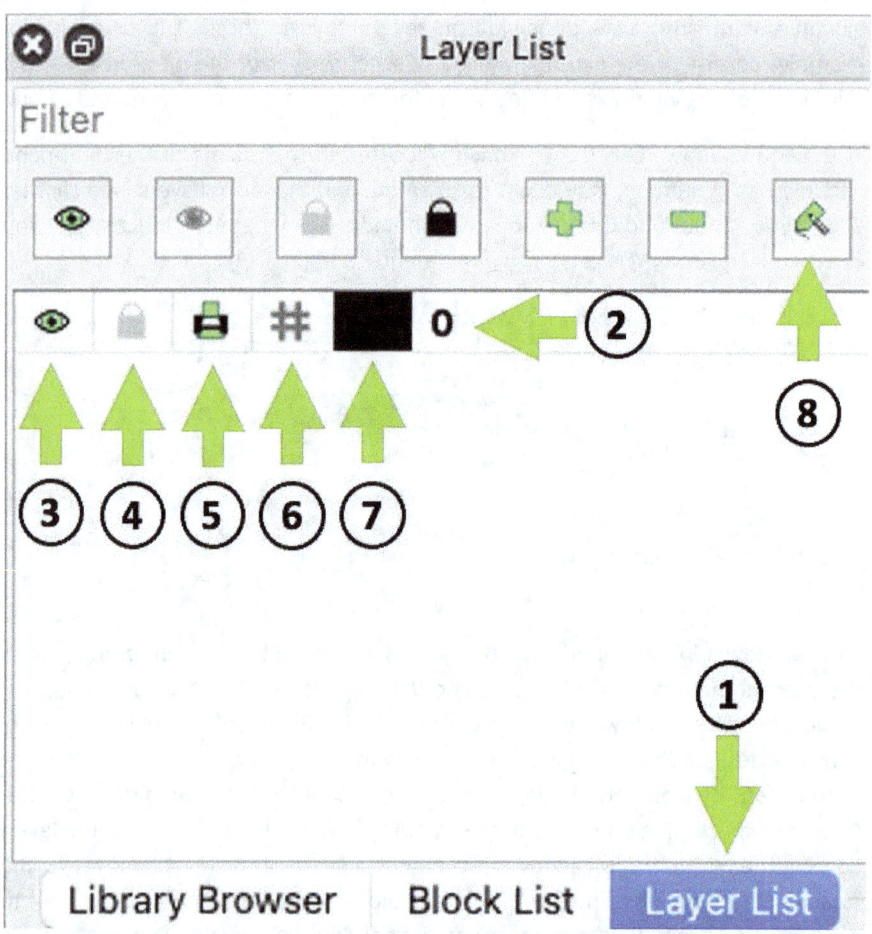

A settings window appears, in which you can change the name of the layer ①. On the other hand, the line color ② and other properties of the line type ③ can be changed or set centrally for all geometries of the entire layer. The name of the default layer 0 <u>cannot</u> generally be changed. The field is therefore grayed out in this case. It is best to get into the habit of giving each layer a meaningful name right from the start. This will help if you later work with a large number of layers or if other users are to make changes to your drawing.

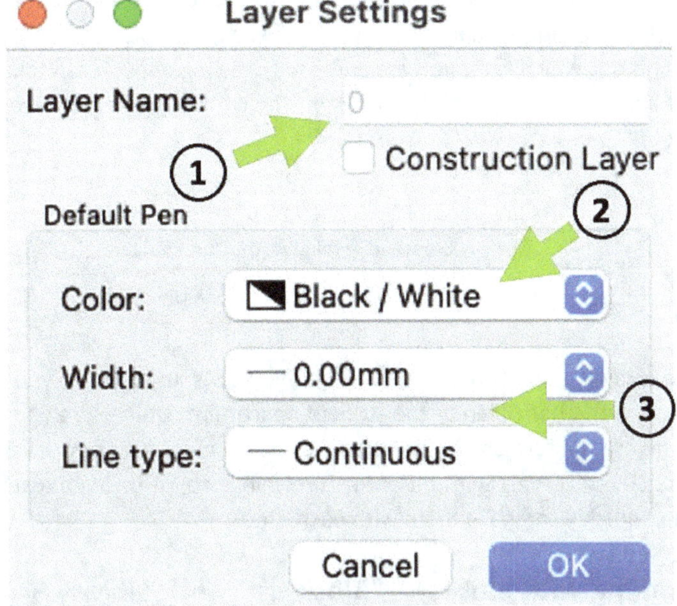

This setting window also always appears when adding a new layer. You can create a new layer by clicking on the + symbol ① and remove it by clicking on ② after selecting the layer. Once a layer has been added, it appears below the previous layer ③. You can lock or unlock all layers in the list with ④ and show or hide them all with ⑤. And using the search bar at ⑥, you can use a search term to filter for specific levels.

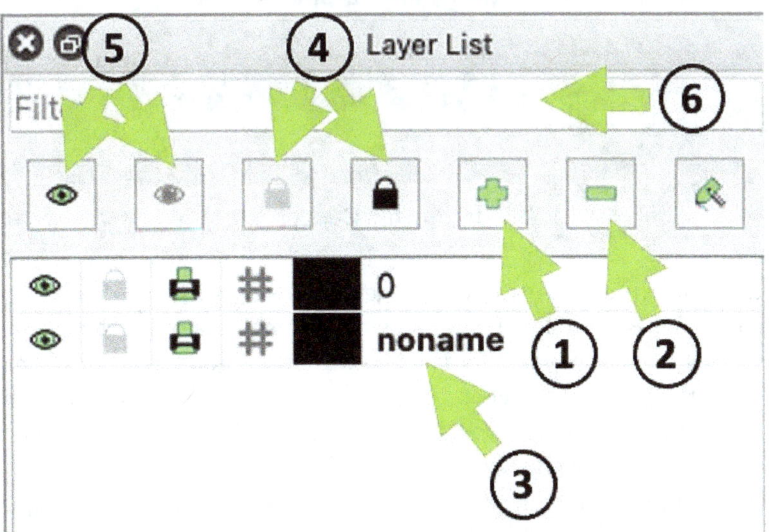

All geometries that are drawn are created on the respective layer that is currently selected. The selection is made in "Layer List" with a simple click on the desired layer. To find out which layer you are currently drawing on, you can take a look at the status bar at the bottom of the program. The currently selected layer is shown to the left of "Grid Status" at "Current Layer".

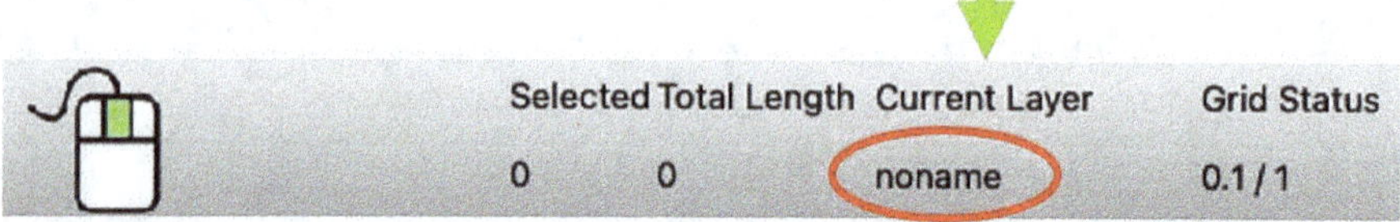

Otherwise, drawing works the same on every level. As an exercise, you could, for example, open the floor plan of the student apartment again. Here you could, for example, delete the furnishings and draw new furnishings on a new layer. You can also create several levels with different furnishings to go through a selection of options and quickly compare them with each other.

4.3 Working with Blocks — "Block List" and "Library Browser"

In the same area — next to "Layer List" — you will also find the tab "Block List". This window is used to create and manage blocks. If you cannot find this window, you should again check whether it is activated. You can also do this at "Dock Widgets" ② in the menu "Widgets" ①. Also check here whether "Library Browser" is also activated.

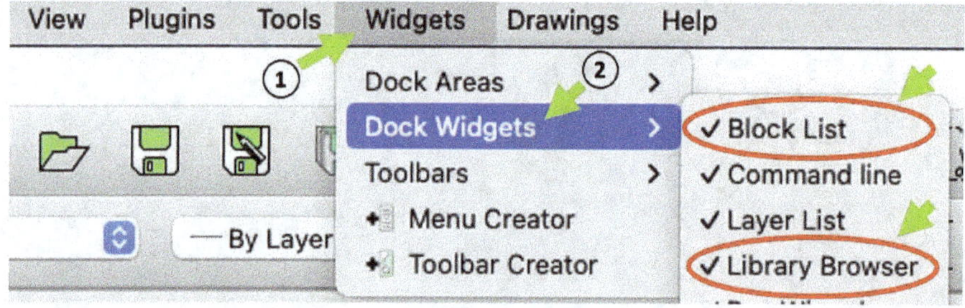

In "LibreCAD" you can save drawn geometries (consisting of lines, circles, rectangles...) as a block. In this context, a block combines the selected geometries into a single unit. If you are familiar with the Group function from "MS PowerPoint", then this is a good comparison. By creating a block, you combine different elements into one unit and can then use this unit as an independent object. This is helpful if you want to use an object repeatedly or insert it in several places in a drawing. You can also import these blocks into another drawing so that you can create a library of furniture, for example, which you can then use again and again in a floor plan. Another advantage is that you only have to change <u>one</u> block when making changes. Let's take a look at the example of the student apartment. For example, let's create a block for the toilet and a block for the bathroom sink. To create such a block, the first step is to select the lines and arcs of the object by clicking on them or using a selection window.

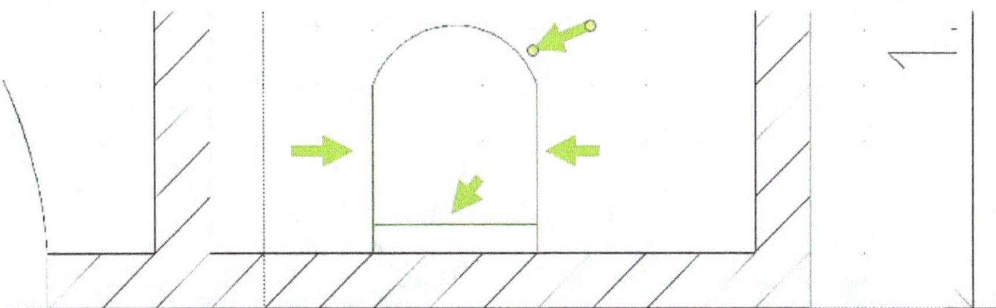

Then we click on the button "Create Block" ② in the window "Block List" ①. We then have to specify a reference point. In principle, we can determine this freely and choose it as we wish. However, it makes sense to select a corner ③ of the geometry, for example. The reference point is also used to position the block later when inserting. A settings window ④ now appears, in which we still have to enter a name for the block. The block is then created by clicking OK.

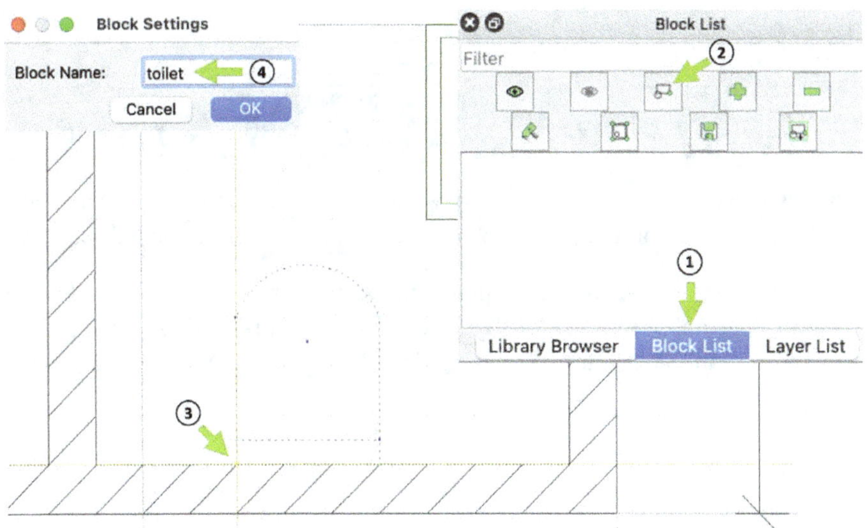

The generated block ① then appears in the "Block List". You can show or hide it by clicking on the eye symbol ②. This always applies to all identical blocks in a drawing. That means in this case, that all "toilet" blocks in the drawing will be hidden. If you want to hide all blocks in the list, you can do this using the buttons in area ③. To save a block to an external file, select it by clicking on it and press the symbol ④ for the save process. You can then import this block into another drawing later. Use the ⑤ symbol to insert the selected block into the drawing.

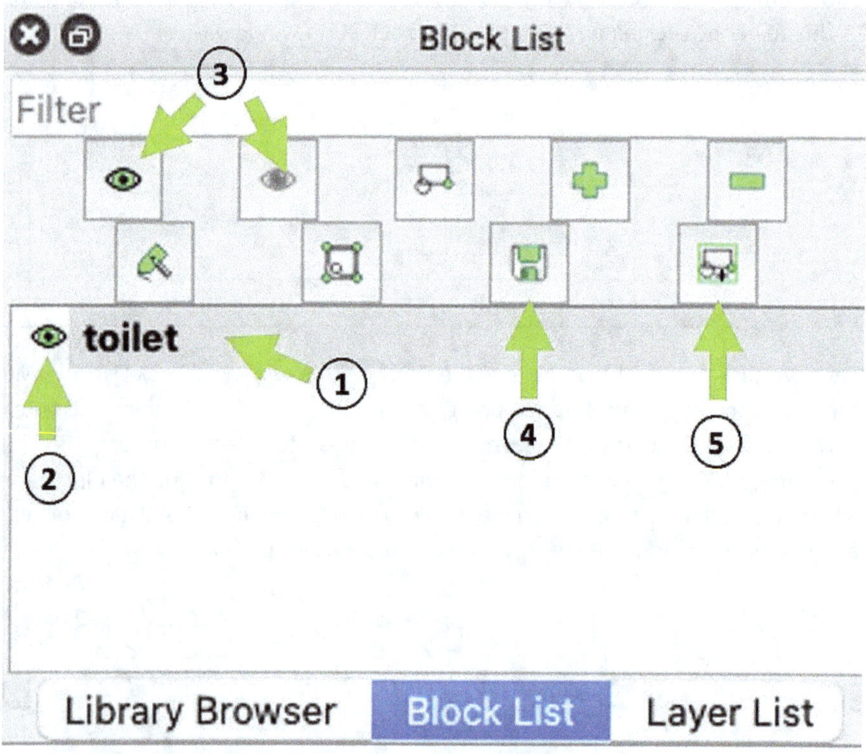

We will try inserting a block later. First, we would like to save the sink as a new block. You are welcome to try this on your own first. The resolution follows now.

Once we have selected all the geometric elements of the bathroom sink ①, we click on the symbol for creation ②. We then enter a reference point, e.g. the corner ③ of the sink. In the settings window that then appears, we enter a name ④.

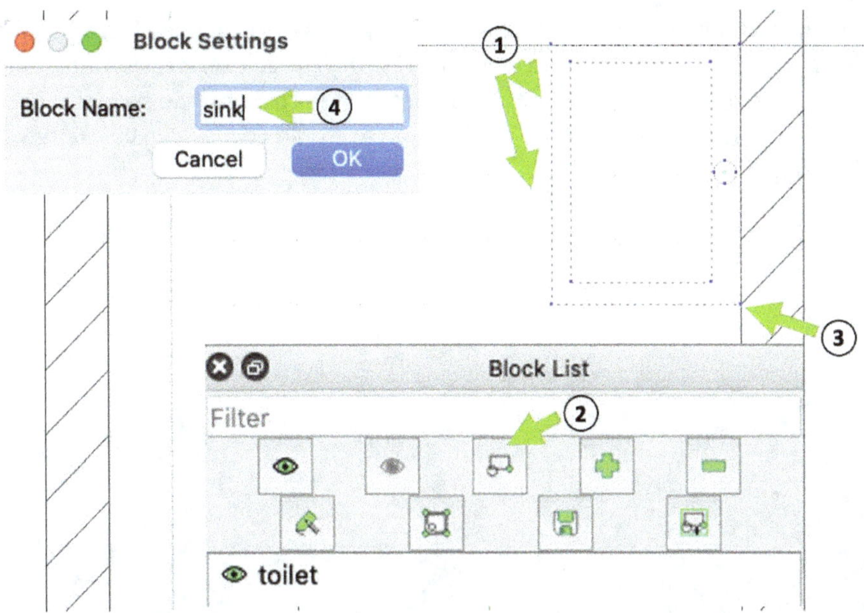

The new block "sink" ① then appears above the previously created block "toilet". If we select the new block and click on the button ②, we can edit the name again. You can delete a selected block by clicking on the minus symbol. Now let's try to insert the block "sink" into the drawing. To do this, first click on the symbol ④.

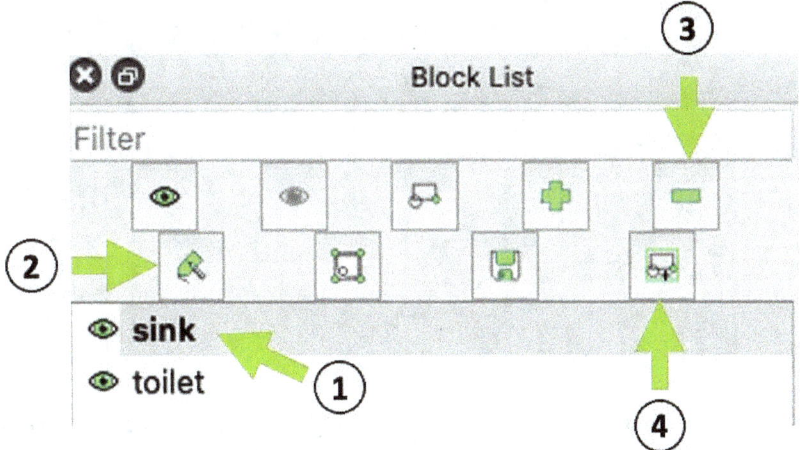

A placeholder ① then appears, which we can move with the PC mouse using the reference point ② selected when creating the block and position with a click. Settings can be made in the menu bar at the top of the program. This allows you to insert a block rotated, for example, by entering an angle in the field "Angle" ③. You can also insert the block scaled, i.e., in a smaller or larger form. To do this, enter a factor in the field ④. In the ⑤ field, you have the option of inserting the block multiple times — in the form of an array. This can be imagined as a table with rows and columns. The first number stands for the columns, the second for the rows. The distance between the blocks — in x and y direction — can be entered at "Spacing".

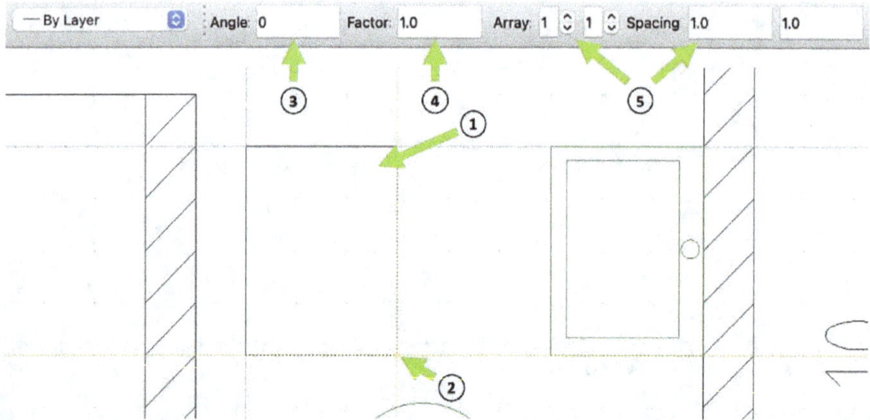

In our case, a rotation of 180 degrees makes sense (enter "Angle"). We can then position the block on the opposite wall using the reference point (which is also rotated) and obtain the following result.

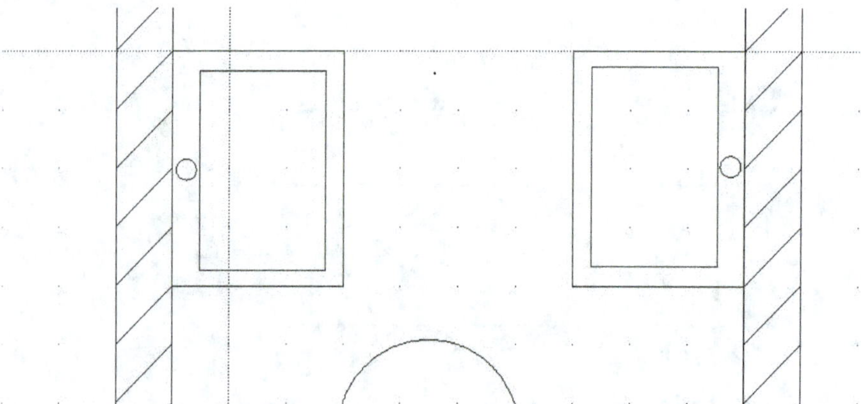

To edit a block, select it ① and click on the icon ②. This opens a new window in "LibreCAD" in which you can edit the block. If we edit the block in this window, the changes are applied to all blocks with the identical name in the drawing.

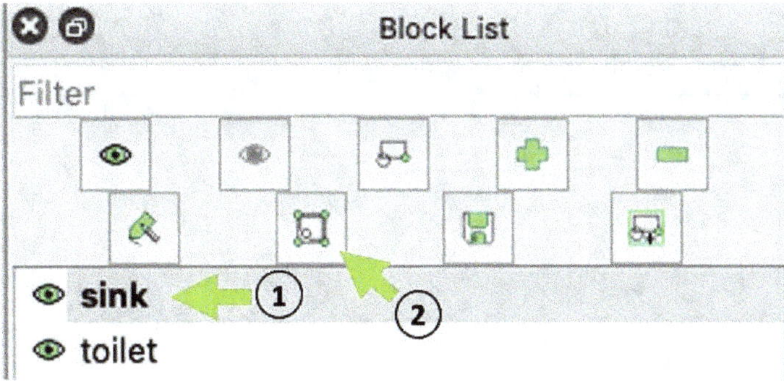

For example, we can add a drain with a slope. When we have finished editing, we can simply close this window.

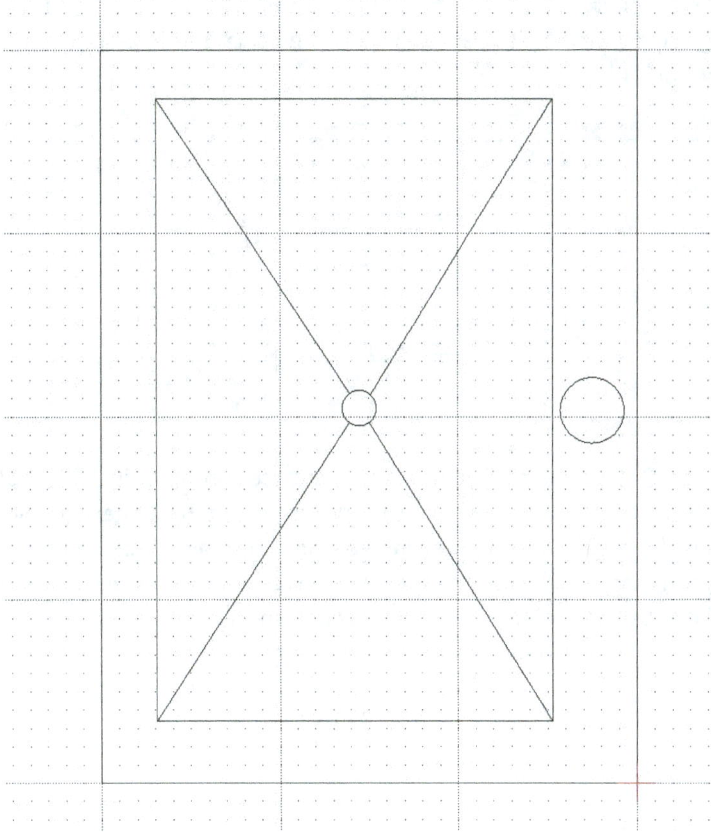

Now we can see in our original document that both sinks have actually been given the new geometry.

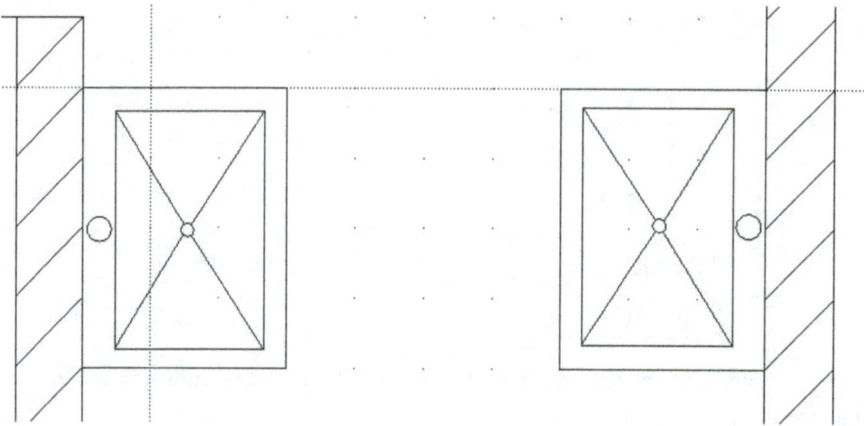

If you save a block using the button ①, you can later insert it into another new drawing using "Import" (② - ④). When importing, the first step is to define a reference point.

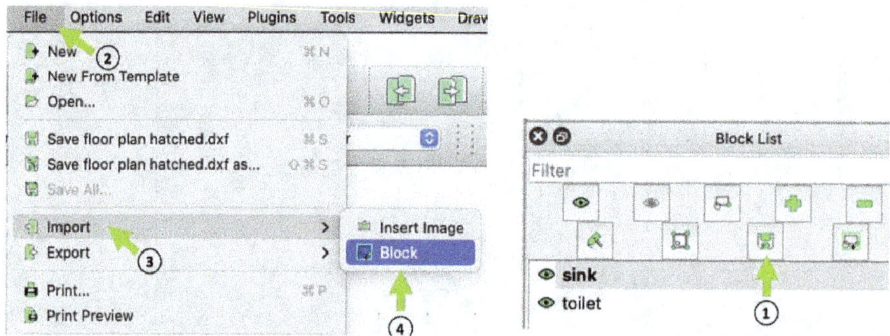

In "LibreCAD" there are also many ready-made blocks on a wide variety of topics. These blocks can be found in the "Library Browser" tab ① next to "Block List" sorted in folders ②. Here you will find, for example, electronic symbols, furniture, arrows, and ready-made drawing sheets as well as many other blocks. A preview is displayed in the area ③. Use the "Insert" button ④ to insert the selected block into the drawing. To do this, simply click on the drawing layer.

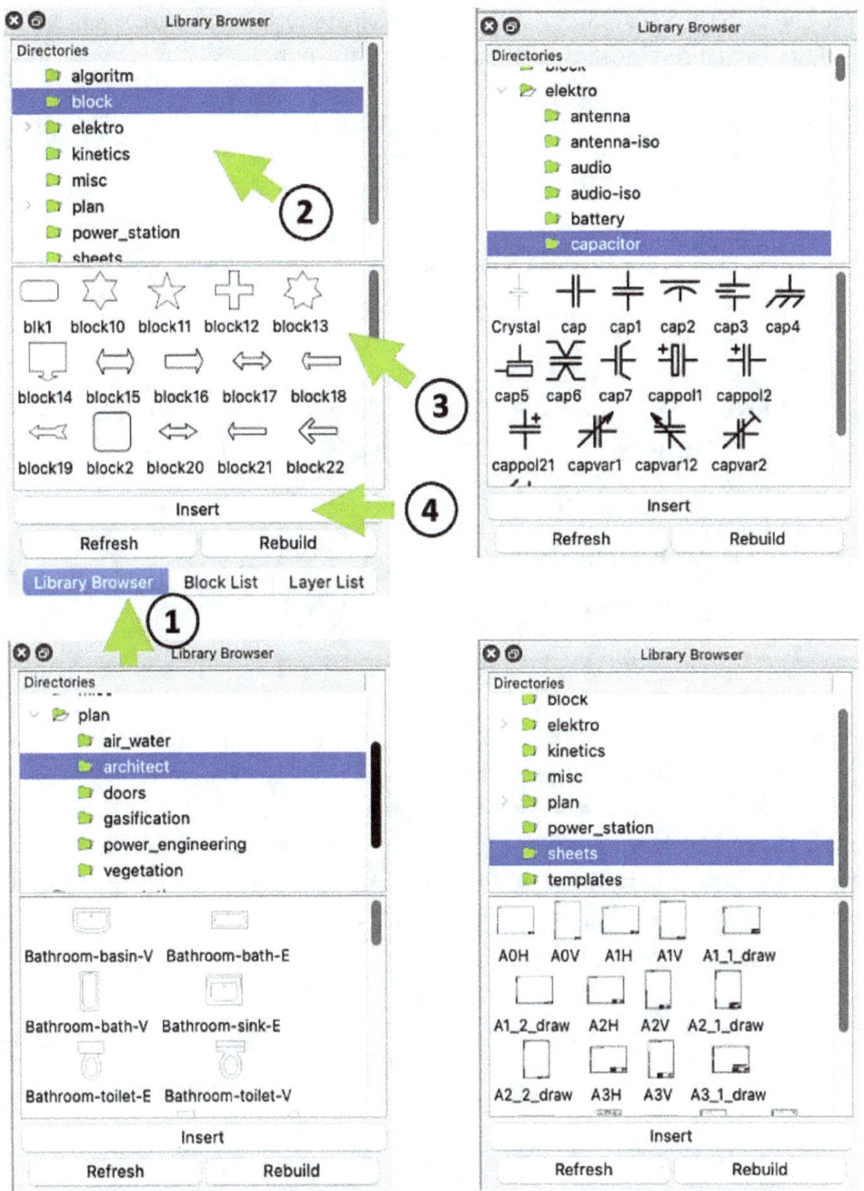

4.4 Working with the Color palette — "Pen Wizard"

Using the "Pen Wizard", you can save line colors as favorites in "LibreCAD" and apply them to geometries. The window is located on the right-hand side at the top of the program by default. If it is not active, it must be activated as shown in the previous chapters.

You can select a color either via the drop-down menu ① or the color palette ②
and then add it to the list of favorites ④ using the button ③.

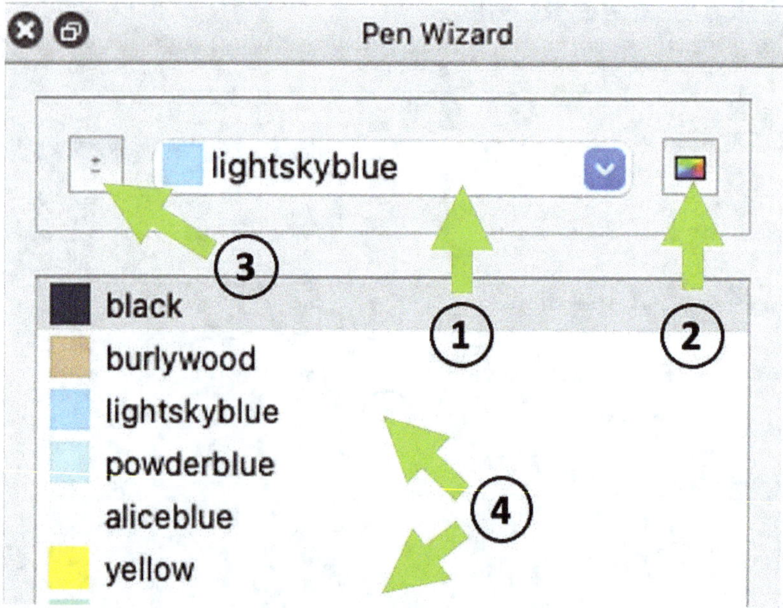

If you right-click on one of the colors (e.g. "black") ①, you can choose between
two helpful commands. On the one hand, you can use "Select objects" ② to select
all geometric elements of a drawing that have exactly this color. On the other hand,
you can use "Apply to selected" ③ to assign the selected color to one or more
elements. To do this, the geometric element (e.g. line) must first be selected in the
drawing. With "Remove" you can remove the color <u>from the favorites</u>.

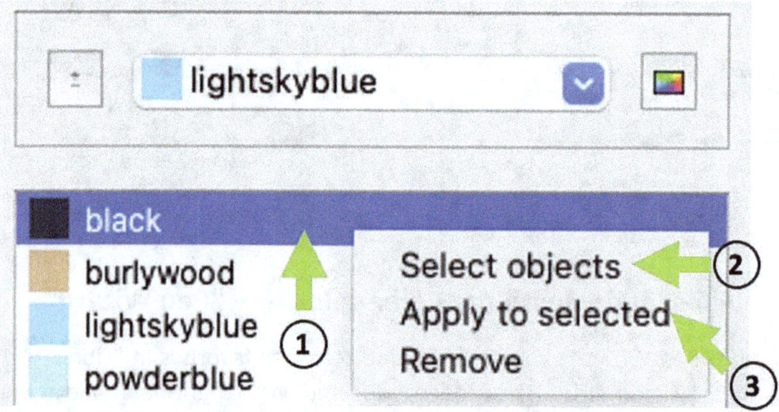

4.5 File Output and Printing

Excellent! In this penultimate chapter, let's take a look at file output and printing a drawing.

Before we learn how to output drawings to scale, we will first look at importing and exporting files. These two options can be found at the top of the menu bar in the tab "File" ①. As we already know, we can import a "Block" at "Import" ②. We can also import an image here with "Insert Image" ③. This can be very helpful if, for example, you want to create a technical drawing of a real 3D part based on a photo. You can then simply trace it.

In the menu "Export" ④ you have the option of exporting the drawing as a PDF, as an image or as an SVG file for production ("CAM" = "Computer-Aided Manufacturing") ⑤.

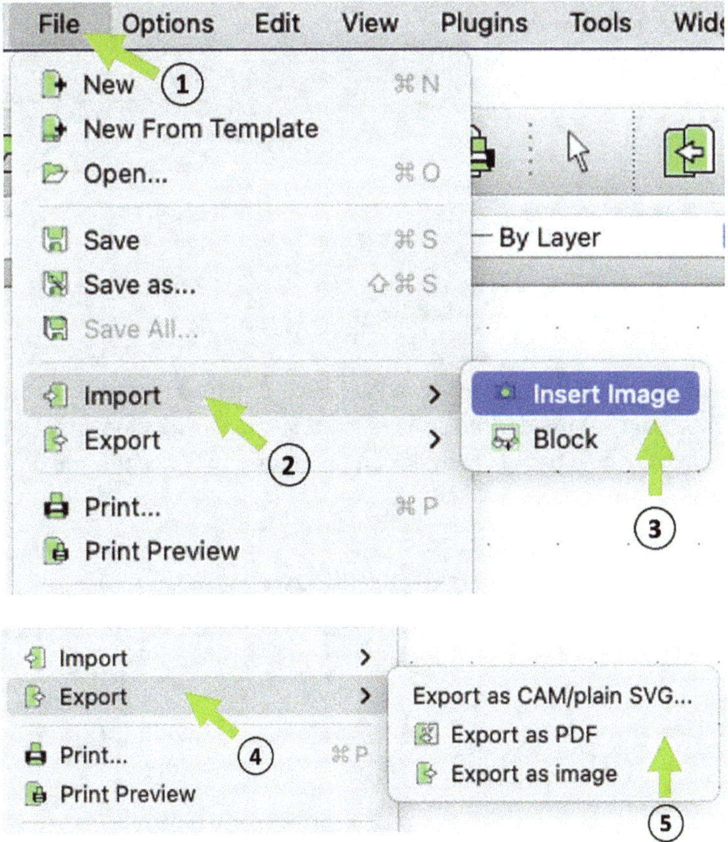

Now let's move on to printing to scale. As an example, let's try to save the floor plan of the student apartment at a scale of 1:25 on A4 paper as a PDF.

To do this, it is essential that we have already created our drawing in the correct unit and the correct "Grid Status" at the start. After opening the drawing, we can check whether the desired paper format and the units of the drawing are set correctly in the "Current Drawing Preferences". In the tab "Paper", set the correct paper format, here e.g. DIN A4 ③ in the orientation "Portrait" ④. In the tab "Units" ⑤ we check whether the unit "Meter" is set. We must have drawn the lines of the floor plan in "Grid status: 0.1/1" to match this unit. The floor plan is 3 m wide, so the width in this "Grid status" must extend over exactly three boxes or 30 grid points. If you still have some catching up to do here, *chapter 2.2* is particularly helpful.

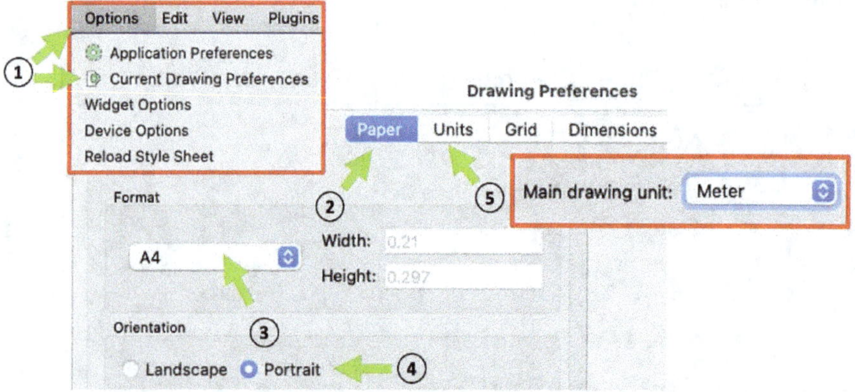

Now we can click on the button "Print Preview" ① to switch to the print preview, in which we can set the desired scale (e.g. 1:25; drawing 25 times smaller than in real life) in the menu bar ② and click on the button ③ to center the drawing on the sheet.

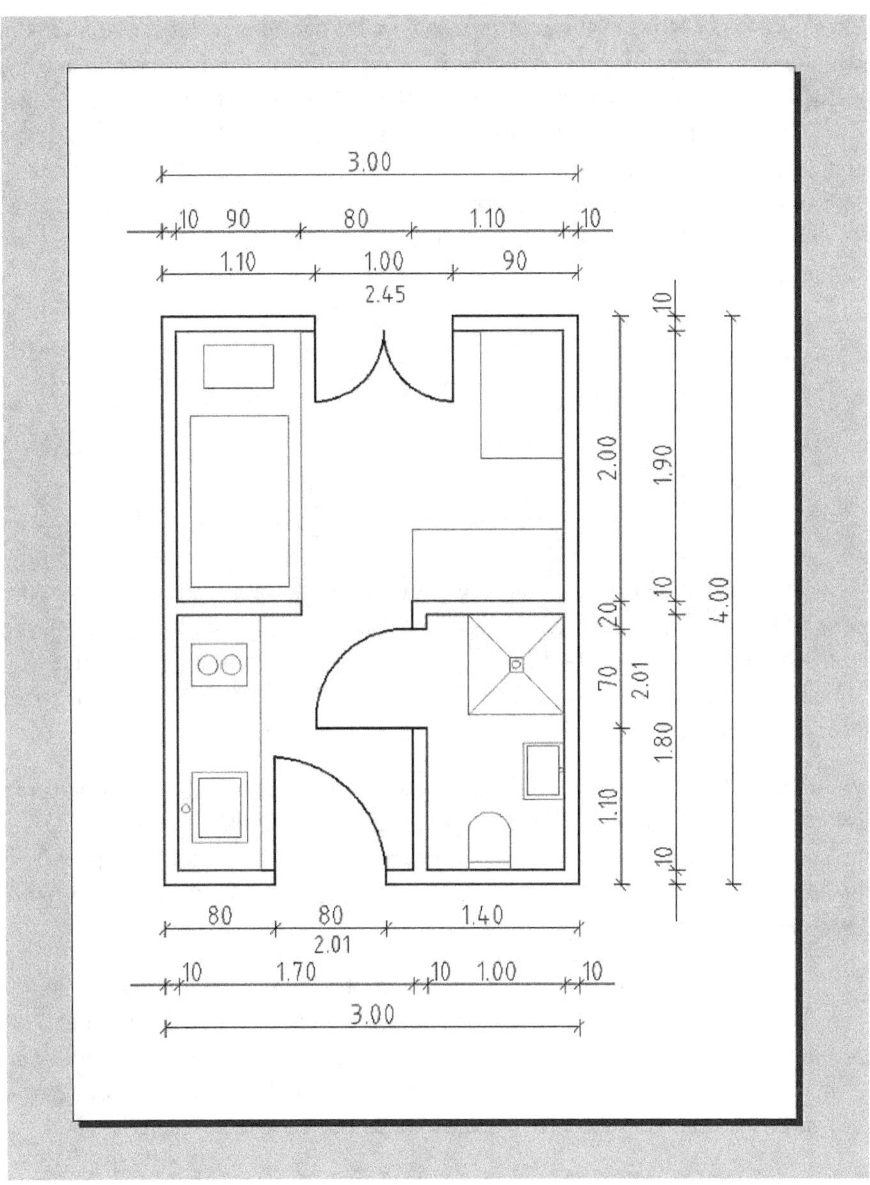

Alternatively, we could have set the unit "Centimeter" or "Millimeter" instead of "Meter" in the "Current Drawing Preferences" at the beginning of the drawing. However, to ensure that the scale is still correct when printing, we would then have had to draw in a different "Grid Status". For example, with the unit "Centimeter" in "Grid Status: 1/10". In this case, the 3 m wide wall (= 300 cm) would be 30 boxes long. So always make sure you use the correct "Grid Status" — depending on which unit is set and which dimension you are drawing.

There are other icons in the print preview menu bar. Finally, let's take a look at what we can do with these. If you check "fixed" ①, you can no longer make any changes to the scale. Using the command "Apply Print Scale to line width" ②, we can also apply the scale to the line width. Just try this out. The button ③ colors the drawing in black and white style. With the button ④ you can fit the drawing into the paper format, whereupon the scale changes. The drawing will be as large as the paper is. And with the ⑤ button, you can calculate how many pages are required to reproduce everything for large drawings.

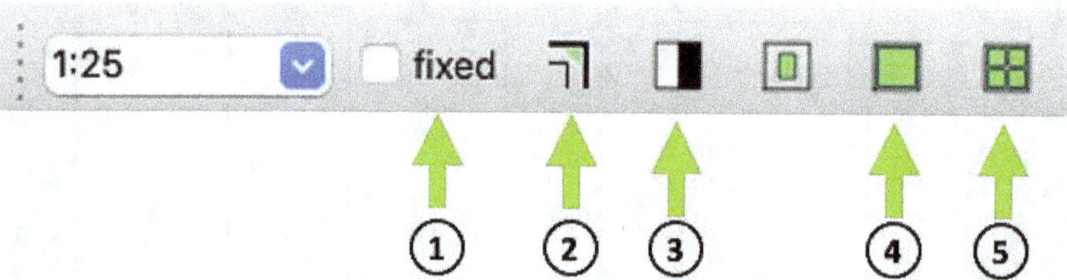

As already mentioned at the beginning of the course, different line thicknesses are only visible in the print preview. In addition, design geometries <u>are not</u> displayed in the print preview by default. Try out both. If you want to print the result, you should note the scale on the printout. You can do this in "LibreCAD" with a text field (command "MText" from the menu bar; *see chapter 3.4*).

You can start the actual printing process with the button "Print". Here you can select your printer or alternatively save the drawing as a PDF. In both cases, you must set the correct paper format. In this case DIN A4. For more complex floor plans, DIN A0 is used and for technical drawings, DIN A3 or DIN A4 format is recommended.

Let's also try to output the technical drawing of the machine component in the correct scale. For example, after opening the document, we set the format to "DIN A3" in the settings. We had set the unit to "Millimeter" when drawing. Now we can switch to the print preview, e.g. select the scale 2:1 (part is twice as large in the drawing as in reality) and center the drawing on the paper by clicking on ②.

This should show us the following result.

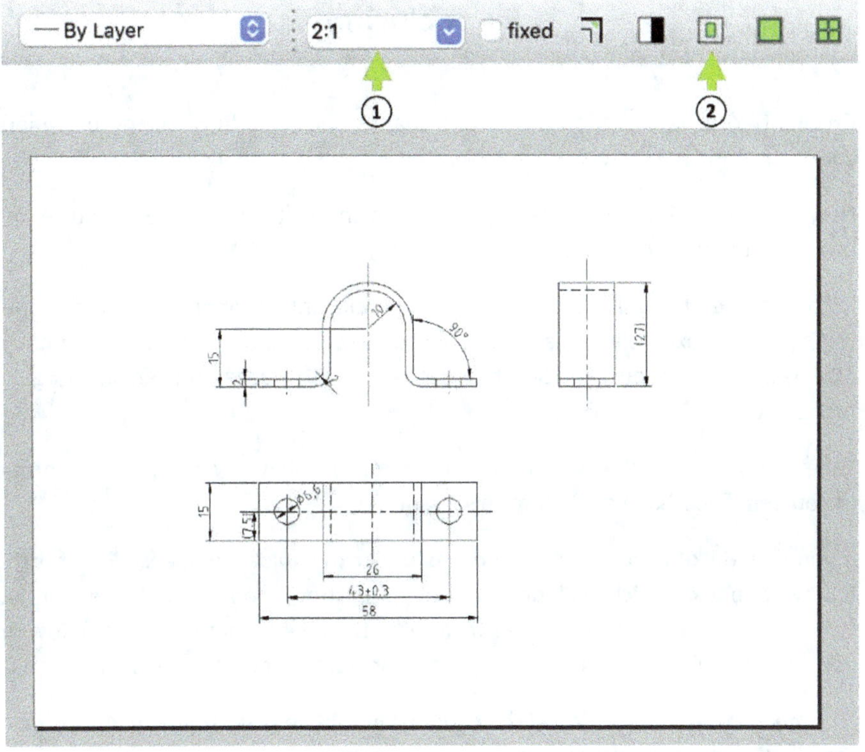
— By Layer
2:1
fixed
1
2
15
2
10
90°
(27)
15
Ø6,6
7,5
26
43+0,3
58

5 Conclusion

Excellent! You have made it; with this chapter we have finished the beginners' course for the CAD software "LibreCAD"!

Now you know all the important functions of the software and can venture into new projects and CAD designs on your own!

In this course, you will have learned all the relevant commands and techniques using practical examples. This will enable you to create 2D drawings and isometric 3D views for various specialist areas such as mechanical engineering or architecture.

Together, we have achieved a lot in this course! You have every right to be proud of yourself if you have made it to this lesson!

If you would like to design more objects under my guidance, please look for the follow-up book, which will probably be published soon and will be entitled "LibreCAD - Projects" or will get a similar title. However, whether such a follow-up book will be published also depends largely on your feedback on this book.

This means that if you enjoyed the course, I would be pleased if you would leave me a rating on amazon.com, and a short feedback as well as recommend the book to others! Thank you very much!

If you are also interested in 3D CAD software, such as the free program "FreeCAD" or "Fusion 360" from Autodesk, then you will also find step-by-step books. In any case, this book has given you a good introduction to the world of CAD and taught you the basics of 2D drawings and 3D views. However, "LibreCAD" is only a 2D CAD program. But designing directly in three dimensions in a 3D CAD program changes a lot, so it's worth it! You will find an overview of all my books on the following pages. Be sure to take a look and order your copies today!

Thank you very much!

Books on topics you might also like

All books are available online on the usual sales platforms. It's best to just search for the title, or feel free to visit my author page. Some books may not be published yet and will be released or found soon. Take a look at the books of your choice and your copy as e-book or paperback!

3D Printing:

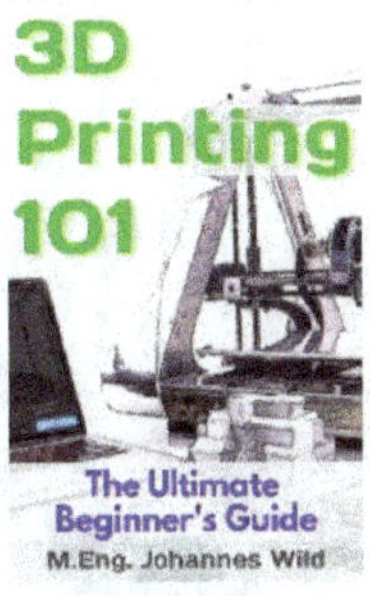

CAD, FEM, CAM (3D Object Creation, Design, Simulation):

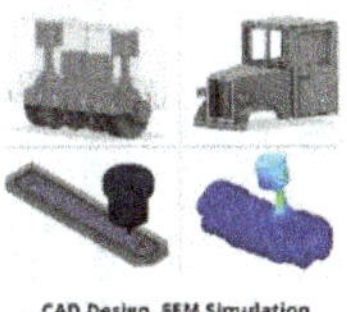

Electrical Engineering:

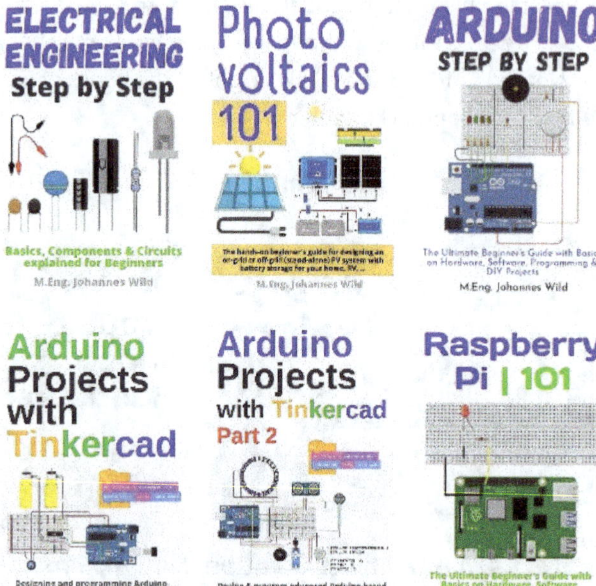

Programming and other Software:

There are also identical video courses for some of these books:

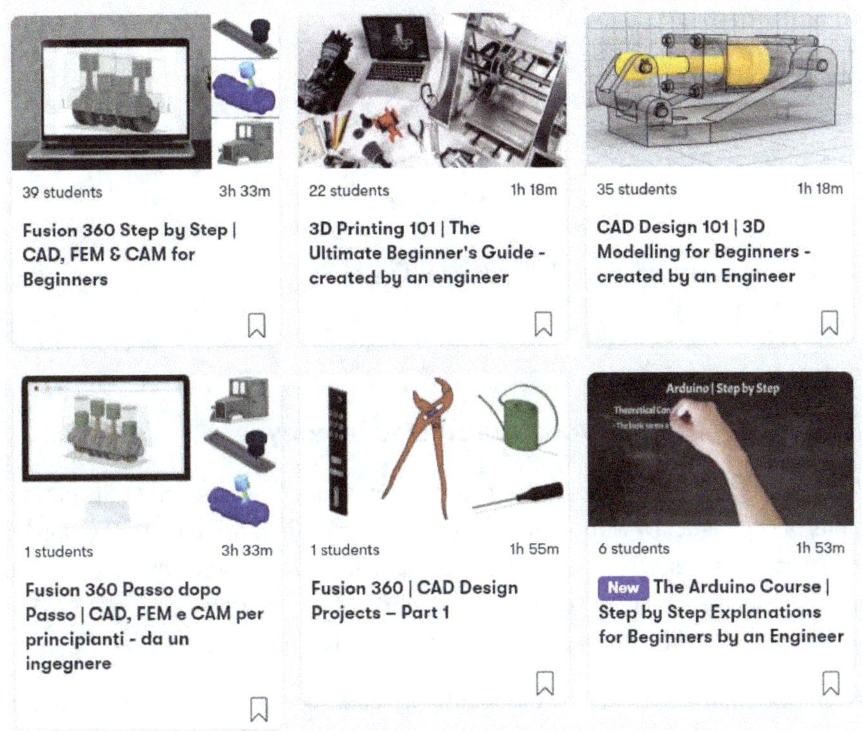

They are hosted on the learning website: skillshare.com

Be sure to use my following friends & family referral link to get a month of membership for free!

(I will get a little bonus if you choose to stay, so we will be both happy. Thanks in advance!)

https://www.skillshare.com/r/profile/Johannes-Wild/854541251

It is best to copy the link in your browser to access the free month!

Sign up today and deepen your knowledge!

Imprint of the author / publisher

© 2024

Johannes Wild
c/o RA Matutis
Berliner Straße 57
14467 Potsdam
Germany

Email: 3dtech@gmx.de

Thank you so much for choosing this book!